Claiming God

Claiming God

Essays in Honor of Marilyn McCord Adams

Edited by
CHRISTINE HELMER *and*
SHANNON CRAIGO-SNELL

◆PICKWICK *Publications* · Eugene, Oregon

CLAIMING GOD
Essays in Honor of Marilyn McCord Adams

Copyright © 2022 Wipf and Stock Publishers. All rights reserved. Except for brief quotations in critical publications or reviews, no part of this book may be reproduced in any manner without prior written permission from the publisher. Write: Permissions, Wipf and Stock Publishers, 199 W. 8th Ave., Suite 3, Eugene, OR 97401.

Pickwick Publications
An Imprint of Wipf and Stock Publishers
199 W. 8th Ave., Suite 3
Eugene, OR 97401

www.wipfandstock.com

PAPERBACK ISBN: 978-1-6667-3588-8
HARDCOVER ISBN: 978-1-6667-9351-2
EBOOK ISBN: 978-1-6667-9352-9

Cataloguing-in-Publication data:

Names: Helmer, Christine, editor. | Craigo-Snell, Shannon Nichole, editor.

Title: Claiming God : essays in honor of Marilyn McCord Adams / edited by Christine Helmer and Shannon Criago-Snell.

Description: Eugene, OR : Pickwick Publications, 2022 | Includes bibliographical references and index.

Identifiers: ISBN 978-1-6667-3588-8 (paperback) | ISBN 978-1-6667-9351-2 (hardcover) | ISBN 978-1-6667-9352-9 (ebook)

Subjects: LCSH: Adams, Marilyn McCord. | Theology. | Theodicy.

Classification: BJ1401 .C47 2022 (print) | BJ1401 .C47 (ebook)

11/07/22

Scripture quotations marked (NRSV) are from the New Revised Standard Version Bible, copyright © 1989 the Division of Christian Education of the National Council of the Churches of Christ in the United States of America. Used by permission. All rights reserved.

Scripture quotations marked (KJV) are taken from The Authorized (King James) Version. Rights in the Authorized Version in the United Kingdom are vested in the Crown. Reproduced by permission of the Crown's patentee, Cambridge University Press

Contents

Acknowledgments | vii

Part I: Evil and Horror-Defeat

1. "Striving into God" | 3
   SHANNON CRAIGO-SNELL AND CHRISTINE HELMER

2. Claiming God after Auschwitz | 12
   SARAH K. PINNOCK

3. Gratuitous Evil and Anselm | 29
   MICHAEL BARNWELL

4. Spiritual Friendship and Sexual Violence | 45
   DANIELLE TUMMINIO HANSEN

5. A Beautiful Love: Compatibilism, Theodicy, and Limited Agency | 56
   JESSE COUENHOVEN

Part II: Individuals in Community

6. Friendship, Human and Divine | 75
   SHANNON CRAIGO-SNELL

7. Claiming God at the Intersection of Ethics and Climate Change | 94
   WENDY PETERSEN BORING

8   Scotus on Common Natures | 110
    JT Paasch

9   Queering Worship | 132
    Ruthanna B. Hooke

Part III: Knowing God

10 Why There Wasn't, and How There Can
    Be, a Latin Social Trinity | 153
    Scott M. Williams

11 God as the Form of the Intellect or, Beatific Union in
    Thomas Aquinas and Giles of Rome, with a Concluding
    Christological Postscript Wherein Is Proposed a
    Novel Account of Uncreated Grace | 175
    Richard Cross

12 Carnal Knowledge of God | 192
    Rebecca Voelkel

Contributors | 207

Marilyn McCord Adams's Bibliography | 211

Bibliography | 223

Index | 231

Acknowledgments

To ALL OF US, Marilyn McCord Adams (1943-2017) was teacher, priest, and friend. She guided and mentored many of us over decades. She taught us that rigorous thinking honors God, that God delights in creativity, and that friendship expresses the divine love. Marilyn never wanted disciples. Instead she was committed to forming long-lasting friendships, taking seriously our fears, hurts, and questions, and showing us that embodied love is restorative. This book is our testimony to the ways in which she encouraged our distinctive joys and talents, and empowered us to cultivate our particular vocations, academic, pastoral, and activist. Some of the papers included in this volume emerged from a session dedicated to Marilyn's impact on our lives sponsored by the Society of Christian Philosophers at the November 2017 American Academy of Religion Annual Meeting in Boston. We thank the authors in this volume for their contributions.

One question arising during the course of our editing had to with how to refer to Marilyn McCord Adams. We decided to use her first name, "Marilyn," in contexts of personal reference, and to use "McCord Adams" when referring to her as a scholar and priest.

We thank Northwestern students Molly Van Gorp and Paul Bernhard for editorial assistance, and Northwestern University URAP (Undergraduate Research Assistant Program) for funding, also Haakon Black for help with the final stage of manuscript production. We thank Robert Merrihew Adams for his support of this project from its inception and particularly for assistance with the bibliography of Marilyn McCord Adams's published works. We also thank Charlie Collier, Matt Wimer, and George Callihan for publishing this volume in the offerings of Pickwick Publications of Wipf and Stock.

Christine Helmer and Shannon Craigo-Snell

PART I

Evil and Horror-Defeat

1

"Striving into God"

SHANNON CRAIGO-SNELL AND CHRISTINE HELMER

THIS BOOK IS A testimony to the generative power of the scholarship, teaching, and priesthood of Marilyn McCord Adams. In each of these aspects of her vocation, McCord Adams was focused on God.[1] In conversation, she stated, "God is infinitely fascinating." In an academic text, she wrote, "Between birth and the grave, the human assignment is to strive into God with all of our powers."[2]

McCord Adams sought to bring God back into the variety of professional vocations that characterized her religious and intellectual interests. She wanted to bring God back into religious studies, a discipline characterized by the "absence of the gods." She wanted to bring God back into the church, which seemed to be focused on a much smaller reality than the God of Jesus Christ. She preached of a God whose gospel was more radical, edgier, and more diverse than people could have imagined in the 1980s. She brought God into church politics, advocating on behalf of LGBTQ folk who too were created in God's image. She brought God back into philosophy, making sure that volume two of her Ockham book included extensive discussion of Ockham's philosophical theology

---

1. Passages within this chapter were first published in two essays: Helmer, "Marilyn McCord Adams"; Craigo-Snell, "Wrestling with God."
2. McCord Adams, "Truth and Reconciliation," 21.

of God, Christ, and the sacraments, and more recently the metaphysics of the Eucharist with explicit claims about the metaphysics of God incarnate in flesh and bread. And she brought God into theology in new ways, self-reflectively drawing biblical claims into the work of theodicy and arguing that prayer is a fundamental aspect of theological work.

McCord Adams brought her commitments to God to the different constituencies of her work and life. Academics and priests, Franciscans and liberal Protestants, colleagues in philosophy and religious studies, parishioners and students were the different groups with whom she engaged her intellectual and pastoral ministry. Yet professional relationships sometimes developed into friendships. One of McCord Adams's key theological ideas was seeing salvation in terms of friendship with God. Anselm of Canterbury was the inspiration for this idea. Yet the idea became reality in her capaciousness for cultivating friendships. Those of us represented in this volume attest to this capaciousness—her rigorous academic mentoring in different disciplines of theology, philosophy, and ministerial studies and her cultivation of friendships with us.

Her brilliance was institutionally recognized. McCord Adams became the first woman occupying prestigious chairs in theology, first the Pitkin Professor of Historical Theology at Yale Divinity School and then the Regius Professor of Divinity at Christ Church Oxford. She was fiercely courageous through these academic "firsts," and throughout, she continued to struggle on behalf of the ecclesial rights of queer people and the ordination of women bishops in the Anglican Church. We knew her as both Professor Adams and Mother Adams.

1. PHILOSOPHY

The work for which McCord Adams first became known was a two-volume study of William Ockham, the fourteenth-century nominalist philosopher. This work changed the way that philosophers understood Ockham's innovations. It would also change the way that theologians at Yale and beyond would regard the importance of philosophy for theology. Since the late nineteenth century, Protestant theologians had policed the boundary between philosophy and theology. "No metaphysics, no mysticism in theology," the German theologian Albrecht Ritschl had pronounced. For one hundred years, theologians insisted on protecting theology from philosophical danger. Theology's truths were based on revelation and scripture. Philosophy was based on human reason. Any encroachment by philosophy onto theological terrain called theology into question. Yet Marilyn McCord Adams introduced medieval philosophy into Protestant theology. The results were transformative for her students and for the field.

McCord Adams taught Protestant theologians that philosophy is an ally, not an enemy. Philosophy can help theologians make better arguments. Protestants trained in the continental theological tradition of German Idealism can benefit from medieval doctrinal insights and paradigms. Anselm of Canterbury should be consulted alongside the seminary's required readings in Hegel and Moltmann. McCord Adams saw that theologians who carefully avoided philosophy and, especially, metaphysics, were often simply refusing to be self-reflective about their underlying assumptions. Even if he could not admit it, Barth made use of philosophical resources from Hegel's metaphysics and Kierkegaard's existentialism. She argued theologians must be honest about the philosophical commitments they inadvertently smuggle into their theological work. Philosophy has always been part of the theologian's métier. Why not reflect seriously on this inevitable connection?

2. THEOLOGY

McCord Adams' later became known for her work in theodicy—addressing the problem of evil in relation to God. The logical problem of evil can be distilled into four statements that appear incompatible.

1. God is omniscient (all-knowing).
2. God is omnipotent (all-powerful).
3. God is omnibenevolent (all-good).
4. Evil exists.

If God wills the good, knows the good, and has the power to enact the good, it makes no sense that evil exists. Some find this quandary to be sufficient evidence to reject the existence of God altogether. Many provide explanations that fudge a bit on point 1 or point 2, nuancing either the knowledge God has in a world that is still unfolding, or the kind of power God has or chooses to use. While few theologians would claim God's goodness is limited, their views include specific angles on how goodness is maximized.

McCord Adams shifts the terms of the debate in ways that shatter these alternatives. From the outset, she focuses on what she calls "horrendous evils." These are "evils the participation in which (that is, the doing or suffering of which) constitutes prima facie reason to doubt whether the participant's life could (given their inclusion in it) be a great good to him/her on the whole."[3] In other words, evils that make it seem that it would be better for the people involved if they had never been born. She rejects definitions of evil that focus on morality, injustice, or mass suffering in order to focus on the least explicable events. It is precisely their inexplicability—their destruction of the meaning-making potential, capacities, and frameworks of those involved—that identify them as horrendous evils. "What makes horrendous evils so pernicious is their life-ruining potential, their power prima facie to degrade the individual by devouring the possibility of positive personal meaning in one swift gulp."[4] Horrendous evils would then include "the Bible's Job, the father who nonnegligently runs over his beloved child, and those who suffer from schizophrenia or deep clinical depression."[5]

Many theodicies fall into one of two categories: Best of all Possible Worlds (BPW) and Free Will Defense (FWD). Best of all Possible Worlds theories argue that evils are an integral aspect of the best world that God could possibly make. McCord Adams takes biblical theological content into account, merging philosophy and theology.[6] She affirms, "Divine love for created persons must mean that God knows how and intends to be good to us."[7] For these horrendous evils to be truly defeated, they must be defeated in the life of each person, such that their own life becomes a very great good to them. Positive meaning must be made for each who has suffered. A general solution, such as those offered in Best of all Possible World approaches, might be sufficient for generic theism, but it is inadequate to Christian claims about the goodness of God.

Free Will Defenses argue that evil results from the misuse of human free will. Put simply, God makes a good world, and we mess it up. The value of creatures with free will is so great that it is worth the risk, or even the actuality, of evil. Yet the problem of evil is much worse than what free

---

3. McCord Adams, *Horrendous Evils*, 26.
4. McCord Adams, *Horrendous Evils*, 28.
5. McCord Adams, *Horrendous Evils*, 28.
6. McCord Adams, *Horrendous Evils*, 206.
7. McCord Adams, *Christ and Horrors*, 45.

will can explain. On this point McCord Adams is part of a chorus of theologians who insist that free will is too thin a reed to bear responsibility for personal blessedness, let alone the world's. Humans are too limited: individuals who perpetuate evil on others cannot fathom, in most cases, the extent of suffering they inflict on others.

If human free will cannot explain why horrendous evils exist, then who is responsible? When posed in this way, there is only one answer: the one who created this world, God. In the Christian theological tradition, few theologians have dared to assign responsibility to God by arguing against free will. Luther, with his idea of double predestination, assigned responsibility of both damnation and salvation to the divine eternal will. Friedrich Schleiermacher too insisted on the claim that God is responsible for sin. While this runs the risk of misunderstanding God as capricious or cruel, this claim has a deeper theological point that McCord Adams makes clear for today. God does not watch as humans make what they can in a difficult and dangerous world. Rather, the God who created a world in which horrendous evils exist is ultimately the one who can "make good" on creation. Traditional theodicies aim, in blunt terms, to get God off the hook for evil. In contrast, McCord Adams's theology recognizes that God is implicated in the origins of evil and claims that God will accomplish its defeat.

Divine goodness not only requires but also enables God to make life good to each person. God is great enough that intimate relationship with God overwhelms, swamps, and defeats all horrors. This view includes two contested points: there is an afterlife and salvation is universal.[8] Horrendous evils are not defeated in the lifetimes of many who die in suffering. Post-mortem, all horrendous evils can be integrated into a meaningful whole in intimacy with God.

McCord Adams proposes that God defeats evil in three stages.[9] In Stage I, Divine-human intimacy is insured through the incarnation of Jesus Christ. God identifies with humanity and leads a human life of vulnerability to horrendous evils. This cancels the dishonor of the human condition and wipes out the stains of defilement. In Stage II, humans begin to appropriate and understand the friendship God offers. Because Jesus participated in horrendous evils, even those horrors can become meaningful parts of an individual's relationship with Jesus. Shared

---

8. McCord Adams, *Horrendous Evils*, 162.
9. McCord Adams, *Christ and Horrors*, 47–48.

suffering becomes a point of contact. Evil and suffering are not needed for salvation but can be integrated into the larger story of a human life such that, "from the vantage point of heavenly beatitude, human victims of horrors will recognize those experiences as points of identification with the crucified God, and not wish them away from their life histories."[10] Stage III of horror defeat is post-mortem, when humans are no longer vulnerable to horrors and the goodness of friendship with God becomes permanent, fully known, and inviolable.

3. CHURCH

While teaching philosophy at UCLA, McCord Adams discerned a call to the priesthood and eventually took two brief turns at Princeton Seminary to complete two master's degrees. McCord Adams also began assisting in the adult education programs at Trinity Episcopal Church in Hollywood. Participants in her Sunday School classes included gay men living and dying with AIDS. When asked directly how God evaluates same-sex love, McCord Adams started a study group on the Bible and sexuality to learn more. Through such study, but much more so through her witnessing of incredible faithfulness and sacrificial love among gay couples and friends, McCord Adams became utterly convinced that erroneous Christian taboos have "blinded us to the image of Christ in gay and lesbian Christians" and that same-sex love can be a reflection of Divine Trinitarian giving and receiving.[11]

McCord Adams preached at Trinity, developing a distinctive and compelling homiletic style that was deeply biblical, radically honest, and unrelenting in declaring God's fierce love. She reflected, "Preaching the Gospel to people whose gray-green skin tells you that they won't be there in six months creates a pressure to tell as much Truth as one can."[12] Her sermons display a lack of inhibition that was surely forged in those days at Trinity. Tell the truth; ask the questions; demand that God be present; assure that God loves us! McCord Adams wrote out precisely worded sermons, which she then delivered from memory without a manuscript, looking the congregation directly in the eye.

---

10. McCord Adams, *Horrendous Evils*, 167.
11. McCord Adams, "Love of Learning," 137–61.
12. McCord Adams, "Love of Learning," 157.

Several of McCord Adams's sermons were published later, during her time at Oxford, in a volume titled *Wrestling for Blessing*. Here she specifically commends Jacob as a model for faith, and wrestling with God as a pattern to emulate.[13] One of the three sections of the book addresses themes related specifically to same-sex love. With characteristic style, McCord Adams points out that traditionally masculine language for the Holy Trinity portrays a same-gender ménage à trois and concludes a sermon for Pride Day declaring, "Gay Pride Sunday is a day of gospel reversals: a day for old Mother Church to come out of the closet and confess her failures, to receive absolution from her priestly children, to parade with them behind Christ our Drum Major, onward to Zion; that beautiful City of God!"[14]

While at Oxford, McCord Adams also served as canon of Christ Church Cathedral. In 2008, she published a collection of brief prayers, most of which were written for liturgical use at Christ Church, in a volume titled, *Opening to God: Childlike Prayers for Adults*.[15] This book is a treasure for any worship leader, layperson, or seeker. The prayers are direct and truthful, topically arranged and indexed in correlation with biblical passages. As McCord Adams intuited that "doing philosophical theology itself is a form of prayer," it ought not be surprising that her intellectually sophisticated work can be conveyed in prayer.[16]

4. CLAIMING GOD

The authors in this volume aim to honor McCord Adams by elucidating the topics that were important to her and how her commitments have been taken up in the specific trajectories of each author's thinking. The style of writing is academic, without being technical. Because this volume is interdisciplinary, the articles are written with the intention to communicate respective interests across the disciplinary divisions that characterized McCord Adams's own thought. While McCord Adams was attuned to linguistic clarity, she developed a coherent language between theology, philosophy, and pastoral ministry that allowed for communication between these disciplines. The work she did in biblical interpretation

---

13. McCord Adams, *Wrestling for Blessing*, 22.
14. McCord Adams, *Wrestling for Blessing*, 39, 140.
15. McCord Adams, *Opening to God*.
16. McCord Adams, "Love of Learning," 153.

became central for the understanding of God she identified in theology. The ideas she worked out in philosophy became significant in theology and preaching. And her experience as a priest informed her philosophy. The title of the book, *Claiming God*, attests to McCord Adams's different ways of claiming God in her work and life, which were both varied and profoundly coherent. This book is divided into three sections: Evil and Horror Defeat, Individuals in Community, and Knowing God. The work of philosophers, theologians, and ordained clergy appear in all three sections.

"Part I: Evil and Horror-Defeat" comprises essays that engage McCord Adams's work on horrendous evil, illustrating the generative influence of her work for both theology and philosophy. Two chapters wrestle directly with her description of horror-defeat: Sarah K. Pinnock's chapter contrasts McCord Adams's work with Jewish perspectives on the Holocaust; Danielle Tumminio Hansen argues that McCord Adams's life demonstrated an additional step in the process of horror defeat that is unacknowledged in her writings. Philosophers Michael Barnwell and Jesse Couenhoven parse issues of human freedom and ability to choose. Both authors highlight how McCord Adams brought the resources of medieval theology into contemporary philosophy in ways that continue to resonate throughout the field.

"Part II: Individuals in Community" explores the ways McCord Adams conceptualizes individual persons in relationships with their communities: social, ecological, and liturgical. The diversity in this section reveals the wide and generative influence of McCord Adams's work. JT Paasch draws on Duns Scotus to explore the uniqueness of individuals, both human and divine. Shannon Craigo-Snell elucidates and extends McCord Adams's emphasis on friendship as central to divine and human life. Identifying climate change as a horrendous evil, Wendy Petersen Boring draws on McCord Adams's liturgical writings and practices as a path to respond. Ruthanna B. Hooke addresses the exceptional creative license McCord Adams took in re-wording Bible and liturgy, specifically the Book of Common Prayer, in a liturgical context. From philosophy to weekly worship, McCord Adams claimed the gift of divine presence such that unique individuality allows for new forms of communal being.

In "Part III: Knowing God," authors address who God is and how we claim this knowledge. Scott M. Williams's chapter takes its cue from McCord Adams's description of the persons of the Trinity as co-lovers and mutual friends. Richard Cross focuses on theologians about whom McCord Adams wrote extensively: Thomas Aquinas and Giles of Rome.

He argues that beatific union is not a case of the believer claiming God, but rather a case of God claiming the believer. Finally, Rebecca Voelkel explores how people of faith claim God in their bodies, through lived experience and advocacy, in ways that both express and form particular truth claims about God.

This array of chapters is intended to offer a glimpse of the many ways in which McCord Adams's thought, work, mentorship, and friendship shapes and energizes the work of many philosophers, theologians, pastors, and activists. The words on these pages necessarily fail to communicate the blessings and joy McCord Adams freely gave to her students and colleagues. Her intellectual generosity was limitless, as she was always willing to discuss ideas and read drafts. Her liturgical creativity was legendary, as she worked in cahoots with students, colleagues, and parishioners to design worship services to disrupt harmful theologies, heal those hurt by the church and the world, and delight in God's presence. The Adams's home was a port of refuge and place of delight for many, as Marilyn and Bob hosted celebrations for friends and students on their graduations and ordinations, invited mentees for writing retreats, and provided a space of peaceful hospitality. For some of the authors of these chapters, the Adams's home was the safest and most welcoming space ever experienced, offering a taste of divine welcome. Among the many gifts McCord Adams offered was a sense—conveyed through intellectual discourse, liturgical mischief, pastoral presence, and chocolate chip cookies—that in a world where evil is obvious, God is with us and God is good.

Marilyn McCord Adams had a refrigerator, the front of which was completely covered with photographs of friends. In the midst of the smiling snapshots was the quote: "If God had a refrigerator, your picture would be on it." One of the central ways she claimed God was by proclaiming, in word and deed, God's love for all of us. Including you.

2

Claiming God after Auschwitz

SARAH K. PINNOCK

YALE UNIVERSITY HIRED MARILYN McCord Adams to replace George Lindbeck in my first year of the Religious Studies doctoral program. Although my area of specialization was continental philosophy of religion, and McCord Adams was an analytic philosopher, I eagerly signed up for her seminar on the problem of evil. I found myself enthusiastic about McCord Adams's objections to the theodicies advanced by Christian philosophers. I strongly agreed with her that the abstract and global approach to evil in philosophy of religion does not pay sufficient attention to the experiences of individuals who suffer, and it fails to address horrendous evils such as the Holocaust. Yet, I had some objections to the analytic approach to theodicy that included McCord Adams's own proposals. To me, it seemed that logical solutions were not sufficient to resolve the difficulties posed by horrendous evils and I found these theodicy solutions morally problematic in the face of severe suffering. As I read widely about theodicy for my dissertation, I gravitated toward the strong statements against theodicy in post-Holocaust writings, such as Richard Rubenstein, *After Auschwitz*, John Roth, "A Theodicy of Protest," and Emmanuel Levinas, "Useless Suffering." I decided to focus on responses to the Holocaust, which I saw as the most difficult theodicy challenges of our era. Given our shared sphere of interest, McCord Adams agreed to be my dissertation advisor, even though I engage with Jewish and Christian continental post-Holocaust thinkers. In the dissertation, I develop two types of practical responses to evil, existential (dialogue) and political (liberation), corresponding to individual and collective dimensions of suffering.[1] I consider the Holocaust as a benchmark for evaluating the adequacy of religious responses to evil which I see as consistent with McCord Adams's critique of abstract theodicy.

McCord Adams and I both finished major projects in 1999. I submitted my dissertation, and she published a volume that drew together decades of reflection entitled *Horrendous Evils and the Goodness of God*.[2] When her book appeared in print, I discovered that in her chapter "The Praxis of Evil" she offers a critique of practical responses similar to those in my dissertation, based on the writings of Holocaust and liberation theologians who object to theodicy. Despite our differences, I remain convinced that there is a practical side to McCord Adams's response which attends to making individual lives overwhelmingly good despite suffering. I also find points of contact between McCord Adams's position and Holocaust thought. Like McCord Adams, Holocaust thinkers agree that it is not satisfactory to claim that suffering is a test or lesson sent by God to deepen faith or punish sin.[3] Like Holocaust thinkers, McCord Adams's theodicy addresses a two-pronged crisis: doubts about God's goodness in allowing the Holocaust and doubts about God's ability to make each Holocaust victim's life good on the whole.[4] McCord Adams trains her gaze on the second part of the crisis by examining how God can repair the damage of suffering. In her view, a God who creates a world containing horrendous evils is exonerated if God can make each individual person's life overwhelmingly good as a whole—a plot resolution that ultimately requires a postmortem intervention. In this essay, I shall consider how to claim God after Auschwitz, bringing post-Holocaust theological responses by Jewish and Christian thinkers into dialogue with McCord Adams's ideas and direct references to the Holocaust in *Horrendous Evils*.

---

1. Pinnock, *Beyond Theodicy*.
2. McCord Adams, *Horrendous Evils*, ch. 9.
3. McCord Adams, *Horrendous Evils*, 26.
4. Scott, *Pathways in Theodicy*, 166.

1. CLAIMING GOD WITH PROTEST

It is a truism to remark that the Holocaust challenges faith in God. While philosophical theists typically concern themselves with how God's perfect attributes are compatible with evil, Holocaust thinkers focus on history: in particular, how genocide against the Jews can be reconciled with God's covenant in the Hebrew Bible. Scripture, rabbinic writings, and modern Jewish texts affirm the binding relation between God and the Jewish people. However, Jewish post-Holocaust authors struggle with the idea of claiming a God whose narrative of redemption permits mass death against the covenant people.

One key early Jewish response to the Holocaust is formulated by philosopher Martin Buber who fled Germany for Palestine in 1938. His seminal book published before the war, *I and Thou*, makes dialogue central to faith and this relational framework shapes his response to the Holocaust.[5] He addresses the Holocaust crisis of faith in a 1949 essay by means of reflection on the biblical book of Job. Buber praises Job for refusing to be comforted, since there is no justice accorded to the suffering of Holocaust victims. What Job longs for, according to Buber, is God's presence rather than any explanation. In the end, Job hears the voice of God which brings him to silent acceptance of affliction.[6] Buber develops his ideas further in *The Eclipse of God*, which expresses the crisis in Jewish life post-World War II. Although God seems absent, this eclipse or exile is not the final word. Buber expresses the anticipation that "after all security is shattered. . . . Through this dark gate . . . the believing man steps forth into the everyday which is henceforth hallowed as the place in which he has to live with the mystery."[7] After the Holocaust, God's absence and mercy remain paradoxical but, one day, people will once again resume I-Thou dialogue with God. Buber's response is practical in centering on dialogue that claims God in paradox and mysticism.

Yet Richard Rubenstein insists that it is not enough to wait for the God of Abraham to reappear after Auschwitz. He argues that one must interrogate who God is and abandon unacceptable concepts of deity. In a visit to Berlin in the 1960s, Rubenstein had a conversation with Protestant German clergyman Dean Gruber which cemented his conviction that biblical interpretations of God's role in history become offensive in view

---

5. Buber, *I and Thou*.
6. Buber, *The Prophetic Faith*, 234.
7. Buber, *The Eclipse of God*, 36.

of the Holocaust. Rubenstein rejects the notion of divine providence and justice. If God is guiding history, Rubenstein considers it unavoidable to conclude that Hitler was God's henchman. However, he does not give up on claiming God. He develops a mystical understanding of God indebted to Kabbalistic ideas and the philosophical theology of Protestant theologian Paul Tillich. In his view, God is the ground of being, an ontological reality, present, but transcendent.[8] In his later work, Rubenstein refers to God as Nothingness, having no substance or finitude, beyond human reasoning. In rejecting God's direct role in history, Rubenstein claims a mystical divine presence.

The struggle to claim God after the Holocaust also foregrounds John Roth's "Theology of Protest" where he offers an anti-theodicy. As a Protestant theologian, Roth is in close conversation with Jewish authors, such as Elie Wiesel, whose writings particularly shape his attention to the trial of God. In his fiction and nonfiction, Wiesel continually raises theological questions, not giving in to despair, neither exonerating nor denying God. Faith lies in questioning and never reconciling with horrendous evils. If God calls creation good in the book of Genesis, why then is history a slaughter-bench with so much waste? To claim God is to handle the tension between God's promises for redemption and evil on earth. Roth considers the words of Job pivotal: "Though he slay me, yet will I trust in him" (Job 13:15 KJV). Roth, with Wiesel, finds resistance in Job's final concession before God's majesty. There is continuity with the New Testament, Roth points out, where Jesus Christ is rejected, mocked, forsaken by God, and crucified. Roth warns Christians not to succumb to cheap triumphalism by claiming victory, and suggests reaffirming Jewish voices and struggles. Antitheodicy and protest combine with unknowing and hope in claiming God after Auschwitz.

2. HOLOCAUST VICTIMS

Horrendous Evils interests Holocaust scholars because of its emphasis on the most extreme cases of evil. Its prominence propelled John K. Roth to add a direct response to McCord Adams in the revision of his influential essay "A Theodicy of Protest" for the twentieth anniversary edition. On the one hand, Roth finds McCord Adams's objections to theodicy amenable. Nevertheless, he disagrees with her "optimism" that God can

---

8. Rubenstein, *After Auschwitz*, 141.

overcome the evils wrought on severely damaged lives. Roth remarks critically that McCord Adams intends to discuss the concrete reality of evil but she "scarcely mentions the Holocaust, let alone genocide."[9] McCord Adams insists that it is possible to transcend suffering for everyone, including Holocaust victims, and she uses the phrase "happy ending" to describe postmortem horror-defeat.[10] For Roth, the Holocaust is an example of massive destruction of lives and "this unjustifiable waste" cannot be wiped clean by divine resourcefulness, no matter what overwhelming good occurs later on. While McCord Adams claims God's goodness to all, Holocaust thinkers like Roth claim God by means of protest rather than falsify the past with "utopian illusions."[11] In my view, Roth is incorrect in faulting McCord Adams for bypassing the Holocaust. A close reading of her work reveals frequent mentions of the Holocaust, which I shall consider as a point of contact for Jewish Christian dialogue.

In the pivotal early sections of *Horrendous Evils* where McCord Adams defines the scope of her investigation, the Holocaust is mentioned repeatedly. While chastising analytic philosophers for their abstract approaches to evil, McCord Adams mentions "the horrors of Auschwitz" as an example of a concrete evil that theodicy must certainly address.[12] In her critique of American philosopher Alvin Plantinga's free will defense, the various intractable examples of evil she considers are: "lingering death by leukemia or cancer of young children or their mothers, the ironic evil of a father accidentally running over his beloved child, and the demonic evils of the death camps where a mother is forced to choose which of her children will live"—these are situations where "we cannot even conceive of any plausible candidate reasons" why God permits these evils.[13] This latter example refers to the dilemma posed in the well-known novel and film, *Sophie's Choice*, where novelist William Styron tells the story of a Polish Christian survivor of Auschwitz living a tortured and eventually self-destructive existence in the United States, a role for which Meryl Streep won an Academy Award for best actress. *Sophie's Choice* is a paradigm example of what Lawrence Langer calls "choiceless choice" where there is no good alternative: either the mother chooses one child

---

9. Roth, "A Theodicy of Protest," 2.
10. McCord Adams, *Christ and Horrors*, 48.
11. Roth, "A Theodicy of Protest," 12.
12. McCord Adams, *Horrendous Evils*, 14.
13. McCord Adams, *Horrendous Evils*, 25.

to live, or she refuses the decision and both children die.[14] In interviews, Styron has remarked that his choice to portray a Christian Holocaust victim in the novel reflects that not only Jews were victims and that Christianity should not bear guilt for the genocide.[15] In using this reference to Sophie's plight alongside other examples in *Horrendous Evils*, McCord Adams does not consider the social identification of the victims of evils, such as whether they are Jewish or Christian, or a member of a persecuted minority. All horrendous evils perpetrated require God to heal the individual victim.

Further along in the chapter, McCord Adams mentions the Holocaust when she defines horrendous evils as situations where a person's life may be irreparably damaged such that the victim is unable to consider his/her life as good on the whole. As an example, she comments that the Nazi death camps "aimed not merely to kill but to dehumanize their victims ... to break down their personalities and reduce their social instincts to raw animal aggression and self-preservation."[16] The camps destroyed the victims' value as persons and made victims unable to find goodness in their lives. Similar to Sophie's choice, McCord Adams presents evils as situations that can happen to anyone, irrespective of identity. However, since the social and political causes of evils are not raised, neither are means of protest or resistance. Treating the identity of victims without social context, from a Holocaust perspective, bypasses an opportunity to reflect on prejudices that cause genocide, such as Christian anti-Judaism. It may also seem to dismiss this-worldly restitution in offering a post-mortem theological solution of recompense to victims.

3. HOLOCAUST PERPETRATORS

Although primarily focused on those who suffer, McCord Adams also considers the impact that evildoing has on perpetrators. Although perpetrators are pictured as hardened criminals, they also bring negative consequences of evil upon themselves. Using the Holocaust as an example, McCord Adams points out that the dehumanization of victims caused

14. Langer, "The Dilemma of Choice," 222–32.

15. William Styron's novel *Sophie's Choice* was the basis for the film *Sophie's Choice*, directed by Alan J. Pakula. Styron is criticized for removing the Holocaust from the context of Jewish and Christian history and universalizing it in Rosenfeld, "The Holocaust according to William Styron."

16. McCord Adams, *Horrendous Evils*, 27.

even more suffering than simply killing them; it made them broken and traumatized. Nevertheless, it also damaged the lives of the Nazi commanders, administrators, and guards in charge of the camps. Referring to Auschwitz, McCord Adams remarks that, "Organizing and running such institutions also degraded the Nazis, who caricatured human nature by using their finest powers the more imaginatively to transgress the bounds of human decency."[17] She speculates on the internal damage wrought by the guilt of their actions and the public damage of their shame and rejection by society after the war.

Not only do perpetrators suffer from committing evils, they may not foresee the results of their actions. In the same passage, McCord Adams mentions the scientists who created the atomic bomb and Hitler as examples of how suffering of great magnitude can be engineered by a small number of evildoers. Her point is that the capacity to produce evil can far exceed the perpetrator's comprehension.[18] When reflecting on the fall of humanity into sin in the book of *Genesis*, it becomes clear that Adam and Eve are not fully responsible for the effects which trigger evil of gigantic proportions in history. Analogously, McCord Adams points out that Hitler had only a "generic grasp of genocide," but he could not have conceived the magnitude of that horror experienced by victims.[19] Perpetrators of evil are not necessarily in control of the evils they release. By accentuating the weakness of humans and the metaphysical size gap between God and humanity, perpetrators seem more like hapless agents rather than sinister plotters. Since God made human beings fallible, free will can explain sin but does not exonerate God. Given human entrapment in sin, a loving God would not condemn any of his creatures to hell or eternal punishment, not even a perpetrator of genocide. McCord Adams remarks that "putting Hitler in a medieval hell of eternal torture would only guarantee the defeat of good by evil in his life."[20] Even for Holocaust perpetrators, God's victory over evil involves making each person's life a great good with no exceptions. The goodness of God includes perpetrators as well as victims.

Horrendous Evils contains frequent mention of the Holocaust together with examples of individual and collective suffering. Without

---

17. McCord Adams, *Horrendous Evils*, 27.
18. McCord Adams, *Horrendous Evils*, 36.
19. McCord Adams, *Horrendous Evils*, 38.
20. McCord Adams, *Horrendous Evils*, 43.

specific consideration of the social dimensions of evil, the Holocaust becomes one amongst many horrendous evils, despite the fact that genocide involves ethnic prejudices and mass violence that are historical and preventable. McCord Adams casts a wide net for horrendous evils. Her use of Holocaust examples shows how her approach seems abstract, not in rising above the level of the individual, but in taking horrendous evils as a general category, a criticism she levies against other analytic philosophers.[21] For Holocaust scholars, McCord Adams's inclusion of Hitler as someone potentially unaware of the results of his actions might seem almost an excuse or an evasion of responsibility.

Hitler is mentioned again in *Horrendous Evils*, Part II, where McCord Adams makes her constructive proposal for how God makes individuals lives overwhelmingly good despite horrendous evils. She proposes three conceptual enrichments that offer models for how God might accomplish this overwhelming goodness: purity and defilement, honor and shame, and aesthetics. These three proposals are presented as distinct and separable, which gives McCord Adams's response to evil a heuristic quality. It seems that she is most interested in the aesthetic model dealing with mysticism and develops it further in her subsequent book *Christ and Horrors: The Coherence of Christology*.[22] In examining aesthetic approaches to evil, she distinguishes between internal (victim) and external (perpetrator) points of view to observe that aesthetic valuation is not necessarily moral. From a perpetrator perspective, she remarks that "Hitler may have seen positive value in the lives of his soldiers who expended their energies and died as cogs in the war machines of *der Führer's* mythological designs" but for those under Hitler's command, some perpetrators surely "felt their lives contaminated beyond cleansing by their participation in the Holocaust."[23] In the aesthetic valuations of perpetrators, mass death would accomplish important goals in wartime but some of them would later regret the evils undertaken. McCord Adams makes the point about aesthetic valuation a different way, commenting that the Union Jack or Nazi swastika might symbolize either danger or security depending on one's point of view.[24] Applied to God's redemptive agency, she argues that

21. The list of examples in ch. 1 includes rape and dismemberment, betrayal, child abuse, child pornography, parental incest, starvation, and nuclear bomb casualties. McCord Adams, *Horrendous Evils*, 26.

22. See n10 above.

23. McCord Adams, *Horrendous Evils*, 145.

24. McCord Adams, *Horrendous Evils*, 150.

God can make good on horrors only if God's external point of view is accompanied by the individual's internal point of view joined together to make the individual recognize overarching patterns and values. In the end, these threads combine to make a tapestry that is overwhelmingly good to the sufferer overall.[25] Aesthetic contemplation of divine beauty and the beauties of creation are overriding features of life's positive value and allow genocide victims and perpetrators to claim God's mercy.

McCord Adams accentuates the need for individuals to seek positive meaning but recognizes that some persons are too decimated to recover after the damage wrought by horrendous evils. The Holocaust is a prominent example of how individual efforts to find meaning in atrocity may not be possible due to psychological damage or premature death. She remarks that "the Nazi death camps show how, in our world, horrors are not selective, visiting only the morally prepared."[26] It is possible to find God in horrendous evils but not for everyone. For instance, the examples of medieval mystics show how human suffering can become participation in Christ's suffering. Therefore, God must participate in the process of meaning-making to ensure than each life is a positive good as appreciated by the individual.[27] McCord Adams rejects what she sees as the elitism of some mystics and ancient Stoic philosophers, for whom overcoming suffering relies on spiritual elevation and strength of character. Recognition of the brokenness or helplessness of victims leads McCord Adams to insist on the necessity of a postmortem experience to claim God.

4. JEWISH-CHRISTIAN DIALOGUE

Given the importance of Jewish responses in post-Holocaust thought, it is significant to note that McCord Adams leaves an opening for possible connections between her constructive proposals and Jewish ideas of God and evil. She makes the provocative claim that the three conceptual enrichments, based on value categories of purity, honor, and aesthetics, are not "exclusively Christian" and that "versions of each would constitute satisfactory responses within Judaism as well."[28] It seems such elaboration

---

25. McCord Adams, *Horrendous Evils*, 146.
26. McCord Adams, *Horrendous Evils*, 158.
27. McCord Adams, *Horrendous Evils*, 149.
28. McCord Adams, *Horrendous Evils*, 164.

would involve fitting Jewish understandings of God into her framework. Her first proposal based on definitions of purity and defilement draws on ideas of sin and holiness in the Hebrew Bible. Secondly, her discussion of shame and honor considers the narrative of the Exodus from Egypt as an "exquisite" example of the honor code where God, alongside Moses and Aaron, challenges Pharaoh's power and reputation.[29] Thirdly, in discussing aesthetic value, she mentions Mount Sinai where God's glory descended on Moses so intensely that Moses's face shone when he descended the mountain and he had to cover it with a veil.[30] The Hebrew Bible is an importance source for McCord Adams's reflection on how to claim God amidst horrendous suffering.

The bridges she builds with Jewish writings, however, remain incomplete given her approach to theism. McCord Adams dismisses the standard monotheism of Abrahamic religions as too minimalist to suffice for reconciling God and evil. Rather, her proposal mines the conceptual resources of Christian theology to understand how God transmutes evil into a greater good. As a counterpart to her project, a Jewish author could arguably build on her framework drawing variously on Jewish biblical interpretation, rabbinic writings, philosophers Philo or Maimonides, Hasidic masters, or the mystical Kabbalah. However, there is not one agreed upon understanding of afterlife in the Jewish tradition. The early books of the Hebrew Bible do not develop the notion of heaven as an afterlife for souls, an idea which gradually emerged under the influence of Platonic philosophy in the Hellenistic period. In response to death, the Pentateuch and the prophets appeal to the endurance of the people of Israel as overcoming death.

With a variety of notions of afterlife in contemporary Judaism, and the emphasis on the collective rather than individual postmortem survival, McCord Adams's ideas appear without Jewish equivalent, and are bound to Christian tradition. Between *Horrendous Evils* and *Christ and Horrors*, Adams makes a significant shift. In part, this refocusing arises from dissatisfaction with treatments of theodicy in analytic philosophy. She finds concepts of God's attributes too sparse when honed according to the logic of perfection. In *Christ and Horrors*, she expands her reliance on confessional doctrine in the service of Christian philosophy. In so doing, she does not intend to be narrow or parochial or exclusive. McCord

---

29. McCord Adams, *Horrendous Evils*, 114.
30. McCord Adams, *Horrendous Evils*, 136.

Adams remarks that she is "not out to prove that Christianity is superior to other religions" but rather to offer a "robust Christology as a viable competitor in the marketplace of religious and theological worldviews."[31] While purity, honor, and aesthetics, might be concepts potentially used in other religious frameworks to respond to evil, it seems that such proposals are not satisfying to McCord Adams for claiming God's goodness.

In post-Holocaust Jewish-Christian dialogue, Christology undergoes examination. In particular, interest turns to salvation and the understanding of the Abrahamic covenant between God and the Hebrews. Christianity has a history of denigrating the Jews for rejecting Jesus and adhering to the commandments of God's covenant with the people of Israel. Holocaust thinkers object to Christian claims to superiority and offer critiques of Christian supersessionism with its view that the covenant in the Hebrew Bible has been surpassed. Theological denigration of the Jewish covenant contributes to European anti-Semitism leading to the Holocaust. The superiority denoted by the symbol of the cross, carried by missionaries and colonial settlers, also indicates triumphalist attitudes. The cross represents the power of Christian institutions, empires, and nations. It is not a symbol of God's mercy for Jews subject to ghettoes, expulsion, and pogroms. In responding to evil, the cross seems to propose divine meanings for the suffering of others.

In contrast, Holocaust thinkers take the arbitrariness of suffering seriously. For Jewish victims, it was frequently chance or luck that allowed them to escape or survive, while others were exterminated. In his essay "Useless Suffering," Jewish philosopher Emmanuel Levinas argues that pain, suffering and horrendous evils, should be viewed as useless. It is immoral to impose religious reasons, explanations, or meanings. Referring obliquely to the Holocaust, Levinas states, "For an ethical sensibility—confirming itself, in the inhumanity of our time, against this inhumanity—the justification of the neighbor's pain is certainly the source of all immorality"[32] He rebukes religious attempts to make suffering "which is essentially gratuitous or absurd, and apparently arbitrary" seem bearable or make God seem innocent.[33] Such views might make bystanders feel better, according to Levinas. They perhaps reduce the horrors of suffering,

---

31. McCord Adams, *Christ and Horrors*, 13. Although restricted standard theism offers more common ground with Jewish thought by defining God simply as all-powerful and all-good, McCord Adams finds such theism too minimalistic.

32. Levinas, "Useless Suffering," 163.

33. Levinas, "Useless Suffering," 161.

while also softening the moral impetus to protest and resist. Like Levinas, McCord Adams distances herself from theodicy because it blames the victim or makes God seem cruel. Moreover, no one knows God's reasoning except tentatively and partially.[34] Rather than see suffering as useless, she offers a hypothesis about how God redeems horrors. Still, it seems that McCord Adams has offered a justifying reason for suffering, namely, that it is acceptable because God will make it good post-mortem.

5. HOLOCAUST LITERATURE

McCord Adams engages with the writings of Holocaust survivors in *Horrendous Evils* to consider the relevance of her conceptual enrichments. In the final chapter, "The Praxis of Evil," she addresses existential, liberation, and post-Holocaust objections to theodicy. She assures her readers that she endorses practical measures to prevent or remedy evil, alongside God's assistance to victims. When McCord Adams enters into dialogue with Jewish Holocaust literature, it is clear that she does not intend to appear facile in her assurances that God defeats all horrors. Yet Holocaust literature illustrates how it may be impossible to repair the life of a person shattered by torture and dehumanization. McCord Adams refers to the novels of Israeli writer Aharon Appelfeld portraying the lives of survivors. She observes how effective Appelfeld is in conveying the irreparable horrendous suffering of many Jewish victims. Born in Romania, Appelfeld survived the Holocaust as a child separated from his parents and moved to Israel, thinking both parents had perished. Not until 1960 did his father find him. Appelfeld's novels, such as *The Immortal Bartfuss* and *For Every Sin*, offer plentiful examples, as McCord Adams puts it, that "liberating the concentration camp prisoners and resettling them in Jerusalem or New York City were certainly necessary but scarcely sufficient to restore psychic wasteland to fertile garden."[35] In such cases, she points out that praxis may be ineffective regarding evils caused by events long past. She also insists, appealing to Holocaust literature, that questions about meaning will arise, perhaps not always during suffering, sometimes much delayed, but eventually. It is then the victim will wonder why God allowed it or how life can have positive meaning afterwards. Even if victims do not give suffering meaning, McCord Adams does not

---

34. McCord Adams, *Horrendous Evils*, 55.
35. McCord Adams, *Horrendous Evils*, 187.

conclude that suffering is meaningless or useless, but as evidence that a postmortem process is necessary to claim a good God.

McCord Adams considers the writings of Elie Wiesel more extensively. She quotes various examples of evil in Wiesel's memoir *Night* encompassing a range of incidents including the degradation of camp inmates and the murder of a fellow prisoner for a scrap of bread. As a counterpoint to horrors, McCord Adams also points out passages in *Night* that depict moments of self-transcendence, such as Yom Kippur prayers and fasting in the camps, or how a Jewish prisoner played a fragment of a Beethoven violin concerto the night he died on the evacuation march from Auschwitz to Buchenwald.[36] She finds these episodes support the potential for meaning making and the need to discover God in all situations.

As a caveat, McCord Adams acknowledges that Wiesel does not see self-transcendence as making a prisoner's life good on the whole or overcoming the horrors of the camp by an act of the will. Wiesel is not optimistic in the manner of survivor Viktor Frankl who planned out a book manuscript about logotherapy in his mind to distract himself from suffering and remain optimistic in Auschwitz.[37] However, her insistence that there can be meaning despite horrendous evils does not seem to reconcile with the pained and unhopeful testimonies in such memoirs. In *Night*, Wiesel portrays a bleak ending where Eliezer looks at his face in the mirror and sees a corpse. The death of Wiesel's little sister and his mother in the gas chambers upon arrival at Auschwitz has no positive religious aspect.[38] The hanging of two adults and one child, in a central chapter in *Night*, is followed by a dialogue implying that God is dead and the remark that the soup tasted like corpses. Where one prisoner remarks apparently cynically that God is hanging on the gallows, some theologians have interpreted this image as symbolic of the crucifixion that displays God's presence. I agree with John Roth who observes that McCord Adams seems to impose redemption onto Holocaust situations.[39]

Referring to *The Town beyond the Wall* by Elie Wiesel, McCord Adams makes a statement about the universality of evil after the Holocaust. The setting is very loosely autobiographical in that it is about a

---

36. McCord Adams, *Horrendous Evils*, 183.

37. Frankl, *Man's Search for Meaning*, 46.

38. Wiesel, *Night*, 115. For a critique of her hopeful attitude toward the Kingdom of Night, see Roth, "Theodicy of Protest," 3.

39. Surin, *Theology and the Problem of Evil*, 116.

Hungarian Jewish concentration camp survivor living in Paris after the liberation of Auschwitz. In this novel, the protagonist Michael decides to travel back to his village, which lies in communist Eastern Europe. As Michael revisits familiar places, he sees the face of a spectator at a window overlooking the town square where the Nazis had forced the Jews to gather. He recognizes the face as the same man who watched the Jews rounded up for deportation to Auschwitz. This Christian spectator sums up the enigma of the bystander for Wiesel, a person who sided with perpetrators in indifference. Boldly, Michael confronts him hoping for him to express some emotion. But the man only stammers that he did nothing, and calls the secret police to arrest him. Looking back on what happened, Michael reflects to himself: "Deep down, I thought, man is not only an executioner, not only a victim, not only a spectator: he is all three at once."[40] This memorable quotation can be interpreted as an existential statement reflecting Michael's inner state. It can also be taken historically in situations where distinctions between perpetrators and victims might become blurred, such as where the Nazis gave certain Jews official roles.

But within the authority structure of the camps, where the separation of guards and prisoners was definitive, there was no equivalence between Jews and non-Jews.[41] As interpreted by McCord Adams, this statement universalizes the Holocaust and blurs the moral status of perpetrators and victims. It is striking that Michael's journey back to his home village in Hungary, which seems like an imagined return for Wiesel to his hometown, does not lead to identification with the spectator at the window. McCord Adams does not include this part of the narrative where Michael suddenly discovers that the purpose of his journey back to his village was to protest and accuse the spectator. Michael shouts angrily at him: "The dead Jews, the women gone mad, the mute children—I'm their messenger. And I tell you they haven't forgotten you. Someday they'll come marching, trampling you, spitting in your face. And at their shouts of contempt you'll pray God to deafen you."[42] McCord Adams does not pay attention to this incident of retaliation in the novel or issues of justice. She locates perpetrators alongside the victims, all of whom, including Hitler, need divine resourcefulness to overcome evil. Consideration of narratives by Wiesel and Appelfeld attests to McCord Adams's concern for reflection on the Holocaust.

40. Wiesel, *The Town beyond the Wall*, 163; McCord Adams, *Horrendous Evils*, 200.
41. Surin, *Theology and the Problem of Evil*, 120.
42. Wiesel, *The Town beyond the Wall*, 162.

6. CLAIMING GOD AFTER THE HOLOCAUST

Jewish and Christian responses open up productive avenues of conversation about McCord Adams's response to horrendous evils. Attention to the voices of victims is one example. McCord Adams pays close attention to victims and how God shows love for them, but Holocaust thinkers are cautious about understanding God in ways that silence victims by imposing extrinsic meanings. McCord Adams objects to such warnings. She objects to Rabbi Irving Greenberg's rule that "After the Holocaust, no statement, theological or otherwise, should be made that is not credible in the presence of the burning children."[43] Similarly she disagrees with Johann Baptist Metz who claims that "Faced with Auschwitz, I consider as blasphemy every Christian theodicy . . . and all language about meaning when these are initiated outside this catastrophe or on some level above it."[44] These statements seem to shut down philosophical discussion. She remarks that there are always some philosophical statements about evil that "would be inappropriate to voice in the presence of burning children because participants in horrors are not always in the presence of burning children."[45] McCord Adams seems to take this point spatially to advocate separating academic and pastoral activities. However, Holocaust remembrance brings up the presence of burning children here and now. Moreover, the trauma of horrendous evils transmits to subsequent generations.[46] There seems to be a misunderstanding since Holocaust thinkers do not forbid theological statements or responses to victims who ask questions. But they recommend modest, situated claims taking into account the varieties of situations and reactions. Given the unrepresentable quality of the Holocaust, religious responses must recognize the poverty of conceptual resources. To respect this incommensurability points towards a mystical approach to claiming God.

Protest against God and evil continually appears in Holocaust reflection. While *Horrendous Evils* focuses on God's goodness to victims, McCord Adams's position on God's metaphysical grandeur leaves room for protest. Her ideas converge in notable ways with those of Jewish philosopher Martin Buber. In *The Eclipse of God*, Buber develops the idea of God's hiddenness to express divine absence after the Holocaust. He

---

43. Greenberg, "Cloud of Smoke," 9.
44. Metz, *The Emergent Church*, 19.
45. McCord Adams, *Horrendous Evils*, 188.
46. Leys, *Trauma*, 3.

considers two valid and complementary moments of faith: affirmation of God's goodness and experience of God's silence.[47] McCord Adams moves toward a similar insight in an essay she wrote for a conference in Israel, "In Praise of Blasphemy," centered on the book of Job. She considers how Job is militantly opposed to the neat plot resolutions regarding suffering proposed by his friends. Theodicy explanations are rejected. Echoing the language of Buber, McCord Adams expresses the view that for Job "suffering is unremitting; the eclipse, silence of God apparently permanent."[48] She praises Job's act of protest against suffering as elevating and a form of self-transcendence. It leads Job to overcome the eclipse and hear God's voice at last. McCord Adams connects Job's apparent blasphemy that leads to mystical encounter with the words of divine blasphemy spoken by Jesus Christ on the cross that bears witness to Job's horrors, "why hast thou forsaken me" (Matt. 27:46 KJV). Paradoxically, God is redeemer and blasphemer. It would seem that McCord Adams could enter into dialogue with Holocaust responses about shifting perceptions of God in the mystery of divine eclipse.

Another issue is who speaks. How can Christians, associated as a group with perpetrators, address Jewish victims' suffering? Referring to the gallows scene in Wiesel's *Night*, Johann Baptist Metz argues that only a Jew imprisoned in the camps facing terror and death "can speak of a God 'on the gallows,' not we Christians who sent the Jew into such a situation of despair or at least left him in it."[49] Metz objects to theological claims that Christ's suffering on the cross is comparable to the suffering of Holocaust victims, who were tortured and psychologically broken, leading to nothing but shame, torture, and dehumanization.[50] Nor is the Holocaust suffering of Christians comparable to Jews as a group destined for extermination under National Socialism. Christian responses should include self-awareness of privilege and its historical legacy. In examining theodicy, Jeannine Hill Fletcher draws parallels between anti-Semitism during the Holocaust and white supremacy in the United States connected with slavery and the extermination of indigenous peoples. Prejudice may be embedded in Christian responses to others' suffering,

---

47. See n7 above.
48. McCord Adams, "In Praise of Blasphemy," 46.
49. Metz, "Facing the Jews," 29.
50. Metz, "Theology as Theodicy?," 70.

and function to assuage guilt for evils committed under Christian dominance.[51] Holocaust theologians have examined Christian doctrines that propagate exclusion towards Jews, as well as supersession and supremacy. In situations where Christians are identified with perpetrators, it may be that resisting the suffering of others is an important way to claim God. Ultimately, Christians must do the difficult work of reflecting on associations with perpetrators, collaborators, and bystanders before claiming God on behalf of victims.

Protest and mysticism are promising spaces for McCord Adams to enter in dialogue with Holocaust thinkers. Both suffering and resistance to suffering can be understood mystically. Dorothee Soelle follows Buber in emphasis on alternating states of religious experience. She also examines Christian identity, prejudice, and responsibility for evil.[52] Speaking from her subject position as a German Protestant, Soelle considers how resistance can be mystical and include prayer, letting go of the self, and the discovery of an aesthetic dimension that includes joy.[53] Like McCord Adams, she understands suffering as a place where God may be found intimately. Soelle insists, borrowing from medieval Saint Teresa of Avila, that God has no other hands than ours.[54] Mysticism offers a meeting point between Jewish and Christian thought, between eclipse and affirmation in claiming God. Pointing toward mysticism in response to horrendous evils, it seems fitting to give the last word to McCord Adams, citing Saint Anselm:

> The mystery of divine goodness is permanently inexhaustible by us and permanently partially inaccessible by us; exploring it will keep us fascinated for eternity.[55]

---

51. Fletcher, *The Sin of White Supremacy*, 105.
52. Soelle, *Suffering*.
53. Soelle, *The Silent Cry*, 181.
54. Soelle, *The Silent Cry*, 275.
55. McCord Adams, *Horrendous Evils*, 54.

3

Gratuitous Evil and Anselm

Michael Barnwell

I DECIDED TO SPECIALIZE in medieval philosophy after I heard Marilyn McCord Adams explain St. Anselm's argument that God must be the "Highest Good" while enrolled in her "Christian Doctrine 451–1650" course at Yale Divinity School. My decision that day was undoubtedly caused by Marilyn's unique, infectious love for Anselm—an intense love that inspired her to publish numerous articles about Anselm's work which she eventually planned to collate into a book.[1] I believe her affection for Anselm was largely due to the Anselmian claim of God as the "Highest Good." This claim undergirded McCord Adams's approach to theology and philosophy in general and to horrendous evils in particular.

As alluded to in the previous chapter, horrendous evils are those evils that are so extreme they call into question the overall goodness of life for those suffering them. It was the Anselmian claim of God as the "Highest Good" that motivated McCord Adams to reject traditional theodicies that paid scant attention to lived experience of individuals suffering horrendous evils. An Anselmian God would not simply "balance out" goodness on a global scale (which is the approach most theodicies take). Instead, McCord Adams understood that an Anselmian God would "defeat" horrendous evils for those individuals suffering them.

1. For a list of McCord Adams's publications, see the bibliography.

Lives that are good on the whole to all individuals—even those suffering horrendous evils—are the only sort of lives worthy of an Anselmian, "Highest Good" God.

Given Anselm's key role in McCord Adams's claim of God against horrendous evils, it is not surprising to find that Anselm's insights shed new light on a closely related issue within the realm of the problem of evil: the debate over the existence of gratuitous evils. This debate takes place within the larger context of the "evidential problem of evil." I will begin by offering a brief explanation of the evidential problem of evil. This will allow me to turn to the debate between two prominent philosophers (Klaas Kraay and William Hasker) over the existence of gratuitous evils.[2] As will become obvious, the debate is at a standstill largely due to differing intuitions over whether God would intentionally keep humans ignorant of certain of God's actions. I will then argue that a wholly different aspect of Anselm's philosophy that McCord Adams particularly loved—his discussion of the fall of the devil—can help break the deadlock. In particular, Anselm's insights regarding the devil's fall support the claim that God can intentionally keep humans ignorant of certain of God's actions. This will indirectly support the claim that there are no gratuitous evils. More importantly, the discussion of Anselm and gratuitous evils will provide hope that God will defeat horrendous evils despite our ignorance over why horrendous evils exist.[3]

1. THE EVIDENTIAL PROBLEM OF EVIL AND GRATUITOUS EVILS

The evidential problem of evil is an argument against the existence of an all-good, omnipotent God. It proceeds as follows:[4] First, if God is all-good and all-powerful, then God would only permit evil that was *absolutely necessary* to prevent a greater evil or to achieve a greater good. In other words, God would only permit an instance of evil when it is the *only way*

---

2. The debate under discussion can be found in the following two works: Kraay, "Theism"; Hasker, "God and Gratuitous Evil."

3. As chance would have it, the last time I saw Marilyn was at a conference where Klaas Kraay was objecting to Hasker's argument.

4. Perhaps the most famous version of the evidential problem is William L. Rowe's presentation in his "Problem of Evil." It should be noted that the "evidential" problem differs from the "logical" problem, the latter of which most consider to have been solved. Space prevents me from elaborating on the distinctions.

to achieve the best world.[5] To permit evil when there is an alternate way to achieve a greater good or prevent a greater evil would, by definition, not be "all-good." Any evil that is not absolutely necessary to achieve a greater good or prevent a greater evil would be considered "gratuitous." The "evidential problem of evil" continues by claiming there is good evidence (thus the name) that gratuitous evil exists. The significant amount and severity of evil in this world does not seem absolutely required for God to achieve the best possible world.

For an example of a gratuitous evil, consider the case of a young person who was accidentally buried alive in an unmarked grave in my hometown during the colonial period. In a later period, gravediggers found that grave, exhumed the casket and discovered that the deceased woman's hair had been pulled out. What had happened? It turns out that she had regained consciousness after having been buried alive and in those terrifying, panicked moments tore out her hair before passing away.

For discussion's sake, let us set aside whether it was absolutely required for a greater good that this young lady die in the first place. Instead, let us focus on those horrible moments when she had regained consciousness in the buried coffin. The pain and fear she suffered during those moments must have been unspeakable. More importantly, it is difficult to see how that suffering was absolutely necessary for some greater good or the prevention of some greater evil. It certainly did not lead to her being rescued. The horrible evil she suffered in those moments seems to have led to nothing except conscious, unbearable pain. Similar to McCord Adams's diagnosis of horrendous evils, it is difficult to even think of a plausible candidate reason why a good God would have needed to let her regain consciousness so as to achieve a greater good or prevent a greater evil. Such suffering seems completely gratuitous and would be exactly the sort of evil a good God would prevent. The existence of such gratuitous evil provides strong evidence against the existence of an all-good, omnipotent God.

---

5. An example of this type of reasoning may be found in the "Free Will Theodicy." In general, the Free Will Theodicy holds that the best world requires free will. Free will, in turn, leads to the possibility (and, as it turned out, the actuality) of misusing one's will and creating evil. Thus, permitting the evil that arises from free will is necessary to achieve the greater good of the best world.

2. TWO RESPONSES: SKEPTICAL THEISM AND NECESSITY OF GRATUITOUS EVIL DEFENSE

There are two ways theists respond to the evidential problem of evil. The first goes by the name "skeptical theism," a view advocated by prominent philosophers such as Ryerson University professor Klaas Kraay. Kraay and skeptical theists point out that it has never been *proven* that any one particular evil is indeed gratuitous.[6] Some evils may *seem* gratuitous because it is difficult to imagine how they would be necessary to achieve greater goods or prevent greater evils. The inability to imagine how they could be necessary, however, does not mean that these evils are not absolutely necessary to achieve a greater good or prevent a greater evil. Skeptical theists emphasize the limitations of the human mind compared to the divine (thus the name "skeptical"). Given the finitude of human understanding, it is reasonable to think there is some necessity for these evils that we just cannot fathom. God's infinite intelligence, on the other hand, understands all the cosmic connections that make these evils absolutely necessary.

A second way to respond to the evidential problem is championed by prominent philosopher of religion William Hasker, Professor Emeritus at Huntington University. In contrast to skeptical theism, Hasker claims gratuitous evils not only exist but that they are necessary given a belief in God. His position is called the "necessity-of-gratuitous-evil defense" (hereafter, "NGE defense").

To explain Hasker's NGE Defense, consider the following formulation of the evidential argument from evil:

1. If God exists, no gratuitous evil occurs.

2. Gratuitous evil occurs

   Therefore,

3. God does not exist.[7]

As mentioned above, Hasker's NGE Defense denies (1) and claims God would permit gratuitous evils.[8] But why would an all-good God possibly

---

6. Advocates of the evidential problem readily concede there is no proof. Indeed, the name "evidential" comes from their claim that they seem to have "evidence," but not proof, that there are gratuitous evils.

7. This is a formulation of the argument offered in Kraay, "Theism," 32–33.

8. Skeptical theists, by contrast, accept (1) but deny (2).

permit such evils that have no necessity for achieving a greater good or preventing a greater evil? Hasker's answer in the NGE Defense is largely based on the claim that if God did indeed prevent all gratuitous evils, humans would know that God prevents all gratuitous evils. Since this is the key claim for this chapter, let's formalize it as Hasker's Thesis (hereafter, "HT").

> Hasker's Thesis (HT): "If God were to prevent gratuitous evil, [humans] would come to know" that God prevented gratuitous evil.[9]

Hasker then proceeds to assert that it would be a negative state of affairs if humans knew that God prevented gratuitous evils. As a result, Hasker argues that God does *not* prevent gratuitous evils.

One may reasonably wonder why would it be a negative state of affairs if humans knew God prevented gratuitous evils. Hasker answers that humans would, in that case, lose two important motivations: the motivations (i) to act morally and (ii) to respond to/prepare for natural evil. For example, if one knew that God would never permit a gratuitous evil, then she need not worry about acting morally. She could rest confident that whether she acted morally or immorally, God would prevent the result of that action from making the world any worse overall: "After all, why refrain from . . . moral evil when you are confident God will ensure that any moral evil that occurs is non-gratuitous."[10] Likewise, humans need not worry about working together and increasing their knowledge so as to prevent natural disasters if they were confident that any actually occurring natural evil is non-gratuitous and thereby does not detract from the overall goodness of the world.[11] Since (according to Hasker) maintaining the motivations to be moral and to prevent natural disasters are of utmost importance and these motivations would be undermined if we knew God prevented gratuitous evils, God cannot let us know God prevents gratuitous evils. But given Hasker's Thesis ("HT"), we *would know* God prevents gratuitous evils if indeed God did. To preserve the moral and natural-disaster-prevention motivations, therefore, God must not prevent gratuitous evils.

Even if Hasker is correct that knowledge of God's prevention of gratuitous evils would undermine these motivations, one may reasonably wonder why HT—the claim that if God prevented gratuitous evils,

---

9. Kraay, "Theism," 36.
10. Kraay, "Theism," 37.
11. Cf. Hasker, "Necessity of Gratuitous Evil," 38–39.

humans would know that God did so—is true in the first place. Why would God not simply keep humans ignorant about the prevention of gratuitous evils so as to preserve these moral and disaster-preventing motivations Hasker believes are essential?

Hasker gives two reasons to believe HT is true and that God could not keep humans ignorant of the fact that God prevents gratuitous evils. The first is based on a view of God's purpose for humans. Hasker asserts that "clearly it is an important part of God's creative purposes that his rational creatures should come to know what God is like. And, by hypothesis, he cannot achieve this purpose without our also coming to know that he prevents all gratuitous evil."[12] In other words, God wants us to know what God is like. And for Hasker, that means we must know that God prevents gratuitous evils (if indeed God were to prevent gratuitous evils).

Hasker's second reason for accepting HT rests on the assumption that if God did prevent gratuitous evils but somehow kept humans from knowing this, God would be acting immorally by deceiving us: "This concealment would amount to a pervasive policy of deception on God's part, which in itself is morally objectionable."[13]

Hasker has hereby offered two rationales for his claim in HT that if God were to prevent gratuitous evils, humans would know that fact. They can be formalized as follows:

> $HT_{rationale1}$: It is part of God's purpose for humans to know God's nature. Knowing God's nature includes knowing whether God prevents gratuitous evils.

> $HT_{rationale2}$: God would be acting immorally if God deceived humans. If God prevented gratuitous evils but led us into thinking God did not, this would be immoral deception by God.

3. KRAAY'S OBJECTIONS TO HASKER'S NGE DEFENSE

There are many ways to object to Hasker's NGE defense. For example, one might claim that maintaining these motivations is not worth the occurrence of gratuitous evils. Maybe the world would be better off without gratuitous evils even if that meant there were no true motivations to be

---

12. Hasker, "O'Connor on Gratuitous Natural Evil," 391. For the location of both these reasons, I am relying on Kraay, "Theism," 36.

13. Hasker, "Necessity of Gratuitous Evil," 37.

moral or prevent natural disasters. Alternatively, one may wonder whether Hasker's argument undermines itself. If these evils are needed for these motivations, then it seems the evils are not (*contra* Hasker's claim) gratuitous after all. While Kraay thinks Hasker may have adequate replies to these objections, he considers two further objections that I want to spend more time on.[14] The first questions the plausibility of HT in the first place (let us call that objection "Obj$_{\text{HT-Plausibility}}$"). And even if HT is plausible, it is still not clear that knowing God prevents gratuitous evils does indeed impede moral action as Hasker asserts. This leads to a second objection questioning the implication of HT ("Obj$_{\text{HT-Implication}}$").

Obj$_{\text{HT-Plausibility}}$: This objection targets HT specifically and asks why we would have to know "or reasonably believe that God prevents all gratuitous evil" if God were to prevent gratuitous evils. If humans do not need to know that God prevents all gratuitous evil, then God could still prevent gratuitous evil without our moral motivations being thereby undermined. We could then be motivated to act morally since it would *seem to us* that our actions are important for making the world better overall. In other words, this objection is simply questioning why HT would have to be true in the first place.[15]

Obj$_{\text{HT-Implication}}$: The second objection questions the implication that moral and disaster-prevention motivations would be undermined if humans knew gratuitous evils were prevented. The considerations in support of this objection are two-fold. First, it is possible that God could simply prevent us from making the inference from the fact that God prevents all gratuitous evils to the conclusion that there is no need for us to the act morally. Alternatively, it might be true that the motivation to be moral is independent of the consequentialist claim that the purpose of being moral is to make the world better. Indeed, the predominant foundational view of ethics (which goes by the name of "deontology") claims that one is supposed to do the moral act morally *simply because* it is the moral act; otherwise, it is not truly a moral action. Morality itself, and not the consequences of the moral action, is the prime moral motivator. If this is correct, then knowing God prevents gratuitous evil should have no bearing on our moral motivation. This should then, contra Hasker, free God

---

14. Note that in Kraay's article they are the third and fourth objections to NGE.

15. Interestingly, Kraay ultimately defends Hasker on this point. Unfortunately, space limitations prevent me from considering Kraay's defense and explaining why I find it insufficient.

up to prevent all gratuitous evil.[16] Ultimately, Kraay thinks $\text{Obj}_{\text{HT-Plausibility}}$ and $\text{Obj}_{\text{HT-Implication}}$ call into question the viability of the NGE Defense as a whole.

4. HASKER'S RESPONSE TO $\text{OBJ}_{\text{HT-IMPLICATION}}$

Let us momentarily set aside $\text{Obj}_{\text{HT-Plausibility}}$ and look at how Hasker responds to $\text{Obj}_{\text{HT-Implication}}$. In response to the consideration that God could prevent gratuitous evils, let us know it, and simply block our inferences from that fact to the implication that there is no need to act morally, Hasker claims "there is something troubling in the idea that God would, as a matter of policy, systematically inhibit the proper functioning of our cognitive faculties in this way."[17] Not only is this troubling, but Hasker also thinks it leads to a "quick and easy disproof of God's existence!"[18] Essentially, he points out that both he and Kraay agree that there have been some theists who have indeed drawn the inference that there is no motivation to act morally from their belief that God prevents all gratuitous evils. But if God is understood as systematically inhibiting such inferences, and if some people have indeed made such inferences, then it would follow that no such God exists! If there were indeed a God who systematically inhibited such inferences, those persons would never have been able to have made those inferences. The fact that such persons exist shows either that God would not inhibit such inferences or that there is no God in the first place.[19]

In response to the consideration that morality itself brings along its own motivation independent of consequences, Hasker essentially responds by asserting that those who are so motivated are acting irrationally because they "have not thought through the implications of holding that God prevents all gratuitous evils." In other words, Hasker thinks such persons are irrational and proceeds to claim that "it is unseemly to suppose that the fulfillment of God's purposes . . . depends on this sort of irrationality."[20] His point is this: if God prevented all gratuitous evils and people realized this, then (Hasker believes) most people would lose their

16. Kraay, "Theism," 43–46.
17. Hasker, "God and Gratuitous Evil," 58.
18. Hasker, "God and Gratuitous Evil," 59.
19. Hasker, "God and Gratuitous Evil," 59.
20. Hasker, "God and Gratuitous Evil," 60.

motivation to act morally and help their fellow humans. And given this assumption, God would have to rely upon *those* people (i.e., the ones who would lose their motivation) acting irrationally by not thinking through the implications of the fact that God prevents all gratuitous evil. If they did not act thus irrationally, they would not act morally. As a result, God's desire for us to act morally would depend on the irrationality of human beings. And Hasker finds this claim—the claim that God's purpose to preserve morality in the world depends on irrationality—objectionable.

5. ANSELM TO THE RESCUE

At this point, one might consider the debate between Hasker and Kraay at a standstill. Part of the deadlock seems largely due to differing intuitions over the plausibility of Hasker's Thesis (HT) in the first place and over the possible implications that would ensue from HT if it were true. To help resolve this impasse, I propose turning to a relatively obscure text: Anselm's *De Casu Diaboli* ("On the Fall of the Devil"). I will show how its insights shed light on this debate and indirectly support Kraay's two objections ($Obj_{HT\text{-Plausibility}}$ and $Obj_{HT\text{-Implication}}$).

De Casu Diaboli is perhaps less known than Anselm's other works, but it is especially loved by those who work on Anselm, including McCord Adams.[21] The treatise is an exploration of the interaction between the will and the intellect of rational beings, and it is ultimately concerned with explaining how sin could be possible in the first place. Anselm pursues this question by focusing on the following puzzle: if the angels were created by God and received everything they have from God, then how could it come about that some of them abstained from sin while the devil and other angels sinned? What could explain the difference between the sinning and non-sinning angels if they were created identically?[22] Anselm answers by appealing to a thought-experiment concerning God's creation of an angel's will.

After noting that newly-created angels cannot will anything of themselves without first having been given some disposition to will, Anselm

---

21. Coincidentally, it was through a paper I wrote on *De Casu Diaboli* (*DCD*) that I first caught Marilyn's attention, so to speak. My dissertation, which I wrote under her direction, was in many ways dependent upon ideas in this text.

22. Technically, Anselm and his student discuss this issue in terms of whether all the angels received "perseverance" in keeping their upright wills. This detail is not of vital importance for the purposes of this chapter.

ponders what sorts of dispositions or inclinations God would grant these angels.[23] Since no creature can be happy without willing their own happiness or benefit (*commodum*), it makes sense that God should give them a specific inclination to desire and will their own happiness. He calls this a "disposition-for-happiness."[24] But if they received only a disposition-for-happiness, Anselm reasons that happiness would be the *only* thing they could will. This would give rise to several bad consequences. Possessing only the disposition-for-happiness would entail that the angels would will the maximum amount of happiness they could recognize, up to and including willing to be like God. While such a willing would be inappropriate, it would be difficult to hold the angels accountable for it since they would be doing it necessarily (because their only inclination would be the disposition-for-happiness). In addition, possessing only a disposition-for-happiness would paradoxically not permit the angels to be happy. If a creature can will only happiness, such a necessitated willing can be neither just nor unjust. But true happiness can only be attained by being just. As a result, the possession of only a disposition-for-happiness permits neither ultimate happiness nor justice.[25]

Given these problems, Anselm wonders whether God should give the angels a disposition-for-justice instead of a disposition-for-happiness. Once again, however, this would lead to a paradoxical result that the angel could not be just by willing justice. Willing justly requires that the angel will the just thing *for its own sake*. But if the angel possessed only the disposition-for-justice, the willing of justice would be because the angel was necessitated to will justice. Such willing of justice would not be for its own sake.

As a result, Anselm posits that God must give the angels both dispositions. By having both dispositions, there is no necessitated willing. The angels can will either in accordance with only their disposition-for-happiness, or they can decide to temper their willings for happiness when such willings conflict with their disposition to will justice. In other

---

23. In *DCD*, these "dispositions" are technically called "wills" (*voluntates*). That these "wills" are meant to refer to dispositions is clear throughout the text (specifically *DCD* chs. 12–14). References to *DCD* are taken from the following critical edition: Anselm, *S. Anselmi Cantuariensis Archiepiscopi*. In his later work, *De Concordia Praescientiae et Praedestinationis et Gratiae Dei Cum Libero Arbitrio*, Anselm clearly indicates he intends them as dispositions by naming them *affectiones* of the will.

24. *DCD*, ch. 12.

25. *DCD*, ch. 13.

words, the possession of both dispositions grants the angels options. They thereby receive a measure of self-determination through which they can simply will happiness or refrain from willing their maximum happiness when doing so would conflict with justice. In this way, they could will justice for its own sake.[26]

Despite this progress, one problem remains. It would seem as if having these dual dispositions do not, contra the initial intention, actually permit the angels to have options. Not only would their disposition-for-justice incline them to will the "just" act, but so also would their disposition-for-happiness. To explain: recall that the only way to be truly happy is to be just. Realizing that the way to maximize their happiness is to will justly, it would follow that the angels' disposition-for-happiness would also incline them to will justly. But if both dispositions dispose the angels to will justly, the angels' wills would once again be necessitated and they would be unable to will justice for its own sake. As a result, they could never be truly just and thus never be truly happy.

God needed to develop a strategy by which the angels could, of their own accord, determine themselves to will justly simply for the sake of justice in abstraction from considerations of happiness. To do this, however, God would need to create a situation in which an angel's disposition-for-happiness and disposition-for-justice would incline toward opposite acts. If such a scenario were created, the angels would then be able to truly determine themselves to will justice for its own sake (and thus be just), or will happiness without regard to justice.

In order to create this seemingly impossible scenario, God engineered a situation in which the angels were forbidden from willing something (call it x)[27] that they thought would make them happy. And in order for the angels to *really* believe that willing x would make them happy when they had been forbidden to will it, God had to make the angels ignorant of the fact that he would punish them. This is, in McCord Adams's words, the famed "planned ignorance" of the angels. Indeed, according to McCord Adams, such ignorance was "necessary."[28] Without such ignorance, the angels would never have had the chance to truly determine themselves to be just. And lacking any self-determination for

---

26. *DCD* ch. 14.

27. Anselm does not tell us what x might have been other than that it was something the devil was not supposed to have willed (cf. *DCD* chs. 4, 22).

28. In person, McCord Adams always referred to this as "planned ignorance." In print, she called it "necessary ignorance." See McCord Adams, "St. Anselm on Evil."

justice, such angels could never be just or happy. It was thus necessary for a greater good that the angels remain ignorant of the fact that God is the type that would definitely punish.

In addition to being ignorant of the fact they would be punished, the angels had good reason to believe they would in fact NOT be punished. Indeed, Anselm spends much of his time in chapter 24 of *De Casu Diaboli* explaining why it would have made sense for the angels to ultimately *misunderstand* God's nature and believe God would NOT punish.[29] If the angels were (mistakenly) convinced that God would not punish them for willing this x that would make them happy, their disposition-for-happiness would have inclined them to will x while their disposition-for-justice would have inclined them to refrain from willing it. In this way, the angels could make a true, self-determining choice either for justice for its own sake (since it *seemed* willing justly would not contribute to their ultimate happiness) or against justice by willing what *seemed* to contribute most toward their happiness.

The key point for our purpose is that Anselm argues it was necessary for God to willingly permit the angels to misunderstand God's nature as a punisher. Without such a misunderstanding, there would never have been true justice or self-determination. This is a classic case of God permitting a misunderstanding of God's own nature in light of a greater good. When one weighs self-determination for justice and true happiness against never misunderstanding God's nature and lacking self-determination, Anselm clearly comes out on the side that God would gladly invite a misunderstanding of his nature for the sake of justice and true happiness.

Incidentally, a similar point can be seen in John Hick's famed "Soul-Making Theodicy," most famously explained in his *Evil and the God of Love*. Put simply, Hick argues that evil is necessary for humans to overcome and thereby "grow up" into the best "likeness of God" possible.[30] Hick proposes that if God's existence were manifest to humanity, human beings would have no choice but to believe and love an all-good God. But loving and believing in God in this manner is, according to Hick, suboptimal. It would be better if humans were allowed to come *on their own* to believe in and love God. It is only if humans believe and love on their

---

29. For example, there had never been an example of God doling out punishment and the angels had no idea humans might be created to replace them in fellowship with God. See *DCD*, ch. 24, for a complete list.

30. I give a concise overview in Michael Barnwell, "Soul-Making Theodicy."

own that they can truly achieve the "likeness of God." And since God is all-good and wants the best for humans, God must have done whatever is necessary in order to permit humans to achieve this likeness. It follows, therefore, that God's existence and goodness must be hidden from humans. In Hick's words, humans were placed at an "epistemic distance" (a distance in terms of knowledge) from God; otherwise, humans would not have been able to believe in and love God on their own and would have failed to attain the likeness of God.

Interestingly, McCord Adams wrote the "Foreword" for the second edition of *Evil and the God of Love* and noted that Anselm's discussion of planned ignorance in *De Casu Diaboli* had anticipated Hick's own solution. In explaining how Anselm's position foreshadows Hick's, she writes of Anselm's angels that "God is responsible for their ignorance."[31] A clearer statement in contrast to Hasker's view would be hard to find.

In both Anselm's *De Casu Diaboli* and Hick's "Soul-Making Theodicy," God keeping creatures "ignorant," so to speak, about essential parts of God's nature is necessary. Indeed, in both cases, ignorance of God's nature is logically required, for it is the only way to permit the best possible results: for the angels to be self-determinedly just and thereby attain their greatest happiness, and for humans to believe in and love God on their own so that they can achieve the likeness of God. Were God to have made God's nature known to these creatures, God would have thereby precluded these greatest possible results. But this would be unbecoming of an all-good God. For Anselm and Hick, there is no requirement that creatures know God's nature. Instead, they argue there is a requirement that creatures do NOT know all of God's nature. Part of God's goodness to these creatures is hiding God's nature from them.

This brings us back to Hasker's Thesis (HT), which stated that "If God were to prevent gratuitous evil, [humans] would come to know this." We noted that Kraay called HT into question in $Obj_{HT\text{-Plausibility}}$ by asking why humans would need to know that God prevented gratuitous evils if indeed God did so. At the time, we did not discuss how $Obj_{HT\text{-Plausibility}}$ can specifically attack Hasker's two rationales in support of the plausibility of HT. In light of Anselm's and Hick's insights, we can now buttress in $Obj_{HT\text{-Plausibility}}$ by specifically addressing these two rationales. In addition, Anselm's *De Casu Diaboli* will lend support for $Obj_{HT\text{-Implication}}$.

---

31. Marilyn McCord Adams, "Foreword," in Hick, *Evil and the God of Love*, xvii.

Recall that Hasker's first rationale in support of HT ($HT_{rationale1}$) was that it is part of God's purpose for humans to know God's nature. The second ($HT_{rationale2}$) was that it would be immoral for God to deceive humans. Anselm's *De Casu Diaboli* gives us reason to simply reject $HT_{rationale1}$. Even if it were part of God's purpose for humans to know God's nature *eventually* (as Anselm's angels eventually did), there is no reason to think that God's creatures should know God's nature at all times. In fact, we have just discussed two important scenarios in which God's overriding purposes were to enable angelic self-determination and human growth into God-likeness. It is these purposes which were paramount to Anselm and Hick, and I see no *prima facie* reason why these purposes should be subordinate to a putative purpose that we know God's nature at all times. Given Anselm's and Hick's arguments that humans need not know God's purpose and nature at all times, Hasker's claim that they do in $HT_{rationale1}$ is far from obvious.

This leads to a rebuttal of $HT_{rationale2}$. Instead of it being immoral for God to deceive humans, Anselm's and Hick's discussions give us reason to think God would have been acting immorally NOT to let creatures be somewhat mistaken about God's nature. If God had prevented the angels from experiencing deception, they could never have been just or happy. And if humans were not epistemically distant from God, they could never grow to be "like" God. Contra Hasker, then, the immoral act would have been God letting rational agents know God's plans and thereby preventing their ability to achieve justice, happiness and Godlikeness—not whatever deception or lack-of-understanding was logically required to achieve those goals.

The considerations just mentioned undermine Hasker's two rationales in support of HT and thereby lend credibility to Kraay's $Obj_{HT\text{-}Plausibility}$. They similarly support Kraay's second objection to the putative implications of HT if HT were true ($Obj_{HT\text{-}Implication}$). $Obj_{HT\text{-}Implication}$ claimed that if humans were to know God prevented gratuitous evils, moral motivation might nonetheless be preserved because either (i) God could prevent us from drawing the inference that our moral acts do not matter with regard to consequences, or (ii) our moral motivations should be independent of a moral act's consequences. As we noted, Hasker replied to the first (i) by stating it was "troubling" to think that God "as a matter of policy, systematically inhibit[s] the proper functioning of our cognitive faculties in this way." But to call something "troubling" is not the same as to call it wrong or incorrect. Indeed, it may be much more "troubling" for an all-good God to permit gratuitous evils than it would be to prevent them and simply keep us from drawing inferences about moral actions. To take a cue from Anselm, God found it much less troubling to let the angels make the wrong inferences about being punished for willing x. Had they not made such wrong inferences, the good angels who obeyed God and refrained from willing x could never have been self-determinedly just and happy.

We must now consider (ii) Kraay's suggestion that knowing God prevents gratuitous evils might have no bearing on our moral motivation since moral motivation may be independent of an act's consequences.[32] Recall that Hasker responded by claiming those so motivated are acting irrationally since they "have not thought through the implications of holding that God prevents all gratuitous evils." Hasker then went on to deny God's purposes would have to depend on such irrationality. Kraay might respond that Hasker is, in some sense, begging the question. I take it that Kraay (and deontology in general) holds that it *is* rational to be moral without regard for the consequences; the rationality of acting morally from a deontological point of view is not necessarily tied to consequentialist considerations. It is moreover important to note that Anselm's explanation of the angels *requires* the possibility of being motivated to act morally independently of the consequences. Those angels who acted morally (i.e., refrained from willing x) also had to think they could maximize their happiness by willing x. If Hasker were correct, it might be said that Anselm's good angels acted "irrationally" in that they had to believe they were acting against their own best interests when they willed morally. But an alternative characterization would be that acting morally can itself be rational independent of the consequences.[33] This supports Kraay's objection that knowing God prevents gratuitous evils would not necessarily undermine morality since moral motivation can be rational in and of itself.

---

32. Space prevents me from dealing with Hasker's claim that a divine inhibition of inference leads to a "quick and easy disproof of God's existence."

33. Perhaps Hasker thinks such moral motivation is not irrational in general but only in light of the specific detail that "gratuitous" evils are prevented. Pursuing this possibility is a task for another time.

6. CONCLUSION

In conclusion, Anselm's discussion of the angels in *De Casu Diaboli* lends support to Kraay's two objections to the NGE Defense and its reliance on HT. The story of "planned ignorance" gives us reason to doubt the truth of HT in the first place. And even if HT were true, it is not clear it carries the implications Hasker claims for it. It must be conceded, however, that these considerations do not conclusively invalidate the NGE Defense.[34] In response to them, Hasker could simply deny Anselm's account of planned ignorance as an accurate understanding of how the bad angels sinned and the good angels became just.[35] Likewise, he may reject Hick's soul-making theodicy and its concept of epistemic distance as veridical. But at the very least, the current discussion has offered some insights to which an opponent of the NGE Defense might appeal. And even if Anselm is wrong about the angels, his claim that ignorance and misunderstanding play an important role for rational agents to make free choices must be taken into account before an NGE Defense can be successful.

I want to suggest that these reflections on ignorance and gratuitous evils shed light on McCord Adams's concern over horrendous evils and the Anselmian claim of God? When one is suffering, it is natural to ask "Why?" Why is God permitting this (or any) particular evil to happen? Hasker and Kraay offer very different responses to this question. But as we have seen, it is not easy to determine which answer, if either, is correct. The inability to clearly determine the nature of evil as gratuitous or not reinforces McCord Adams's claim with regard to horrendous evils: we cannot know "Why" God permits them. Anselm tells us that this ignorance over God's reasoning may not only be okay, but is perhaps even expected. If Anselm is correct, God's purposes have sometimes required rational agents to remain ignorant of certain of God's plans. Despite such ignorance, believers can cling to the claim that God is good. And as an infinitely good being, believers retain the hope, along with McCord Adams, that God will "defeat" horrendous evils (such as the ones discussed in this volume) despite the inability to understand why they may be occurring.

---

34. Space limitations have prevented me from dealing with all of Hasker's rebuttals to Kraay.

35. Incidentally, I have argued in several papers that Anselm's account faces significant problems. As one example, see Barnwell, "Harder Problem."

4

Spiritual Friendship and Sexual Violence

Danielle Tumminio Hansen

INTRODUCTION

Those who knew Marilyn McCord Adams held her in such high regard because she possessed an incisive, analytic mind, coupled with a soul that welcomed senior scholars and children with equal regard and nurtured future scholars into friends. Her books and articles on evil emblematize this commitment to a thriving mind and soul: They present both a highly systematic and quietly personal engagement with theodicy—the cool abstraction of logic bisecting the passion that emerges from experience and the warmth of agapeic love. That body of literature reflects the essence of Marilyn's life and legacy: it inquires as it challenges, all the while insisting upon the presence of a loving and affirming God.

In this chapter, I attempt to expand and further develop some of the work that McCord Adams completed on theodicy. Specifically, I will propose that sexual trauma fits the category of a horrendous evil and then build upon the three stages of horror defeat that McCord Adams names in her published work to add a final one that I refer to as Stage IV Horror-Defeat. In this stage, spiritual friendship manifests through legacy.

1. ON THE THEOLOGICAL SIGNIFICANCE OF EXPERIENCE

To write about the theological significance of sexual trauma is to write about the theological significance of human experience. Yet explicit theological engagement with the concrete events of people's lives is infrequent in a majority of theological discourses for several reasons. First, theologians frequently express skepticism about the extent to which experience can be relied upon as an epistemic source because experience can be highly variable between individuals and even within a single person's life. Relationships, time, culturally normative ways of knowing, personal neurobiology, neurochemistry, and prior experiences all provide a single individual with what essentially amounts to a bespoke interpretative lens. As a result, two people can, and frequently do, participate in the same event together but interpret that event in significantly different ways.[1]

Additionally, reason has historically been normed as the highest mode of rigorous thinking. Those of us trained in the discipline absorb hundreds of years of scholarship that assumes that reason's wisdom must be adopted over and against the threat of emotion and feeling, which distort and disrupt one's ability to see clearly and truthfully. As a result, theologians, along with philosophers, often believe that to craft a compelling argument, counterargument, and rebuttal is to engage the mind at the highest and most complex level. As Bertrand Russell concludes, "The free intellect will see as God might see, without a *here* and *now*. . . . Hence also the free intellect will value more the abstract and universal knowledge into which the accidents of private history do not enter."[2]

Now theologians, of course, *do* seek to see as God sees and to know as God knows. The problem, however, is that reason alone will not do the job, in part because it is often a smokescreen for normed—aka white, cisgender, male, and western—ways of knowing. Moreover, some events appear to defy reason, with trauma falling squarely into this category, for at the heart of a traumatic event is the defiance of both language and logic. Indeed, those with a personal experience of a trauma keenly know the ways in which reason has failed them: They often feel as if time has stopped, even

---

1. For an expanded argument defending the epistemic validity of experience as a form of theological revelation, see Tumminio Hansen, "Remembering Rape in Heaven."

2. Russell, *Problems of Philosophy*, 160.

though their clocks keep ticking.[3] The dogmas taught by their religious leaders may cease to make sense.[4] They find themselves facing the reality that language—the tool designed to allow for human communication—lacks the vocabulary to encapsulate what they mean to say. They may even discover that reason, which they once trusted as the paradigmatic source of wisdom, is no longer as infallible as they once assumed.[5]

If traumas pose a challenge to the value placed on reason as a privileged way of knowing in theology, so does the very foundation of the discipline. Christian theology emerges out of experience, whether it be the experience of Jesus' life, death, and resurrection as reflected through the Gospel writers and their redactors, or the experiences of modern Christians who seek to understand that history in relation to their own lives. Indeed, I would argue that it is both impossible and mistaken to divorce the study of theology from the wisdom of human experience because this is where theology has the opportunity to make the most profound contribution. This is particularly true in regards to the human experiences that we collectively try to avoid, silence, or obscure, among which are many horrendous evils suffered by those who are systemically oppressed due to their gender, race, class, ability, or faith.

Because I believe that theology is fundamentally enriched by concrete engagement with human experience, this chapter utilizes a methodology that adopts a commitment to both reason and realized relationships, to theory and to practice. It is worth noting, however, that McCord Adams and I differ in the privilege that we explicitly afford personal experience. As a philosopher of religion, analytic in orientation, McCord Adams relied heavily on the forces of logic and, in her ministry as a priest, the Scriptures and traditions of the Church. In her academic publications, she generally did not identify personal experiences to justify

---

3. Shelly Rambo theologizes that the space trauma inhabits theologically is a "middle" space in which there are "elisions of time, body, and language." She conceptualizes this traumatic temporal space as akin to Holy Saturday, the time between the death of Christ and the resurrection. See Rambo, *Spirit and Trauma*, 7–8.

4. Studies find that people of faith face particularly intense epistemic challenges depending on the extent to which their faith leaders and dogmas are authoritarian in orientation. See Tumminio Hansen, "Do People Become More Religious?"

5. By way of example, philosopher Susan Brison summarizes her own epistemic struggle following a rape and attempted murder thusly: "It has been hard for me, as a philosopher, to learn the lesson that knowledge isn't always desirable, that the truth doesn't always set you free. Sometimes, it fills you with incapacitating terror and, then, uncontrollable rage." Susan Brison, *Aftermath*, 20.

her abstract arguments, though she referred to experience more openly in her editorials and in her books of prayers and sermons.[6]

However, I would argue that while McCord Adams refrained from explicitly engaging with human experience in her academic work, it was always in the background, quietly informing both her scholarship and her ministry. She was, for instance, quite open in conversation about how her experience of ministering to those who suffered from AIDS and her relationships with those in the LGBTQ community influenced her doctrine of God and theodicy, and late in her career, she wrote in *Theologians in Their Own Words* that the physical, psychological, and sexual abuse that dominated her childhood laid the foundation for her life's work. As she summarizes in that essay, "My problem was how to house God and evil in the same world, and how to contain the experiences of God and horrors within the same self."[7]

It is my belief, therefore, that McCord Adams ultimately valued experience as a source of revelation and, in turn, would not have objected to my privileging it in what follows, at least in part because McCord Adams often said, "God is very, very big, and we are very, very small" or, as she summarizes more formally in *Theologians in Their Own Words*, "God is too big to be a social construction."[8] McCord Adams intended this sentiment to highlight the metaphysical size-gap between humans and God, to remind us to encounter God with humility because, from our ontological location, it is impossible to see the world as God does or to understand God fully. However, it could also be used to defend experience as a source of spiritual revelation because God, in all of God's largesse, likely utilizes all available resources to help us strengthen the Divine-human relationship, so that if a resource is available, God will use it to help bridge the metaphysical size gap. One such resource is human experience.

2. DEFINING SEXUAL TRAUMAS

English speakers use a variety of terms to refer to sexual violations, including rape, sexual assault, sexual violence, gender-based violence,

---

6. An exception to this is Marilyn McCord Adams's brief spiritual autobiography, "Love of Learning."

7. McCord Adams, "Truth and Reconciliation," 17.

8. McCord Adams, "Truth and Reconciliation," 18.

incest, pornography, and sexual harassment.⁹ Parsing the distinctions between these categories can be both colloquially and legally confusing, as there is often significant overlap between them.¹⁰ A definition is therefore in order: Throughout this chapter, I will be using the term "sexual violation" to mean an act of power, using sex, that violates a person's agency, body, and desire. I include "rape" within this definition and "incest" as a subset of it in which the harm done is perpetrated by someone who is part of the victimized party's biological or social family. I consider a "sexual trauma" to be a specific kind of sexual violation that brings about a crisis of meaning which may cause an individual to question the overall goodness of their life.

3. SEXUAL TRAUMAS AS HORRENDOUS EVILS

It may seem like a *prima facie* claim that sexual violations constitute horrendous evils, especially given that McCord Adams includes both "the rape of a woman and axing off of her arms," "child pornography," and "parental incest" in her initial list when presenting the concept to readers in *Horrendous Evils and the Goodness of God*.¹¹ Still, a deeper examination of how individuals experience these events helps explain why their inclusion fits the category that McCord Adams developed.

Those who fall victim to sexual violations do not have a monolithic experience of them due to a variety of factors ranging from the victimized party's age to the pragmatics of the violation, the victimized party's prior history of trauma, and the relationship that the harmed party had with the one who inflicted the violation. What might be broadly said, however, is that many who experience such a violation process it as a form of trauma in which trauma is defined as an event that precipitates a crisis of meaning within the life of an individual or community.¹² This

---

9. Philosopher Linda Martín Alcoff develops the term "sexual violation" as preferable to "rape" in her book-length work on the subject. See Alcoff, *Rape and Resistance*, 12–15.

10. What constitutes "rape" in one state, for instance, may legally be defined as "sexual assault" in another, leading to confusion for survivors about what exactly happened to them and how to speak about it. For more on the significance of this linguistic ambiguity, see Tumminio Hansen, "Absent a Word."

11. McCord Adams, *Horrendous Evils*, 26.

12. Note that processing an event as a trauma and experiencing posttraumatic stress disorder (PTSD) are not synonymous. Posttraumatic stress disorder requires

trauma is, at its essence, epistemic in nature insofar as it causes an individual to question a number of assumptions about the world, including assumptions about their identity, God, truth, goodness, guilt, innocence, and the purpose of life on the whole.

I propose that epistemic crisis embedded within sexual traumas is the locus of overlap with the category of horrendous evils. Recall that McCord Adams relies heavily upon a human's meaning-making capacity to determine whether a horrendous evil occurred. A horrendous evil, in other words, is not defined by external criteria related to the nature of the event but rather by how a given human being understands the significance of it. Therefore, if horrendous evils are, as McCord Adams populates, "Evils the participation in which (that is, the doing or suffering of which) constitutes prima facie reason to doubt whether the participant's life could (given their inclusion in it) be a great good to him/her on the whole," then the key qualifying criteria is not the individual pragmatics of the event but rather a person's epistemic relationship to it.[13] Those who experience sexual violations as traumatic therefore relate to the event in a way that resonates with McCord Adams's definition of a horrendous evil because the harm done deeply challenges their meaning-making capacities to the point that they may question the goodness of life on the whole.

I experienced such a crisis during the first few years that I knew Marilyn McCord Adams, when I was raped by someone I was dating.[14] This event inaugurated a profound epistemic trauma, as I found myself questioning a seemingly infinite number of assumptions about my identity, my relationships with other human beings, and my relationship with God. I was no longer the person I had been before, and it was entirely unclear to me whether the human experience that had come to be mine was—or would ever be—good on the whole.

Marilyn was willing to join me in the epistemic battle that I waged as she listened, offered empathy, insights, reason, books to read, prayers, blessings, and meals. But what always felt most important was that she did not seem shocked. She expressed no pity; she did not look at me any differently than she did before, which was my greatest fear when telling

---

the presence of a variety of criteria from the *DSM*, such flashbacks, irrational outbursts of anger, emotional numbing, and hypervigilance.

13. McCord Adams, *Horrendous Evils*, 26.

14. For a more extensive theological analysis of this particular event and its relationship to epistemology, memory, and experience, see Tumminio Hansen, "Remembering Rape in Heaven" (n1 above).

anyone what had happened. Through her reaction to me, I could understand what God's abiding love must look like. Because of her, I felt emboldened to engage directly with the epistemic crisis I faced rather than try to avoid it.

It is worth noting here that the epistemic dimension of trauma often impacts self-concept in a profound way. Trauma appears to destroy the self as the victimized party once understood it and, in turn, raises profound questions about the way the self exists within the overarching narrative of the person's life, as well as if there will be—or ever was—such an overarching narrative. It raises questions about the essence of the self—is the self essentially good, for instance—and whether the self is constructed, and if so, then how the process of construction occurs.[15]

Many trauma theorists conclude that the process of reconstructing the self in the aftermath of trauma is necessarily a relational process.[16] Theologically, one might argue that it is the work of the Church, insofar as the Church is *imitatio Christi*, following in the healing and reconciliatory work of Christ, with its mission also emerging from the trauma of Christ's death. As I reflect back on Marilyn's work broadly as a priest as well as the times in which she ministered to me as I processed my own sexual trauma, I see that Marilyn's ability to wrestle alongside me was also an exercise in co-constructing the self in the aftermath of trauma. By listening, reflecting, praying, and blessing, Marilyn grounded our friendship in safety, creating a space in which there was no shame in speaking the truth, in which something of God could be discovered and known more deeply, and, in turn, in which the defeat of evil could occur.

I would propose, therefore, that the process of reconstructing the self in the aftermath of trauma is a component of what McCord Adams referred to as "spiritual friendship," in which two individuals are:

> Stabilized in a certain bent, wanting to grow in a certain direction; persons who are so agreed that each can be alter ego to the other, to act on behalf of the other, to give the other constructive criticism and advice to growth towards their common goal. Such intensity of shared purpose and affection trusts without reservation, supports without hesitation, loves the other more

---

15. For an extended philosophical analysis of the effect of trauma on the self, see Brison, *Aftermath*.

16. See Alcoff, *Rape and Resistance*; Herman, *Trauma and Recovery*.

than self, creates such a depth of understanding as to put the one in a position to act and speak on behalf of the other.[17]

In the early years after I was raped, when I was seemingly stuck in an epistemic quagmire, McCord Adams had just published *Horrendous Evils and the Goodness of God* and she was beginning to work on *Christ and Horrors*. Reflecting back on her work and our conversations during that time, I see how her work on theodicy allowed her to "speak on behalf of the other," conceptualizing what was at stake for me and for other survivors of this particular kind of horrendous evils in her scholarship. Her writing and research, in other words, was a profound act of spiritual friendship, even as its enduring presence after her death has become central to her academic legacy.

Yet I would argue that legacy goes beyond the writing that she left postmortem and instead begins during this life and then extends into the life beyond. In what remains of this chapter, I will develop this concept of legacy as being central to the defeat of horrendous evils such that it functions as an addition to the three stages developed by McCord Adams.

3. STAGE IV HORROR-DEFEAT

McCord Adams postulated that evils require defeat by God such that the life of the affected individual is worth living on the whole in spite of the prior presence of a horrendous evil. She suggests that this process of defeat can—but does not necessarily—begin in pre-mortem life and that it compromises three stages, which she outlines as follows:

> 1. *Stage I Horror-Defeat*: God co-experiences horrors in this world alongside us. Here McCord Adams reasons that God must co-experience horrors for two reasons: 1. Divine participation is essential to creating intimacy between humans and God such that human participation in horrors does not happen in isolation from divinity; 2. The groundwork for positive meaning-making from horrors derives from divine presence in this world.
>
> 2. *Stage II Horror-Defeat:* The affected human engages in meaning-making. McCord Adams argues that horrors impede meaning-making capabilities, harming people's ability to derive positive meaning from their lives on the whole. Therefore, for the horror to be defeated, humans must have the opportunity to

---

17. McCord Adams, *Christ and Horrors*, 155–56.

participate in meaning-making in their ante- and postmortem existences in order to heal and rediscover anew what it means for their lives to have positive meaning on the whole.

3. *Stage III Horror-Defeat:* McCord Adams argues that our bodies make us vulnerable to horrors because of their own fragility and reliance upon the earth's scarce resources. Therefore, horror-defeat requires that the body is no longer vulnerable to horrors; McCord Adams postulates that this occurs postmortem.

The elegance of this three-fold formulation is that each part identifies a problem for theodicy and offers a correlating response. The sense that God has abandoned a person in the midst of horrors requires divine solidarity; the surd element needs sense; vulnerability demands inviolability. What remains undeveloped, however, is the necessity of human solidarity both in ante- and postmortem existence. I therefore want to build upon the three stages that McCord Adams developed to propose the addition of a fourth in which legacy, built through ante- and postmortem community, receives recognition as a central feature of horror defeat.

When horrors strike, they impact not only the individual directly affected but also the community of spiritual friends that love that individual. Psychological research provides data to support this assumption: Secondary or intergenerational traumas affect individuals who did not experience a trauma directly but who became exposed to it through a loved one's direct impact. The symptoms of children of Holocaust survivors provide the most well-documented evidence of this phenomenon, illustrating how evils like traumas are much like a storm, with not just a locus but with expansive bands of metaphoric rain that drizzle or drench, depending on where people stand. Either way, they get wet. Spiritual friendship, therefore, transmutes trauma precisely because there is one soul in two bodies, and that shared soul co-experiences the evil that persists beyond the body itself. This might be considered a tax on love because the soul is only shared because of the love that binds the two halves together. It is love that causes a friend to absorb and be affected by another's experience of evil. It is the magnet that keeps the soul's halves bound between bodies. It might be said to be the heart of empathy, as well as that which arms one more body to co-defeat evil.

The transmutation of evil—or trauma—thus leads to a communal expansion of horror defeat, for it is no longer just the individual victim who is affected, who demands defeat and participates in it.[18] It is also

18. I perceive significant overlap between the secular term "trauma" and Adams's

the community of that individual, the friends with whom the affected party shared a soul, that must participate in defeat as well. They draw themselves to the work because if one shares a soul with another, then the cosmic, seismic, intrapsychic pain that categorizes horrors within the individual necessarily transmute to the shared soul of the friend so that when Stages I–III remain unresolved for the individual, they remain unresolved for all.

What I propose, then, is that friends inherit horrors and demand their defeat on behalf of themselves and the one with whom they share a soul. They become co-participants in the defeat of horrendous evils precisely because they, like God, understand what is at stake: the overall value of the victimized party's life, or, put differently, their legacy. In turn, spiritual friends join together in the worthy task of wrestling for blessing, to invoke the language McCord Adams uses (Gen 32:22–32).[19]

My postulation here is that this work of co-defeat is also work that becomes central to the legacy of both the party directly affected by evil as well as those for whom the experience was vicarious or empathic. This may seem like a counterintuitive claim, given that we often consider the term "legacy" to refer to that which remains or endures after a person's death, as if that were a static, proscribed entity. Such an assumption overlooks the way that postmortem existence might shape both the identity of the victimized party as well as their legacy. It also overlooks the way that legacy may manifest prior to a person's death. In Marilyn's case, for instance, her written work and the effect her mentorship left upon her students was all accomplished prior to her death and thus began within her antemortem existence.

Finally, we often assume that legacy is a solitary enterprise insofar as we assume that it is the lasting impact of one person. However, I propose that community is essential to legacy, whether it originates ante- or postmortem. Indeed, when the word "legacy" was first used in medieval English—as it would have been used during the time that Julian of Norwich lived—it meant a body of individuals who were sent forth on a mission. In Stage IV Horror-Defeat, then, friends receive this mission from the individual who experienced the horrendous evil directly, and it becomes

---

term "horrendous evil," as both instantiate an epistemological crisis of meaning and an anthropological crisis of identity. For more on how trauma recovery requires meaning-making and identity construction, see Herman, *Trauma and Recovery*.

19. For a more extensive discussion of what wrestling for blessing involves in Marilyn's own words, see McCord Adams, *Wrestling for Blessing*.

their mission as well. They must believe and act differently because of this mission, because of the legacy entrusted to them. Legacy is, one might say, perichoretic, a dance between those who share a soul and a mission to wrestle for blessing in order to defeat the most horrendous of evils.

4. CONCLUSION

It has been close to twenty years since I first spoke with Marilyn about my own experience of sexual trauma. At the time, I felt very alone in a world where time seemed to move beyond me but without me.[20] And yet, I see now that I had quite a lot of time ahead of me, time to ask many questions and find some answers, to learn and to teach, to grow deeper in knowledge and love of God in large part through the process of enriching my human relationships. My friendship with Marilyn was, and will remain, integral to the self that emerged out of my own experience with horrendous evil. I think, act, and believe differently because of it. But I, of course, am not the only person with whom she shared such a transformative relationship, nor the only one upon whom she had such a transformative impact. Her legacy therefore continues to develop through the bodies of those who remain in this pre-mortem time to co-defeat evil in this world together, as a community, guided by and held within the love of God.

---

20. For a book-length philosophical analysis of time in relation to sexual violations, see Burke, *When Time Warps*.

5

A Beautiful Love
Compatibilism, Theodicy, and Limited Agency

JESSE COUENHOVEN

IT HAS BECOME COMMON for theists to claim that they have a somewhat satisfactory response to the puzzle of how a perfectly good, powerful, and knowledgeable God co-exists with evil—the free will defense. The import of this argument as a ground-clearing exercise, which made room for theists to have a place in the field of analytic philosophy, can hardly be overstated. Theologians who enjoy having conversation partners in fields other than their own should therefore be grateful for the free will defense, and not dismissive of attempts by philosophers of religion to respond to the problem of evil. Nevertheless, the rhetorical success of the free will defense has sometimes blinded philosophical theologians to its inherent limits, and has created what is for Christians a historically anomalous bias towards libertarian accounts of moral agency, which associates human freedom with having undetermined, autonomous choices. A majority of philosophically oriented theists and non-theists alike have apparently concluded that the theological problem of evil is intractable without libertarianism.[1]

---

1. See, e.g., Manuel Vargas's suspicion that most libertarians are theists motivated by a need to hold onto free will defenses. Vargas, "The Runeberg Problem."

It is no surprise, then, that free will theodicies have come under attack by non-theists. (Philosophers commonly distinguish between a "defense," which seeks merely to address the question of whether it is illogical to believe in a perfect God, given evil, and a "theodicy," which takes up the more challenging task of offering good reasons God might have for permitting evil to exist. This essay takes up the latter project). More interesting is the fact that theists have also begun to raise questions about the propriety of such approaches. A particularly prominent theological critic of free will theodicies has been Marilyn McCord Adams. Although she was careful not to undermine the appeal of her project by rejecting libertarian approaches generally, her approach to the problem of evil helped convince me that, contrary to widespread opinion, theists who advocate compatibilist approaches to free will (according to which freedom is compatible with determinations such as divine grace) are no worse off than libertarians. Indeed, McCord Adams's own approach suggests that compatibilists may well be better equipped to offer meaningful reflections on theodicy.[2]

This essay seeks to expand on Marilyn McCord Adams's thoughtful wrestling with the limits of human agency in the face of horrors. My discussion begins by exploring her reservations about free will defenses and concludes by reflecting on the ways in which her theodicy of participation fits Robert Merrihew Adams's suggestion that love itself guides but also places certain limits on divine agency. My argument throughout is, first, that appropriating McCord Adams's unwillingness to shift the blame for evil from God to humans frees us to appreciate neglected theological resources for reflecting on evil, and second, that the sort of view McCord Adams defends can be strengthened by taking advantage of compatibilist approaches that both honor responsible human agency and recognize its limits.

1. SHIFTING THE BLAME, TRAUMATIZING THE VICTIM

In *Horrendous Evils and the Goodness of God* McCord Adams frames her discussion of various types of free will theodicy with a general question: do the ways in which such theodicies highlight the idea of human

---

[2]. I develop this thought in relation to doctrines of predestination in ch. 6 of Couenhoven, *Predestination*.

self-determination appropriately respect human dignity (as adherents of such approaches believe), or do they actually do vulnerable agents a dubious honor? McCord Adams's concern is that although it can seem optimistic to extol a supposed human ability to create one's own identity, doing so can actually be unfair, because it asks too much of us. Whatever the differences among them, she argues, free will approaches share a common and basic flaw. They attempt to shift responsibility for horrors, and corresponding blame, from God to human beings.[3] The tragedy of this move is that attempting to honor human agency by characterizing human beings as autonomous and in control of their lives tends to crush vulnerable and weak finite persons under expectations they cannot meet. Because human beings are creatures formed by their relationships, in histories that have at least as much to do with others' decisions as their own, they tend not to have a great deal of control over or even comprehension of their identities or personal powers.

For that reason, it is a mistake to equate God and human beings as moral peers. Even when in various ways we choose evil, we cannot share equal responsibility for a world full of horrors with the one who elected to create that world in the first place.[4] Think, for instance, of modern consumers' relationship with the many complex technologies they use. Most of us hardly understand the environmental and other implications of our choices, and given the pressures of relationships and jobs, lack the time and energy needed to deeply comprehend the impact of our seemingly mundane economic decisions. Moreover, even those who do have access to knowledge may find it hard to act on it. In these ways and others, human beings are significantly limited in their agency.

Given the "size gap" between divine and created personhood, McCord Adams suggests a different picture of the relation between divine and human agency—that of parents and little children.[5] Children who play with chemicals or put their hands on a hot stovetop may have chosen to disobey parental commands even though they should trust that their parents know best. But if authority figures leave children in harm's way, or stand by and watch while children foolishly injure themselves, one tends to blame the adult much more than the child. Like children, then, we

---

3. McCord Adams, *Horrendous Evils*, 34, 38.

4. McCord Adams, *Horrendous Evils*, 48–49; McCord Adams, *Christ and Horrors*, 37.

5. McCord Adams, *Horrendous Evils*, 49.

have a proper sphere of responsible agency for the horrors we perpetuate on ourselves and others. Yet, like children, that sphere is quite limited.

Some free will approaches exacerbate this problem of blame-shifting more than others. Correspondingly, McCord Adams distinguishes two types of free will theodicy, the "free fall" approach and the "soul-making" approach, and argues that "free fall approaches founder while soul-making theodicies at least teeter on the rock of horrendous evils."[6] Classic free fall approaches contend that God is justified in permitting evil insofar as doing so is necessary to allow created persons the good of making their own undetermined free choices. These approaches tend to emphasize human autonomy, arguing that God must leave human beings to their own devices so that they can choose their own identities without divine interference. A soul-making theodicy, by contrast, assigns somewhat less significance to autonomous human choices and more to divine pedagogy. Such approaches suggest that God makes use of evils to create an environment conducive to soul-making that does not force but invites free creatures to cooperate with God as they mature. Enduring pain or sorrow can, for instance, teach character, including virtues such as empathy or graciousness.

McCord Adams's concern about the free fall approach is that it puts too much weight on human self-determination. This is most obviously the case when a free fall approach makes an original human choice between evil and good a sufficient reason for divine permission for later humans to be placed in a corrupted world in which (at a minimum) significant temptation and suffering are givens (think of some readings of the Adam and Eve story). As is well known, there are also significant questions about the historical and scientific plausibility of such accounts, given typical accounts of evolutionary development, which insist that there was no simple "first human" but rather many gradual steps towards developing the suite of abilities that are now widely associated with human distinctiveness. But even those who insist that "every man is his own Adam" ask too much of humans and their choices. McCord Adams argues that human beings are too limited and fragile in their agency for it to be reasonable or appropriate for God to rest much on their choices. Far from being insightful about their choices, or having significant control of them, ignorant human agents tend to cause chaos and pain that far exceeds not only their intent but their capacity to comprehend. Moreover,

---

6. McCord Adams, *Horrendous Evils*, 33.

they are radically vulnerable to trauma from the earliest ages, and as a result often need healing in order for their agency to be genuinely free in the first place.[7]

Soul-making theodicies are similarly weak on this latter point, concerning the tendency of human beings to accidentally pursue self-destructive paths, since widely experienced horrors appear pedagogically inept given the ways in which they are agency-undermining.[8] Suffering might sometimes open doors for insight or deepening of character, but it often simply traumatizes victims, making it hard for them to open up to the world or other persons, trapping them in cycles of addiction, and short-circuiting their emotional and cognitive processing. It seems cruel to blame victims for not "choosing to grow" under such sadly common circumstances as chronic shame, poverty, famine, endemic disease, or war.

These reservations do not deter McCord Adams from saying that "I assume the desire to have personal creatures who have some free play" is among God's reasons for permitting evil.[9] Readers might wonder, however, what sort of free will theodicy is left over once McCord Adams's reservations are taken into account. She grants that human beings have great culpability for many terrible deeds, but also insists that we are not the competent and well-informed creatures required by libertarian accounts that ascribe human agents the power to be the undetermined sources of their character and actions.

My suggestion is that the best way to balance these claims is to take advantage of compatibilist approaches that honor distinctive aspects of responsible human agency while also recognizing our significant limits. Rejecting the libertarian ideal of "ultimate responsibility" results in less demanding theodicies that seem more adequate to our humble circumstances, and mitigates the blame placed on us. Given their openness to the powerful forces around us, such accounts suit McCord Adams's widely shared intuition that human agency cannot compete with God's agency but is, rather, secondary.

The remainder of this essay sketches out a compatibilist approach to theodicy that takes seriously McCord Adams's concerns about the asymmetries between divine and human agency and the challenge presented by horrors. In an initial section I argue that compatibilists can

---

7. McCord Adams, *Christ and Horrors*, 36.
8. McCord Adams, *Horrendous Evils*, 53.
9. McCord Adams, *Horrendous Evils*, 54.

offer humble analogues to libertarian free will theodicies. I then note that McCord Adams's own suggestions about how God defeats evil by offering participation in the divine life are easiest to defend given compatibilist assumptions. Finally, I contend that Marilyn Adams's views can fittingly be developed by reflecting on Robert Adams's suggestion that God elects to create particular individuals out of love—a predestinarian theme that, again, fits best with compatibilism.

2. ANALOGUES TO THE FREE WILL DEFENSE

Philosophical compatibilists, like libertarians, have typically focused their attention on responsibility for the intentional, voluntary choices of well-informed agents. McCord Adams's emphasis on the relative childlikeness of human agents and the porousness of human selves in their vulnerability to influence by other agents and experiences suggests, however, a less volitionalist picture of human agency.[10] The Augustinian compatibilism I favor might be a good fit (not least because it was developed in part by reflecting on implications of McCord Adams's suggestion that human agency is "radically vulnerable").[11] Augustinian compatibilism is non-volitionalist in thinking of human agency not mainly as consciously chosen acts of the will but as an intrinsic quality of personal beings. On this view human agents are responsible for what they own, and they own their attitudes and emotions, their concerns, values, and interests—and expressions of those attitudes. They have significant agency by inhabiting their attitudes and in acting on them; in doing so they stand for something, and make a difference to the world. At the same time, they are open to influences of many kinds, deterministic or non-deterministic, created and uncreated. These influences need not undermine responsible agency, so long as they are compatible with the powers rational animals have to reason and to love.

But if we can have significant agency under local or global divine determination(s), why would God not simply ordain sinless perfection, without suffering? It is worth noting that compatibilists need not be committed to absolute determinism. Indeed, compatibilists need not rule out the possibility that human beings have libertarian free will (in at least

---

10. McCord Adams, *Horrendous Evils*, 104–5.

11. See Couenhoven, "Problem of God's Immutable Freedom"; Couenhoven, *Stricken by Sin*, ch. 6.

some cases). As we have seen, however, McCord Adams's discussion of human agency suggests a chastened picture of vulnerable agency. A fitting compatibilist approach to theodicy could begin by offering partial answers that appeal not to claims about significant undetermined free choices but to less metaphysically demanding ideas about individual human responsibility and growth in personal character.

One such partial answer appropriates the soul-making theodicy mentioned above. Arguably, there are insights and emotions that human beings can only learn, or only come to deeply own, through a developmental process. Certainly, we see value in watching children grow from ignorance to wisdom, from innocence to virtue, and so on. Personal maturity may not require encounters with personal or natural evil, but it may be that certain kinds or degrees of growth are possible only with such encounters. Undergoing certain kinds of struggle can deepen a person, and make possible strengths one could not otherwise have. For instance, compassion is typically greater in human beings who have themselves suffered some pain. In addition, certain virtues or other goods may be possible only in the face of certain kinds of evil. Courage, for instance, requires facing adversity. Similarly, forgiveness is possible only if moral evils exist.

More generally, it seems reasonable to suggest that divine permission of evil makes it possible for human agents to make decisions and develop commitments of sorts that would not be possible in a world where we had no occasion to fear evil, or to be tempted by it. Facing the possibility of natural or moral evils may offer human agents unique opportunities to attain depth of character and moral and spiritual insight. For example, struggling with the limits of human agency may be the best pedagogue of humility and gratitude, teaching us about our nature as dependent creatures, offering the possibility of advancing in faith and hope, and inspiring appreciation for the delights of union with the divine and other persons who share our joys and sorrows. Enduring some suffering may enable us to become deeper participants in one another's lives.

Compatibilists might further argue that God permits many evils because a world in which God regularly intervened to limit the effects of evil would be one in which certain decisions would become unthinkable, because they were known to be undoable. One cannot be tempted to hit one's sibling if one knows punches do not land. In order for human beings to have proper ownership of their loves, they need to make decisions driven not merely by what they know to be possible but by genuine desires for the good. That requires epistemic options and the ability to do things that make a difference (both of which are compatible with determinism of one sort or another).

Even on a compatibilist view, God would want to maintain boundaries on divine influence on human agency, in order to honor the basic conditions for human ownership of action. Both compatibilist and libertarian accounts of responsible agency require lawlike continuity and regularity in the world in which finite persons act, so that agents can act for the reasons that make sense to them, expressing their personalities in response to past events and in expectation of future outcomes. Constant miraculous divine interventions would interrupt too much, undermining the conditions necessary for persons to have stable identities, act out who they are, or to undergo developmental processes of change. The centrality of memory to human identity might play a significant role here, since whatever prodding God offers to move individuals or worlds toward the good must fit logically with personal and communal histories in order for the changes that take place to be a development of those persons or bodies.

One might think of such trade-offs between the goods God seeks and the evils God permits as making possible certain sorts of narrative arcs (individual and communal). If we are to grow into the sort of persons God desires us to be, God may confront intrinsic constraints on even God's ability to take away suffering. If God wants a certain sort of narrative, say of human development in appreciation for the depths of the meaning of self-giving and redemptive love, God must permit the suffering that goes along with it. And although stories that have the dramatic shape that narratives of development, struggle, regeneration, and redemption have need not be regarded as the very best stories, they may be good enough to play a role in God's creative plan.[12]

3. HORRENDOUS EVILS VS. PARTICIPATION IN SUPREME GOOD

Approaches to theodicy that highlight human responsibility and freedom can be an appropriate element in our attempts to understand why a good God might permit evils—so long as they do not seek to justify evils so awful that permitting them makes God seem intrinsically unloving, or

---

12. These comments appropriate insights from Hick, *Evil and the God of Love*; Lewis, *The Problem of Pain*; Plantinga, "Supralapsarianism."

so devastating that referring to agential development in their context becomes implausible. Agency-oriented theodicies are humane when they do not seek to shift responsibility for evils from God to humans, but rather show respect for the fragile and limited nature of human agency, which is rightly understood in the context of greater powers, especially the divine. Representing human beings as at best partially responsible creatures who characteristically share responsibility for evils with their maker is a task well suited for compatibilist accounts that do not equate responsible agency with having free floating choices or autonomy. Within these limits, as we have seen, compatibilists are able to embrace or develop analogues to a variety of aspects of well-known free will defenses.

It is nevertheless appropriate to echo McCord Adams's suggestion that though agency-oriented theodicies (especially those with a developmental orientation) have a place in helping us understand why a good God might permit some evils to exist, they offer us limited insight, at best. In the course of even normal lives, it is common to face numerous horrific evils. Extreme sorrow, deprivation, or humiliation threaten to overwhelm those who suffer such trauma, pushing them into depression and despair, and undermining their ability to find or make meaning. Such evils cannot be justified by reference to the depth of character they make possible. Here, then, we should take our cue from McCord Adams's thoughtful reflections on horrendous evils.

McCord Adams memorably defined horrendous evils as those which make it difficult for us to see how a person's life could be a good to that person, given what that person has participated in.[13] Less abstractly, paradigm horrors include severe physical suffering, whether inflicted intentionally or not, such as that caused by hunger, genetic disease, or concentration camps; sexual and other forms of personality destroying abuse and trauma; betrayal of one's deepest loyalties; and involvement in genocide, including the loss of one's people.

McCord Adams's argument for the goodness of God in the shadow of such horrors shifts attention from questions about how to justify divine permission of evil, and toward the broader question of whether God can be trusted and admired. Her thesis is that God can be said to love and be good to each individual person God creates if each person

13. McCord Adams, *Horrendous Evils*, 26, offers a more technical definition of horrors as: "evils the participation in which (that is, the doing or suffering of which) constitutes prima facie reason to doubt whether the participant's life could (given their inclusion in it) be a great good to him/her on the whole."

is able to (rightly) accept that in spite of participation in horrors her or his life is good and worthwhile on the whole.[14] Even if the ways of God cannot be fully understood or justified by the likes of us, it makes an important difference if God's creatures are able to regard God as worthy of praise, and to trust that God honors and loves them as well. Notably, embracing these claims commits McCord Adams to both a theodicy and a form of skeptical theism (the view that human beings are not in a good position to understand why God might permit evil). McCord Adams is a skeptic about certain deontic theodical justification projects, which seek to defend God from blame for the existence of evil, but she is not skeptical about the need for believers to trust that God is good, in aretaic and aesthetic terms.

How, then, can God defeat horrors? On McCord Adams's account, God can do so, first of all, by guaranteeing that each created person will participate in an incommensurable good—enjoyment of and participation in the supreme beauty of the divine life itself. Participation in such a great good ensures that horrors are marginalized in each person's life, so that they are not decisively meaning-defining for anyone. Without the perspective supplied by this larger context one might, here and now, wish to cease to exist or never to have been born. From an overarching perspective, however, every person's life is in fact valuable overall, and should be valued as a good gift for which each one is grateful.

Second, McCord Adams argues, because the incarnation permits God to suffer horrors, the horrors we suffer can be endowed with a kind of positive meaning through participation in the divine life. Sharing suffering with God in Christ transforms the defilement and shame naturally associated with horrors, elevating the lowly. In these ways, God is able not just to balance off horror with goodness in each life, but to defeat horrors.

As McCord Adams makes clear, her defense of divine goodness requires commitment to universal salvation. The idea that God universally claims us for participation in the divine life, in turn, fits best with compatibilist conceptions of human agency. This is not to say that there have been no libertarian universalists. Origen, for instance, may well have been both the first Christian libertarian and the first Christian universalist. In his view divine plenitude endlessly reaches out to creatures, rejecting rejection, and eventually bringing all back to that from whence all life

---

14. McCord Adams, *Horrendous Evils*, 155, 167.

emanates.[15] More recently, John Hick has expressed the hope that all will eventually choose union with God of their own accord.[16] It is widely acknowledged, however, that it is difficult for libertarians to offer anything more than the hope that somehow universalism will become true. They must, after all, always leave open the possibility that some will reject the divine offer. Indeed, if God endlessly pressures those who say no, that seems to disrespect rather than honor libertarian freedom. Accordingly, on libertarian views, a God who allows creatures to participate in horrors takes a tremendous gamble, running the risk that they will have lives that are not, on the whole, good to them. For McCord Adams's theodicy to be effective, however, it requires a stronger claim, that all human beings are guaranteed not only a vision of divine beauty but participation in God's own life. Without such assurance her theodicy would make eternal happiness dependent on foolish and uninformed choices, thereby becoming too much like the sort of free fall approach she begins by rejecting.

For these reasons, it does not come as a surprise that McCord Adams appears to endorse the attractiveness of some kind of compatibilism. After writing that "I do not share the worries of free will defenders about how God can make sure to win human cooperation without violating our freedom" she notes that "I flatter the Creator with enormous resourcefulness to enable human agency to work, not only to 'grow it up' in the first place but to rehabilitate it."[17] She adds, "If this should mean God's causally determining some things to prevent everlasting ruin, I see this as no more an insult to our dignity than a mother's changing a baby's diaper is to the baby."[18] Although she does not explicitly mention compatibilist theories of free will or responsibility, they are strongly implied by McCord Adams's embrace of gracious divine determinations that enable and rehabilitate human agency. Such a move makes sense. Independent agency and autonomous choice are not high on McCord Adams's scale of value, but participation and healing are. The best way to ensure that all say "I do" at the divine wedding feast is for God to shape human agency, building into human hearts and minds the wisdom and love that propel and sustain such commitments.

15. For an overview, see Greggs, *Barth, Origen, and Universal Salvation*, ch. 3.
16. Hick, *Evil and the God of Love*, 344.
17. McCord Adams, *Horrendous Evils*, 157.
18. McCord Adams, *Horrendous Evils*, 157.

In summary, McCord Adams's aretaic theodicy of divine victory over horrors through the gift of participation in God's own life is a powerful (if still partial) response to the questions about evil we all inevitably ask as we struggle through this life. The reassurance her view offers, that God is good in ways that make it possible for all creatures to worship, to pray, and to be grateful for their lives, requires a commitment to universal salvation that is difficult to embrace on a libertarian view but natural for compatibilists who hold that necessity and freedom need not be in competition. Compatibilism thus seems to be an advantageous fit for McCord Adams's view.

4. "JESUS LOVES ME"

I have argued so far that one need not be libertarian in order to appropriate significant elements of classic free will defenses. This leaves McCord Adams and others who emphasize the limits of human agency not much worse off when it comes to justifying divine permission of evil, a point that is especially clear when we keep in mind reasonable constraints on the weight one places on free choice, such as historical plausibility and a compassionate estimate of what it is right to make ignorant and wounded creaturely agents responsible for. In addition, Marilyn McCord Adams's God centered theodicy of the defeat of horrendous evils can most easily be developed alongside the compatibilist insight that human freedom need not compete with divine agency, but is compatible with it. In this final section I suggest building on McCord Adams's preferred parent-child metaphor to add another piece to the theodical puzzle, one that further emphasizes the good of participation while reflecting on the potential limits of both human and divine agency. In brief, the idea I develop with help from Robert M. Adams is that the creator's divine love itself may help us understand why God is willing to put up with evil.

Biblical creation narratives suggest that God gives life to creatures so that they can image the divine beauty in various ways, and love God and be loved by God. This idea has been developed in relation to doctrines of predestination with the suggestion that prior to creating, God elected to bring specific creatures into being. As we have discussed, one can speculate about various possible reasons why God would choose to instantiate particular worlds or persons with particular identities—to tell particular stories, perhaps, or to illustrate certain virtues. There might be many overlapping reasons. But from a theological perspective it makes sense to combine McCord Adams's universalism, which emphasizes the good of participation in the divine life, with the idea that God creates for love, and to propose that God elects to give particular persons life because God, even as the prospective author of their lives, already loves them and wants to participate in relationship with them.

As Robert Adams has argued, this need not imply that those who are created are the best, or that God loves them because they are the best.[19] God might choose them, as God famously chose Israel, because they are among the least. It would be cruel for God to give life to beings whose lives were not a great good to them on the whole, but given this constraint it seems acceptable, and in many ways delightful, if God elects to create a variety of persons for reasons that have little to do with value rankings. One reason we might offer to those who ask why their lives are the way they are, is that God loved them as they are.[20]

That raises an obvious question: why could one not be given the gift of life, but a life without suffering, or with less suffering? One possibility is that God has, for all we know, created persons who have such lives. At the same time, it appears that God also wanted to create persons who have lives like ours, as well. Is that defensible?

Robert Adams has offered at least a partial answer to this question, one that echoes the themes of much recent work on moral and other forms of luck.[21] In short, his suggestion is that it is not clear that my own history, and the history that gave rise to me, could have been very different without my losing the distinctive features that make me who I am.[22] To give me life, therefore, might very well require something very much like the actual history that I have had. If God loves me, and wants to build an eternal relationship with me, bringing me into God's own life, God might have to permit many or most of the evils in my history. Repeated often enough, this narrative logic raises the possibility that God, for reasons of love, might have fewer options about getting rid of evil than we tend to think. In order to reject evil God might end up having to reject some of those whom God loves.

19. Adams, "Must God Create the Best?"

20. This theme is developed insightfully and at length in Vitale, "Horrendous Evils." I am indebted to John Churchill and Alex Arnold for introducing me to Vitale's work and for helpful discussions of it.

21. Cf. Couenhoven, *Stricken by Sin*, ch. 5.

22. Adams, "Existence"; Adams, "Love and the Problem of Evil."

These themes are related to deep questions sometimes taken up in the literature on the differently abled.[23] Robert Adams takes Helen Keller as an example. Some have, no doubt, thought that she might have been better off were she not blind or deaf. R. Adams, by contrast, argues that without her blindness and deafness she would not have been who she was.[24] It could not, therefore, be better for *her* not to have been blind and deaf, because those are constitutive features of her. Human identities are often so closely tied up with our histories (personal and communal) that our particular identities simply could not exist without those histories being fundamentally what they are.

Of course, that point does not settle the question of whether certain features of our histories are good or bad. Advocates for the differently abled now commonly argue that deafness and other "disabilities" are not simply a loss, and should not be seen as intrinsically evil. Other identity constituting features of a person's life might indeed be evil, however, such as physical or psychological abuse. The fact that R. Adams's point about identity applies in both cases might seem to lead to a problematic collapsing of intrinsic goods and bads into a flat "needful for me." In response, R. Adams suggests that his view should not foster an attitude of complacency, in which everything that is part of our histories is taken to be justified or good (a characteristic mistake of popular pieties of predestination or providence, at least in some traditions). Rather, R. Adams suggests, we should regard the negative aspects of our lives with a complex ambivalence, in which we regret the acknowledged evils in each life but regard the life itself with love and thankfulness. This admixture of regret and gratitude is appropriate, he argues, if we regard each life from within the framework of a world that we consider comprehensively good:

> It may be hard in the end, however, to see any all-things-considered gladness as justified except in a religious context, and a certain sort of religious context at that. What I have in mind is an eschatology, and a theology of history, that would support us in believing that what is given us to love is so good that the totality of our history with God will provide a framework of gladness in which all our just regrets can be contextualized.[25]

---

23. I want to thank Kevin Timpe for his insightful comments on especially this part of my discussion.

24. Adams, "Love and the Problem of Evil," 246.

25. Adams, "Love and the Problem of Evil," 251.

Here it is natural to draw on McCord Adams's suggestion, discussed in the previous section, that imperfect lives that participate in divine goodness and beauty can not only be worth living but can be occasions for praise and thanksgiving. In the context of the defeat of horrors described by McCord Adams, in which a person's life is good to him or her on the whole, it seems reasonable to follow Robert Adams in arguing that God can be seen as good even when permitting evil, if participation in that evil is crucial to the identity of a beloved person, for whose life and existence we are grateful. In this context we may reasonably both sorrow over evil and accept that it is, in a certain respect, necessary. It is necessary not simply pedagogically, or for the sake of some greater good to exist in creaturely lives, but for the sake of those particular lives themselves.

It might not be obvious how this theodicy of a divine love that claims us for participation in God's life is related to my contention throughout this essay that compatibilism offers certain advantages to those who seek theological answers to the questions raised by evil. Consider, however, what would be necessary for God to elect and will a world and its particular history, so that it can give rise to and support the lives of the specific individuals who have the particular identities that God loves and wishes to give birth to. Prior to creation, God would need to know with a very high degree of certainty that the story of the world would include the specific lives in which God would love to participate. This would seem to require, or at the very least fit best with, some sort of (perhaps partial) divine determinism.[26] Without divine shepherding of at least crucial developments in the story of the world writ large as well as of particular persons, God would simply be gambling with creation, perhaps forced to create multiple worlds in order to find the beloved God originally had in mind. If God is to be parent of particular children, of us, then the events that make us who we are must come to pass.

The widely used metaphors of God as author and world history as a story are helpful here. If, having imagined specific characters in a particular story, God loves them and wishes to bring them to life, God is under certain constraints in doing so. The persons we know in this world exist within a context of evil and are who they are because of the histories they have. Even if God destines humanity for eternal happiness and joy, a framework of gladness that will re-contextualize all our sorrows, God cannot make *us* without those sorrows. For that would be to

---

26. A related possibility that I am unable to discuss here is that of divine "middle knowledge." For one relevant discussion, see Vitale, "Horrendous Evils."

make others—also good, but different. If, however, for whatever reason God loves us and wants our stories to be told, certain things in history must come to pass. It may be that certain things in my or your life could be different without the loss of anything very important to our identities. A great many things, though, are crucially formative, necessary elements of our stories. Writing our stories thus requires that God determine significant aspects of history. It would be ironic if that were to mean that we are therefore not free and responsible agents who are capable of loving God in a manner similar to the way in which God loves us. Compatibilist views allow us to welcome the idea that God destines *us* for existence, we who are free to claim God as parent just as God claims us as children, and that being under such a divine determination gives great meaning and excellence to our lives in spite of certain tragic necessities.

5. CONCLUSION: WRESTLING WITH EVIL

There is a sense in which the problem of evil is intractable. We cannot justify all the suffering we see in our own lives, in lives around us, and throughout human (and animal) history. It remains unclear whether many individual evils really need to be permitted in order to attain definite goods. For these reasons, McCord Adams was right to be skeptical about some common theodical projects, which seek to explain too much. It is possible, however, to honor her skepticism and embrace her emphasis on the limits of human agency and understanding, while also building on the positive themes introduced in her own theodicy, if we attend to the theological resources made available by an Augustinian compatibilism.

To fit each of us for participation in the divine life God might elect to permit some evils that shape us and our stories in certain ways. The role of horrendous evils in our lives remains mysterious, but given the ways in which our identities are tied up with horrors, it might not be possible for God to give *us* life without also making room for suffering, even horrendous suffering. This does not explain or justify horrors, in the traditional sense of offering a reasonably satisfactory explanation for why they happen or how it is in certain respects better that they did. Nevertheless, it does re-contextualize the ugliness of evil while offering us a way to see the God who permits such evil as caring rather than heartless. Electing to create a world like ours, and people like us, seems permissible if God cannot have us any other way, and if God elects and destines us for relationships of love, and thus for lives that are a blessing to those who live them and to those who share in them. From such a perspective, evil remains foul, unattractive, and much to be regretted. Perhaps even God might wish for less suffering. Yet there is also beauty and grace in a love that seeks the beloved in spite of these limitations.

PART II

Individuals in Community

6

Friendship, Human and Divine

Shannon Craigo-Snell

This essay analyzes the role of friendship in the theology of Marilyn McCord Adams, particularly in regards to claiming God. Setting her work beside that of theologians Natalia Marandiuc and Karl Rahner clarifies the very particular space that McCord Adams carves out for human friendship. These theologians are representative of theologies that ascribe human relationships power to make or break human development (Marandiuc) or individual salvation (Rahner). McCord Adams avoids both options, prioritizing Divine-human friendship as decisive for both human development and salvation. At the same time, McCord Adams grants a different value to human friendship—perhaps even more exalted—as a universal eschatological reality through which humans become part of the Trinitarian friendship of God. Friendship—Divine and human—is both how and why God claims us, and how we, in turn, claim God.

Theologians use a number of different terms to identify positive relationships between humans, each of which taps particular traditions. "Love" is used by many to indicate a wide variety of relationships. Others parse types of love appropriate to particular relationships: agape, eros, and so forth. Karl Rahner uses the term love, hearkening to the biblical commandment to love God and neighbor. Natalia Marandiuc, drawing on "neuro-scientific research and attachment psychology," writes specifically about positive relationships of love and attachment.[1] In her theological works as a whole, McCord Adams speaks less of love—human or Divine—that one might expect of a theologian. Instead, she writes of Divine goodness and of friendship. The term friendship aligns her with discourse of spiritual friendship and friendship with God. In this essay, I will compare these discourses under the shared heading of positive human relationships. While they are each distinctive, their commonalities warrant considering them as part of the same conversation.

1. FRIENDSHIP AND GOD'S PROJECT

In *Christ and Horrors*, McCord Adams draws explicitly on Cicero's vision of human friendship as "one soul in two bodies."[2] Usually such friendships occur between "two persons who are stabilized in a certain bent; wanting to grow in a certain direction" such that each can provide support to the other as they seek a common goal.[3] McCord Adams writes: "Such intensity of shared purpose and affection trusts without reservation, supports without hesitation, loves the other more than self, creates such a depth of understanding as to put the one in a position to act and speak on behalf of the other. . . . Friendship is thus an end in itself, one of the great joys of life."[4] Such friendship can exist within or independent of romantic or familial relationship. McCord Adams embraces this very high view of friendship and uses it to create analogies for "conceptualizing Godhead, Divine-human relations, and Christ's mediating role."[5] Intra-human friendship becomes a metaphor by which to understand God, the universe, and everything: "the whole universe is envisioned as a society of friends, with Christ as center."[6]

Richard of St. Victor contributes a friendship-based vision of the Trinity. God's omnibenevolence would necessarily be other-directed, and the only possible recipient of the no-holds-barred sharing of infinite goodness would be another Divine person. Divine omnibenevolence means a permanent sharing of essence. In order to achieve this, "Divine

---

1. Marandiuc, *The Goodness of Home*, 5.
2. McCord Adams, *Christ and Horrors*, 155.
3. McCord Adams, *Christ and Horrors*, 155.
4. McCord Adams, *Christ and Horrors*, 156.
5. McCord Adams, *Christ and Horrors*, 156.
6. McCord Adams, *Christ and Horrors*, 156.

Goodness 'twins' itself."[7] However, this friendship can only reach its consummation in the mutual love for a common object, so a third Divine person is necessary: the Holy Spirit.[8]

Understanding the Trinity through the metaphor of friendship is not unique to Richard of St. Victor. McCord Adams brings support from Bonaventure and the Johannine writings to buttress and further develop this vision. In Jesus, Divine friendship opens to humanity. Jesus perfectly shares the likes and dislikes, the commitments and outlooks, of the Father. First through Jesus' friendship, and then through the indwelling of the Spirit, Jesus' followers are invited to share the same worldview and purpose and "become collaborators with God."[9] Disciples are invited into the Divine friendship, particularly through the commandment that they love one another. It is in being true friends—which is defined by God's likes and dislikes—that human beings enter into the Trinitarian friendship.

Having described the Godhead in terms of friendship, it is not surprising that friendship plays a large role in McCord Adams's depiction of God's project—that is, God's aim in creation. McCord Adams proposes that "God must love material creation with a love that dual-drives towards assimilation and union."[10] This involves some sub-hypotheses. First, God loves material creation. Second, McCord Adams contends, God is personal.[11] As a personal Godhead, profitably understood as the Triune friendship of infinite benevolence, God wants other persons to love, and particularly material friends. In order to have such friends, God creates and takes on the assimilative goal of making material as God-like as possible. God desires to sanctify matter, to, in a phrase McCord Adams used often in conversation, "knead light into clay." McCord Adams understands human nature as the crown of God's efforts to make material creation God-like.[12]

7. McCord Adams, *Christ and Horrors*, 157.
8. McCord Adams, *Christ and Horrors*, 156.
9. McCord Adams, *Christ and Horrors*, 158.
10. McCord Adams, *Christ and Horrors*, 39.
11. McCord Adams, *Christ and Horrors*, 49.
12. McCord Adams's published theological work focuses on Divine-human relationship without exploring broader interrelations between divinity and creation and with little priority given to understanding humanity as part of creation, rather than its pinnacle. Wendy Petersen Boring's essay in this volume brings out some of the ecological implications found in McCord Adams's unpublished sermons, which offers new ways to interpret the corpus. In her life, McCord Adams delighted in the beauty of nature, especially ladybugs, but did not, to my knowledge, ever have a friendship with an animal. She disliked cats, therefore they sought her out at every opportunity.

> This assimilative aim is a precursor to God's unitive aim. Having made beings who are inextricably material and spiritual—personal animals—God desires to be in unity with them. On the one hand, God wants matter to be as Godlike as possible while still being itself. Like any good parent with its offspring, God wants as far as possible for creatures to be like God and still possess their own integrity. So God makes chemicals and stuffs dynamic, plants and animals vital, human beings personal. Human nature crowns God's efforts to make material creation—while yet material—more and more like God. On the other hand, God's passion for material creation expresses itself in a Divine desire to unite with it, not only to enter into personal intimacy, but to "go all the way" and share its nature in hypostatic union.[13]

God's project, which McCord Adams cashes out more precisely in assimilative and unitive aims, is fundamentally a desire for personal intimacy with another. God desires to expand the (sufficient unto itself) circle of friendship that is the Trinity. Humanity arises due to God's yearning for new friends.

This statement is not benign. McCord Adams is clear that God's aims put humanity in a very tough spot. Light and clay do not mix easily. God's project has created at least three forms of "metaphysical mismatch."[14] The first is within humanity. As personal, humans are all about meaning making and relationships. As animals, we are subject to developmental cycles, external harm, diseases and disorders, and sickness unto death. Our need for meaning-making as persons is easily thwarted by threats or harms to our well-being as animals. Conversely, difficulties that befall us as animals take on greater destructive power as we attempt, often unsuccessfully, to make meaning. The second mismatch is between humanity and our earthly context of real and perceived scarcity, in which meaning-making is easily thwarted by "fear and animal aggression" as we struggle to survive.[15] The third mismatch is between God and humanity. Even if we personal animals do our best to survive and make meaning, the ultimate goal of Divine/human friendship is made difficult by the

---

13. McCord Adams, *Christ and Horrors*, 39.
14. McCord Adams, *Christ and Horrors*, 38.
15. McCord Adams, *Christ and Horrors*, 38.

metaphysical size gap between humanity and God. "What we are and what Divinity is make communication difficult and trust hard to win."[16]

In McCord Adams's reading, God has taken on a very strange project, and the Divine assimilative and unitive aims put humanity directly in harm's way. We are vulnerable to evil. McCord Adams does not take evil lightly, nor is she willing to consider human experiences of evil as sufficiently justified if they are necessary to God's long-term project. In sharp contrast to theodicies that are satisfied with some possibility that evil is necessary for God's cosmic intentions, McCord Adams's work demands that if God put us in the path of evil, God can and will defeat the evils we encounter. She writes, "My claim is that Divine love would not subject some individual created persons to horrors simply for the benefit of others or to enhance cosmic excellence. Divine love would permit horrors only if God could overcome them by integrating them into lives that are overwhelmingly good for the horror-participants themselves."[17]

In *Horrendous Evils and the Love of God*, McCord Adams focuses her theodicy not on evil generally, but on what she terms "horrendous evils." These are "evils the participation in which (the doing or suffering of) constitutes prima facie reason to doubt whether the participant's life could (given their inclusion in it) have positive meaning for him/her on the whole."[18] Setting herself a very high bar, McCord Adams foregrounds evils so destructive that it seems like a person involved in them would be better off if they had never been born. This definition spotlights McCord Adams's understanding of evil as that which destroys human meaning-making. Because of this, McCord Adams's definition is "objective but relative to individuals," meaning that it addresses concrete events and conditions while recognizing that what counts as horrendous varies from person to person, culture to culture.[19] Finally, by focusing on the possibility or impossibility of a participant in evil finding positive meaning in their own life, McCord Adams sets a standard in which the only acceptable responses to evil must do more than justify the existence of evil over the whole of human history, but rather must provide positive meaning for each participant in evil.

---

16. McCord Adams, *Christ and Horrors*, 38.
17. McCord Adams, *Christ and Horrors*, 45.
18. McCord Adams, *Horrendous Evils*, 26.
19. McCord Adams, *Christ and Horrors*, 33.

McCord Adams outlines a three-stage process by which God defeats evil; a process in which friendship plays a central role. Stage I is the incarnation. God participates with us in the horrors of human life as a victim, as one whose life occasioned horrors, and—as part of a broken society and therefore complicit in social harm—a perpetrator of horrors.[20] In the incarnation, God takes a definite step towards the Divine unitive aim in hypostatic union. And, vital for the defeat of horrors, Jesus' metaphysically solidarity with humanity establishes "a relation of organic unity between the person's horror-participation and his/her intimate, personal, and overall beatific relationship with God."[21] Because Jesus is in the horror with us, even the horrors we participate in can be points of connection in our relationship. Furthermore, that relationship is/will be so very good that the horrors themselves take on meaning as a part of that.

It is important to note that McCord Adams is not saying that horrors cease to be horrendous or that horrors are in any way necessary or even beneficial, but rather that they can be integrated organically into a relationship in such a way that their meaning changes. This is something that happens in human friendships all the time. I was fortunate enough to be friends with Marilyn McCord Adams. When I encountered horrors—a series of miscarriages and terrible medical care—she supported me. She did not heal my injuries, restore my losses, or reverse the pain of hopes destroyed. And yet, over time, part of the import of these events in my life was transmuted by her presence. I remember not only the pain, but her care. Not only my anguish, but her endless supply of tea and chocolate chip cookies. These events have taken on the meaning of being part of our friendship—a friendship which is a very great good in my life. If this example resonates, imagine how much more important such transmuted meaning is when the friend—the one who stays and cares in the midst of suffering—is Jesus.

Often, due to the metaphysical mismatch between human and Divine friends, we cannot apprehend that Jesus is present with us in the midst of horrors. McCord Adams preached an Easter sermon in which she addressed this specifically. She instructed,

> think back to the most terrifying experience of your life.... Remember, re-enter those times when you were really convinced it was all over, when you were absolutely certain there was no

---

20. McCord Adams, *Christ and Horrors*, 69–71.
21. McCord Adams, *Christ and Horrors*, 66.

power in you—body, mind, or spirit—strong enough to pull you together, enable you to stand.

But here you are, risen from the bed! You've got yourself to church on Easter Sunday, more or less clothed and in your right mind![22]

Most of the time we interpret such revival as indication that we misjudged the situation. The horrors weren't really that bad; our resources greater than we knew. However, McCord Adams exhorted, a different interpretation is not only possible but demanded by the message of resurrection. Things really were that bad; we really couldn't survive it on our own. We survived because Jesus was with us. God is with us through all our "daily deaths and resurrections."[23]

Realizing that God was with us is part of the second stage of horror defeat, which McCord Adams describes as "healing and otherwise enabling the horror-participant's meaning-making capacities so that s/he can recognize and appropriate some of the positive significance laid down in Stage I."[24] This is the stage within McCord Adams's own work is set: an attempt to make meaning in relationship with God who is with us and for us. Given the extreme vulnerability of humans as personal animals, much of Stage II horror-defeat cannot occur in our ante mortem life. Abuse, disease, and trauma can cause such psychic damage that meaning-making capacities cannot be healed this side of the river Jordan. McCord Adams embraces postmortem life as the setting for much healing and meaning-making, in which one can perceive more clearly God's loving presence even in the midst of horrors.

Finally, for such meaning to be definitive, to hold fast and not crumble, the vulnerability to horrors that marks human life must end. "The plot cannot really resolve into a happy ending unless the relation of embodied persons to our material environment is renegotiated so that we are no longer radically vulnerable to horrors."[25] McCord Adams rejects any vision of eternal bliss that leaves embodiment and matter behind. God's project of kneading light into clay, of creating personal animals that are therefore radically vulnerable to horrors, has been far too costly

---

22. McCord Adams, *Wrestling for Blessing*, 71.
23. McCord Adams, *Wrestling for Blessing*, 71.
24. McCord Adams, *Christ and Horrors*, 66.
25. McCord Adams, *Christ and Horrors*, 48.

to be "a temporary episode to be left behind."[26] Stage III horror-defeat take place in eternal life, where the meaning made in Stage II becomes permanent and inviolable.

Convinced that God "is the only good great enough to defeat horrors and restore us to positively meaningful lives," McCord Adams aims to identify "a transaction" that puts the goodness of God "on our side."[27] To this end, in *Christ and Horrors*, McCord Adams writes extensively about sacrificial understandings of salvation. She describes no less than thirteen forms of sacrifice before creating a taxonomy of three: communion, gift sacrifices, and sacrifices for sin.[28] This seeming simplification turns into a jumping off point for recasting sacrificial roles in layer upon layer. God sacrifices humanity to God and Jesus to humanity; humanity sacrifices Jesus to God; Jesus sacrifices Himself as both priest and victim. The cumulative account of the Christ event and our eucharistic participation in it includes: communion sacrifice, holocaust sacrifice, first-fruits sacrifice, gift sacrifice, hatta't sacrifice, self-sacrifice, covenant sacrifices, and thank offerings.[29] McCord Adams rehabilitates the concept of sacrifice, which has been soundly critiqued in recent decades, by excavating its complexities and the ways in which understanding Jesus as sacrifice includes asymmetrical mutuality between God and humanity.

However, while it is prima facie unwise to disagree with a theologian's representation of her own scholarship, I argue that the concept of sacrifice does very little work in McCord Adams's theology. One could omit the section on sacrifice and the logic of *Christ and Horrors* would still cohere. In my reading, the driving explanatory power of McCord Adams's theology is not sacrifice, but friendship. What is ultimately needed for the goodness of God to be "on our side" is not a "transaction" but a relationship.

The goodness of God requires friendship and is therefore Triune. God desires material friends and therefore creates. Humans are created from the beginning to function in conjunction and friendship with God. And when God's friendship project sets humanity up for horrors, those horrors are defeated through friendship with God. The logic of McCord Adams's theology rests on friendship. In the remainder of this essay I will

---

26. McCord Adams, *Christ and Horrors*, 50.
27. McCord Adams, *Christ and Horrors*, 273.
28. McCord Adams, *Christ and Horrors*, 270–81.
29. McCord Adams, *Christ and Horrors*, 275–78.

draw out implications of McCord Adams's writings on friendship, moving beyond her explicitly stated views.

2. THE PROBLEMS OF HUMAN FRIENDSHIP

While human relationships are often idealized in religious and theological contexts, friendship and attachment are also dangerous and painful. Natalia Marandiuc and Karl Rahner are two theologians who both identify dangers of human love relationships and sill give such relationships decisive power in the development and salvation of the self.

Natalia Marandiuc, in her book, *The Goodness of Home: Human and Divine Love and the Making of the Self*, emphasizes the psychological role of close attachment relationships in human development, as well as what happens when such relationships are missing. Marandiuc is not talking about friendship, in particular, and her primary metaphor is of home and family. Yet she is one of the theologians who best articulates the idea that human relationships are theologically necessary for human development.

Marandiuc argues that such "relations of love and attachment . . . cocreate human subjectivity."[30] In her account, "human love attachments are irreducibly needed for the actualization of the human self"; "love is a source of subjectivity"; and "human attachments produce human selves."[31] "Home consists of love relationships that constitute the human self, a self that is, in fact, "selved" and "actualized through the experience of love."[32] Marandiuc wishes to avoid the possibility that a human who is not provided an appropriate "home" of relations will be stunted beyond repair in a theological sense. She asserts that God is always involved in the process of self-actualization, as Divine and human loves "are never mutually exclusive or binary categories."[33] Further, "the kernel of love that God gives everyone, even when massively undercultivated or shaken, does not disappear."[34] Yet Marandiuc's intent is to emphasize the great harm we can inflict upon one another, going so far as to reduce the un-homed person to not fully a "self."

---

30. Marandiuc, *The Goodness of Home*, 1.
31. Marandiuc, *The Goodness of Home*, 5.
32. Marandiuc, *The Goodness of Home*, 12.
33. Marandiuc, *The Goodness of Home*, 13.
34. Marandiuc, *The Goodness of Home*, 192.

One of the key aspects of human loves that "home" a person and nurture the process of becoming a self is recognition. Mining the work of Charles Taylor, Marandiuc describes recognition as an exchange with another person that "validates who, what, and how the person is."[35] Going further than Taylor, Marandiuc argues that "the self *as such* is formed and actualized in such exchanges."[36] A person who sees herself as kind, for example, is affirmed and encouraged when another recognizes her kindness. This is not, for Marandiuc, simply a matter of acknowledging what is already true. It is through the (ongoing) process of recognition that it becomes true, that a person becomes, in this example, kind.[37] In Marandiuc's root metaphor of home, the process might look something like this: A child is born into a home, which consists of a small number of attachment relationships. The others in this child's life recognize him as a person, worthy and capable of love, and thus create the conditions in which his identity as a self, worthy and capable of love, comes to be.

However, this process often goes awry. The relational home is not present, or perhaps it misrecognizes the child. The process of "selving" or self-becoming is inhibited or distorted. This happens both on a small scale—a particular child is misrecognized as unlovable—and on a large scale—particular groups of people are misrecognized as inferior.[38] It is the danger of misrecognition and thwarted self-actualization that drives Marandiuc's writing, which is a warning and a roadmap towards being "home" to each other.

Theologian Karl Rahner has a very different concern about human love relationships. Put simply, they hurt. Friendship always ends in pain. Either the one you love, a flawed and finite being, turns out to be unworthy of your love, or she dies, leaving you heartbroken. Rahner takes the pain of grief seriously. Recalling friends who have died, he states, "every one of the departed has taken a piece of my heart with him, and often enough my whole heart."[39]

Friendship is dangerous. Misrecognition can impede the full becoming of the self; on a larger scale, it can damage whole groups of people. Even when friendship goes well, it still leads to pain and heartbreak. And yet, for all its dangers, friendship holds a vital role for Marandiuc and Rahner.

35. Marandiuc, *The Goodness of Home*, 53.
36. Marandiuc, *The Goodness of Home*, 53.
37. Marandiuc also references Levinas in relation to this process.
38. Marandiuc, *The Goodness of Home*, 55.
39. Rahner, *Prayers for a Lifetime*, 145.

3. THE IMPERATIVE OF HUMAN FRIENDSHIP

Even though loving human relationships have dangers, for Marandiuc and Rahner, they are still imperative. For Marandiuc, attachment relationships mediate Divine love and are required for the becoming of the self. This is a theological account of human relationships as developmentally decisive. In the context of addressing the "relational poverty" of contemporary life and the mass movement of peoples in the twenty-first century, Marandiuc warns that lack of attachment relationships to "home" the self can thwart the process of becoming. Drawing on Kierkegaard, Marandiuc describes human love as mediating Divine love and argues that "human loves are *necessary* in the making of the self."[40]

Rahner also writes of loving human relationships as being borne by God and as being decisive, although in his case human love is both developmentally and salvifically decisive. In Rahner's theological anthropology, human identity is both a gift and a task. We become who we most truly are when we love God and neighbor. He writes, "One may speak of a commandment of love as long as one does not forget that this law does not command man to do something or other but simply commands him to fulfil himself, and charges man with himself, i.e., himself as the possibility of love in the acceptance of the love in which God does not give something but gives Himself."[41]

Loving one's neighbor is the paradigmatic act of faith for Rahner, presupposing (on some level) the reality of Divine love and that such love includes the neighbor.[42] His logic runs like this: The choice to love another person is neither benign nor reasonable. The only person whom one could safely love unconditionally—without risking disappointment, betrayal, and grief—is Jesus Christ. To open oneself so completely to anyone other than Jesus would be unfounded: "It would be ascribing to the lover, and even more so the beloved, an unconditionality and absolute validity which is simply not attributable to them."[43] It is only with Jesus, who is in union with God and is unconditionally accepted by God, that love has "the right of extravagance."[44]

---

40. Marandiuc, *The Goodness of Home*, 19, 15.
41. Rahner, "The 'Commandment' of Love," 456.
42. Rahner, *The Love of Jesus*, 44.
43. Rahner, *The Love of Jesus*, 40.
44. Rahner, *The Love of Jesus*, 41.

And yet, in Jesus, union with God and acceptance by God have been extended to all of humanity. Each person we encounter is God's beloved. Therefore, it is not unfounded, inauthentic, or self-deceiving to truly love another person, because that love is generated, empowered, and grounded by God. For Rahner, the risk of love does not disappear, but it is borne by Jesus. Neighbor love is a form of recognition—recognizing the other as within the scope of Divine love. It is the way that humans say "yes" to God's grace, and the way that humans fully become themselves.

For both Marandiuc and Rahner, recognition is a key point in positive human relationships, although they differ in who needs to be recognized. For Marandiuc, the becoming self needs to be recognized by attachment loves. For Rahner, it is the self who needs to recognize (consciously or unconsciously) others as beloved by God in order for the self to accept God's salvific grace.

4. DIVINE-HUMAN FRIENDSHIP IN MCCORD ADAMS'S THEOLOGY

While both Marandiuc and Rahner portray God as present in human love relationships, McCord Adams goes straight for Divine-human friendship as the primary and decisive relationship for human development and salvation.

Herself a student of psychology, McCord Adams is aware of much of the knowledge on which Marandiuc's theology draws. McCord Adams rehearses the basics of human development, describes humans as "born with a capacity to be personal" that "has to be evoked by personal contact."[45] Children deprived of caretakers "do not actualize this capacity to be personal," and adults who have become personal can have that capacity damaged by isolation.[46]

If this developmental process goes well, a next step is differentiation. Psychology envisions an ideal in which a child is cared for by others, actualizes her own capacity to be personal, and then successfully differentiates herself from her caregivers, becoming an individuated self who is capable of personal relations.

McCord Adams understands the wisdom of psychology but moves toward theology for a more Divinely centered view of humanity. McCord

---

45. McCord Adams, *Christ and Horrors*, 154.
46. McCord Adams, *Christ and Horrors*, 154–55.

Adams sees God as our primary caretaker, following the works Julian of Norwich, who portrays Jesus and the Trinity as the mother of all humans in two related ways. Metaphysically, God our mother is the ground of our being and we are "deeply set in God."[47] Functionally, God our mother indwells us; the Trinity makes "their home within us at the core of who we are."[48] This mothering enables our capacity to be spiritual persons. However, the goal of self-actualization in regards to God our mother is not total differentiation, but rather functional collaboration within the self. "The goal of spiritual life is for us to become ever more aware of and cooperative with such enfolding presence that we are best seen functionally, consciously as well as unconsciously, as only semi-differentiated."[49]

While McCord Adams values the psychological growth necessary to become an "autonomous ego with adult competences," she argues that it would be mistaken to imagine that as the pinnacle of human development. God intends more for us. Human persons only function at our best when "friendship with God becomes the functional core of who we are."[50] God is always with us, guiding us, loving us. Yet given the size-gap, it takes practice and discipline for us to gain awareness of God's presence and still more to respond with "friendly gestures" of our own.[51] When we do this, we "consciously and deliberately consent" to allowing "our adult selves to be restructured, to tangle us up with the divine life, so that our functional core is not a "solo" (the isolated ego) but a duet or—considering that God is a Trinity—a quartet."[52]

McCord Adams offers a compelling psycho-theological portrayal of human development, in which Divine-human friendship allows the person to become part of the friendship in the Trinity, and the Trinity to become part of the person. Eschewing a singular line of inclusion, McCord Adams depicts a relational "tangle" in which human and Divine live together.

---

47. McCord Adams, *Christ and Horrors*, 160.
48. McCord Adams, *Christ and Horrors*, 160.
49. McCord Adams, *Christ and Horrors*, 160.
50. McCord Adams, "Prayer as the 'Lifeline of Theology,'" 275.
51. McCord Adams, "Prayer as the 'Lifeline of Theology,'" 275–76.
52. McCord Adams, "Prayer as the 'Lifeline of Theology,'" 275.

5. HUMAN FRIENDSHIP IN MCCORD ADAMS'S THEOLOGY

When we cultivate such "cohabitation" and friendship with God, we are shaped "toward holiness."[53] We begin to share "God's passions and allergies."[54]

> Consciously and unconsciously opening to God drops our defenses and makes us vulnerable to sympathetic vibration with God's own passions: with divine delight in Truth and beauty, with God's hunger and thirst for joyful life together with all created persons, with God's blessed rage for justice, with God's apoplectic intolerance of human cruelty and degradation.[55]

In her more technical writing, McCord Adams addresses the sharing of likes and dislikes with the Latin phrase *idem velle, idem nolle*, which is used to characterize true friendship.[56] For McCord Adams, friendship with God is primary. Yet God loves people, so friendship with God necessarily involves friendship with people. *Idem velle, idem nolle*, when cashed out a bit, is profoundly social. It involves "heightened empathetic alertness" to the rest of the world.[57] McCord Adams makes Divine-human friendship primary, and human friendship flows out of that relation.

The choice to make Divine-human friendship primary allows McCord Adams to avoid some of the dangers of prioritizing human relationships. Because she chose to reflect publicly and theologically on her own life, we have the benefit of knowing something about how human relationships influenced her, both negatively and positively. I suggest that her own experience instilled a primary reliance on God's friendship and shaped McCord Adams's faith through a distinctly roundabout form of recognition.

In her essay, "Truth and Reconciliation," McCord Adams describes her childhood home as "chaotic, conflicted, and violent."[58] She was "the

---

53. McCord Adams, "Prayer as the 'Lifeline of Theology,'" 279.
54. McCord Adams, "Prayer as the 'Lifeline of Theology,'" 279.
55. McCord Adams, "Prayer as the 'Lifeline of Theology,'" 279.
56. McCord Adams, *Christ and Horrors*, 162.
57. McCord Adams, "Prayer as the 'Lifeline of Theology,'" 279.
58. McCord Adams, "Truth and Reconciliation," 16.

target of relentless physical and psychological abuse."[59] In this context, McCord Adams's identity as a person worthy of love, as a beloved child of God, was not recognized, to use Marandiuc's term. Indeed, she was misrecognized. That misrecognition made it difficult for McCord Adams to come to know herself as beloved by God. There were steps along the way, including philosophy and liturgy. One of the steps she describes as vital involved a form of recognition rather different than Marandiuc describes.

In the 1980s, McCord Adams ministered to homeless people in Hollywood, California. This was the height of the AIDS epidemic in the U.S. In writings, sermons, and conversations, McCord Adams credited her experiences at Trinity Hollywood as teaching her truths vital to her own meaning-making struggles. She witnessed friends and partners caring for one another in the worst of times, recognizing "sacrificial love and faithfulness persevering to the end" in relationships between others.[60] In those loving relationships, McCord Adams "saw God-with-us at work in the midst of horrendous suffering."[61]

The human friendships McCord Adams witnessed were revelatory for her, in the full theological meaning of the word. In human friendship, she spied Divine love. She then realized that if these men, who were suffering horrendous evils, were loved by God, perhaps she, too, who had suffered horrendous evils, was loved by God. So convinced was she that God loved these men, that she stepped into the pulpit to deliver fiery sermons about the unrelenting love of God, bringing her enduring theology of God's fierce goodness to articulation.[62] Preaching to congregants dying from AIDS, she wasted no time, cut straight to the chase, and proclaimed the wideness of God's mercy with what became trademark urgency. She reflected, "Preaching the Gospel to people whose gray-green skin tells you that they won't be there in six months creates a pressure to tell as much Truth as one can."[63] McCord Adams recognized God's love for others, and in proclaiming that love, began to extrapolate her own beloved status.

This process does not begin with, nor rely on, another person recognizing one's value. It starts in recognizing the value of the other, matures

---

59. McCord Adams, "Truth and Reconciliation," 16.
60. McCord Adams, "Truth and Reconciliation," 25.
61. McCord Adams, "Truth and Reconciliation," 25.
62. McCord Adams, "Truth and Reconciliation," 25.
63. McCord Adams, "Love of Learning," 157.

in claiming that love, and extrapolates the love of God to oneself.[64] McCord Adams was not only clear about the effect of this roundabout process of recognition in her own life; she commended it to others: Begin by claiming the love of God for others and eventually you might include yourself in its scope. This process reflects McCord Adams's own life experience. It also reveals her careful handling of human friendship as a part of Christian life.

While friendship is central to her theology, McCord Adams does not ascribe human friendship a necessary and decisive role in development or salvation. This contrasts sharply with Maradiuc. Emphasizing the great harm we can inflict upon one another, Marandiuc goes so far as to reduce the un-homed person to not fully a "self." McCord Adams understands the harm and is unwilling to let love from others determine whether or not a person becomes fully themselves. Too many people do not experience such loving relational homes.

Marandiuc writes explicitly that while "Marilyn McCord Adams contends that one's sense of value of life and of one's personhood are degraded and defeated when one's meaning-making structures collapse. My claim is that meaning is rooted in love."[65] Marandiuc's theology departs from McCord Adams in two ways here. First, Marandiuc names intra-human love as central to the root of meaning. Second, Marandiuc's understanding of selfhood does not delineate strongly between one's self-understanding, experience, or meaning and their actual human selfhood. McCord Adams does. While we are meaning-making animals, we are still such even if we cannot fully make meaning. This different understanding of human selfhood is a theological guard against the notion that we have the ability to destroy one another fully. We can inflict terrible harm, but for McCord Adams, we do not have ultimately ruinous power.

Recall McCord Adams's description of God mothering humanity. She carefully delineates two forms of mothering: metaphysical and functional. Metaphysically, we are grounded in God and God is with us. We

---

64. While McCord Adams and her husband are more than friends in colloquial terms, their relationship is certainly a friendship in Cicero's exalted description. She credits this friendship with a vital role in her spiritual life that is not recognition. McCord Adams says of her husband, Robert Merrihew Adams, "His strength of character and firm faith have provided the stability and safety I needed to wrestle with God and to venture many things." McCord Adams, "Truth and Reconciliation," 21. Given that McCord Adams understands wrestling with God to be a primary task of human life, this is a very strong statement.

65. Marandiuc, *The Goodness of Home*, 27.

have the capacity to collaborate with God, and this is capacity is part of human nature. Functionally, we can come to collaborate with God in our daily life. Our capacity for collaboration with the Divine passes "from potency to act."[66] When a person begins to collaborate with God, this is a real transformation. However, the person is still a person if it never happens. The dynamic of potency and act applies to meaning-making, as well.

Karl Rahner is also wary of granting other people the possibility of doing ruinous harm to the human person. As noted above, he does make self-actualization hinge on neighbor love, but the key is loving the neighbor, not being loved by them. Scholars such as Jennifer Beste have pointed out that these two things cannot be easily separated. Her research shows that survivors of chronic incest often find loving others difficult, or even impossible, due to the lasting psychological and neurological effects of the abuse.[67] Rahner's strongest guard against other people having theological power over one's self-actualization (and, in his theology, even acceptance of salvation) is his understanding of the human person. His theological anthropology employs a spiritually reinterpreted Kantian framework. As historical and social, we are deeply intertwined with others and shaped by our contexts, vulnerable to the suffering that befalls us. And yet, as transcendental, we have a graced and sturdy freedom that cannot be negated or destroyed by others. Even if a person never loves another in a way that can be humanly recognized, that does not mean it doesn't happen. Such a guard would not work for McCord Adams because her view of the human person is too profoundly embodied to imagine any aspect of the self could be unscathed by horrendous evils.

6. FRIENDSHIP AS ESCHATOLOGICAL

Seen from one angle, the fact that McCord Adams does not claim friendship as developmentally or salvifically decisive is a diminishment of her otherwise exalted view of friendship. However, from another angle, McCord Adams makes friendship far more ultimate than our interlocutors, Marandiuc and Rahner. McCord Adams places friendship—both with God and with humans—squarely in Stage II horror-defeat. Humans are meaning-making beings, and it is in Stage II horror-defeat that we make

---

66. McCord Adams, *Christ and Horrors*, 165.
67. Beste, *God and the Victim*.

positive meaning of our lives through friendship with God and humans. In other words, friendship is how we claim God.

Furthermore, McCord Adams recognizes that for many people Stage II horror-defeat does not happen in earthly life. She banks on postmortem existence—heaven—for the completion of horror-defeat, both arguing and demanding that each and every human being be welcomed into heaven, where horrors are fully defeated. Stage II horror-defeat happens for everyone. This means that, ultimately, every single one of us experiences human friendship. For those of us fortunate enough to experience human friendships during our earthly lives, those friendships become eternal. McCord Adams asserts that the world to come "does not bring an end to the enjoyment of shared creativity in which we collaborate with God and other creatures as friends."[68] For all of us, there is more friendship to come. Heaven is, for McCord Adams, "a state of beatific enjoyment of God and of our fellow human beings."[69] Friendship is not the starting point of being human. It is, instead, the culmination of humanity and its eternal fulfillment.

Her position acknowledges that real friendship, or loving human relationship, is too scarce and fragile to hold decisive power, either developmental or salvific. It is Marandiuc's awareness of the insufficient number of loving attachment homes that prompts her to emphasize how important they are by describing their decisive role. She bites the particular theological bullet of describing homes that are few and fragile as theologically necessary for humanity, issuing a holy challenge to set things right.

Rahner's understanding of neighbor love is incredibly lofty—it is an "all-embracing intercommunication between two infinite mysteries," a "kiss of two eternities."[70] A purely anthropological account of such love would find it exceedingly rare. However, Rahner takes it as an element of Christian faith that, due to the grace of God in Jesus Christ, in every human life "the unfathomable coming to pass of such love does take place, or else such a human being is lost entirely through his or her own fault."[71] Rahner sets the bar for love of neighbor extremely high, so high that it is only possible with God's grace, and makes it decisive for salvation. He

---

68. McCord Adams, *Christ and Horrors*, 240.
69. McCord Adams, *Christ and Horrors*, 227.
70. Rahner, *The Love of Jesus*, 100.
71. Rahner, *The Love of Jesus*, 102.

tempers this, however, by declaring that the incredibly daring and irrational risk of neighbor love can occur in the banality of everyday life. Trivialities such as "the biblical glass of water to someone thirsty, a kind word at someone's sickbed, the refusal to take some small, mean advantage even of someone whose selfishness has infuriated us . . . can be the unassuming accomplishment by which the actual attitude of unselfish brotherly and sisterly communion is consummated."[72] At its best, this is a view of mysticism of everyday life, in which Rahner assures his readers that even the most unremarkable elements of human life are filled with grace. At its worst, this is an unwarranted claim that reduces the elevated ideal of neighbor love to trivia in order to declare it universal.

Both Marandiuc and Rahner realize that friendship—in their corollaries of attachment loves and neighbor love—is difficult. Yet they construct theologies in which such relationships are decisive for the full becoming of the human person. In contrast, McCord Adams's theology, by making human friendship the pinnacle of human becoming rather than the starting point, acknowledges the rarity and exquisite value of such a relationship. Some of us—perhaps many of us—will never have that kind of "two souls in one body" experience in this earthly life, will never be truly recognized by another in all our vulnerable complexity, will never manage to risk our own subjectivity in openness to another. Yet God's goodness provides that each of us will have true friends eventually and eternally. This means that in our present lives, friendship of the kind McCord Adams's describes is a glimpse of heaven. It is part of how we come to recognize God, to claim the love of God for others and ourselves. It is also part of how God claims us, incorporating us into the Trinitarian friendship that is God.

---

72. Rahner, *The Love of Jesus*, 103.

7

Claiming God at the Intersection of Ethics and Climate Change[1]

WENDY PETERSEN BORING

What are the spiritual implications of climate change? I am so hungry for this conversation.

—TERRY TEMPEST WILLIAMS[2]

God calls us to experience the whole universe as a society, a body-politic held together and animated by God, its esprit de corps. God is the One, the only One, Who can underwrite this project.

—MARILYN MCCORD ADAMS[3]

    1. The ideas in this chapter were initially explored in a paper co-written with Emily L. Boring, "God's Self-Diffusing Goodness"; and also in a paper, "Ecclesiology and Climate Change." Many thanks to the organizers and participants of these panels. Special thanks go to Emily L. Boring for continuing to be a conversation partner (and editor) and to Rebecca Voelkel, Ruthanna Hooke, Emily Turner, and Clara Sims for their conversations, contributions, and friendship as the ideas here have taken shape.

    2. Williams, "The Liturgy of Home."

    3. McCord Adams, "Resurrecting the Cosmos," Easter Vigil sermon (2013), Episcopal Church of the Advocate, Chapel Hill, NC. It can be found on McCord Adams's personal website: https://questioninganddisputing.wordpress.com/. Two other

MARILYN MCCORD ADAMS ENGAGED in theology in order to witness to the love of God in the public sphere and to address head on, with grit and precision, the enduring and historically specific reasons it is so very difficult for us to get along and thrive on this planet. Her theology emerged out of her command of the theological and philosophical traditions of the West, her careful study of disciplines from across the social sciences and sciences, and her creative retelling of biblical narratives in the context of a felt and lived faith. I was a student of Marilyn's at Yale University. She advised my dissertation on St. Bonaventure's epistemology and Franciscan spirituality. She was a teacher and a mentor in all respects. She nurtured the deepest parts of me, spirit and intellect.

About eight years ago, I began creating classes that address the historical causes and existential experience of climate change. A hybrid of environmental history, environmental ethics, and philosophy, the classes were designed to address the crisis by asking, "How did we get here?" and "What can we do about it?"[4] Marilyn and I spoke about these classes on several occasions. To follow up, she mailed me a packet of unpublished sermons that focus on diagnosing and responding to the root problems marking human interaction with the natural world.[5] The purpose of this essay is to excavate these and other sermons in order to think alongside McCord Adams about the question: "How, and on what terms, might we 'claim God' in the face of climate change?"

1. CLAIMING

At first glance, the question appears problematic on many levels. Isn't the problem that the public sphere has been "claimed" by climate deniers on the religious right? Evangelical denialists have blessed inaction (why intervene when the world is hurtling towards divine-designated doom?). At

---

sermons, "Bullying" and "Omnibus Benediction" can also be found here. Subsequent references to these online sermons are noted as "online." See also her book of published sermons, *Wrestling for Blessing*.

4. Christensen, "Climate Anxiety Is Real"; Boring, "Sustainability and the Western Civilization Curriculum."

5. The seven unpublished sermons referred to in this essay are: "A Life for a Life!"; "Crucifixion"; "Glorious Challenge!"; "Housing the Holiness"; "Ignorance"; "Interconnection"; and "Terrifying Truths." Subsequent references to these sermons are noted as "unpublished." McCord Adams reworked various themes from these sermons into the sermons that can be found online on her personal website (see n3 above).

the same time, they've allied with climate-change-denying politicians and right-leaning think tanks to create a "carbon-combustion complex" intent on extracting fossil fuels into whatever perpetuity remains after 2°C rise.[6]

How and where a "God claim" might figure in this political landscape remains elusive. Important interfaith and denomination-specific declarations have emerged, naming climate as a moral issue and Creation Care a divine mandate, directing and organizing lobbying and conservation efforts.[7] Despite this work, however, religion has not yet entered climate consciousness on a large scale. People *who believe climate change is human-induced and that we should do something about it say that it's not religion that shapes these beliefs, but rather education, the media, or personal experience.*[8] In the current political climate, religious claims don't appear helpful in the practical work of climate mitigation. "Claiming God" in the midst of filing lawsuits against fossil fuel companies, lobbying for state carbon tax bills, or developing clean energy technology is potentially alienating, counterproductive, and inappropriate. Perhaps best to leave God out of it entirely.[9]

"Claiming God" also seems to runs afoul of what we sense are the unprecedented moral complexities of climate change, planetary in scale and "wicked" in nature.[10] We intuit what environmental ethicists have long described—that climate change is a problem of the global commons that eludes solutions due to a nest of interlocking difficulties: the fact that the responsibility for emissions and the costs of climate chaos are distributed with gross inequality across the globe; a lack of agreement on how to value impact and how to measure obligations; and the fact that it is not us, but future generations that will face the most intense effects, to list just a few.[11] On what terms and in what way could we "claim God" amidst this ethical thicket? Who or what, amid the global scale of the problem, would do the claiming? Besides, isn't a good part of the reason for the inequity in blame and responsibility due to the fact that those who are most responsible have for centuries claimed a divine right to the resources?

---

6. Oreskes, *Collapse of Western Civilization*.

7. See religious and interfaith statements on climate change collected at Faith Climate Action Week, "Religious Statements on Climate Change"; see also Sallie McFague's ground breaking work, *Life Abundant*; McFague, *The Body of God*.

8. Pew Research Center, "Religion and Views on Climate."

9. Keller, *Political Theology of the Earth*.

10. Gardiner, *A Perfect Moral Storm*.

11. Jenkins, *The Future of Ethics*, 35–40.

Theologically speaking, doesn't the question have the grammar backwards? Isn't the real point that God "claims" us in all things, climate included? McCord Adams's theology articulated a saving Love far greater than we have the cognitive or moral capacity to grasp (necessarily so to make up for our impaired thinking). Mother/Father God claims us as God's own from womb to tomb, waiting for us to realize we need the help God offers. It seems the grammar of the question ought to reflect this reality.

And yet, as the essays collected in this volume attest, McCord Adams claimed God, publicly and boldly, in the face of challenges that were morally complex, conceptually unwieldly, and shot through with human suffering. She did so in spheres in which Christian theology was not a central or even a welcome discourse: her work with the AIDS crisis in Los Angeles in the 1990s, and her work on the philosophical problem of evil, are cases in point. How did she do it?

Perhaps a better question is, where did she do it? One of McCord Adams's signature moves was to bring the particularities of Christian story, liturgy, and theology to speak directly to suffering communities and individuals. The result was a theology that both went deeper in its analysis of systemically-caused injustice and oppression and leaned more fully into embodied presence. For McCord Adams, a Generic Loving Presence would not do. She claimed a crucified and risen Christ able to meet broken human bodies and souls at their most vulnerable, and she named the systems that produced the suffering with specificity. Surely one thing McCord Adams meant by "claiming God," then, was bringing Christian theology to spaces of doubt, loss, and pain in order to diagnose root causes of harm, to assuage fear, and to witness to the transforming power of love.

This, I would like to suggest, is a promising strategy for what it might mean to "claim God" in the midst of climate change. If we take a cue from McCord Adams's signature move, it will be as we work in the sites of climate chaos, in the midst of community organizing, migrant advocacy and care, policy-making, legislating, creating new systems of energy, community, and economy that ethical responses and theological creativity will emerge.

2. EMBODIED ETHICS AT THE SITES OF CLIMATE CHAOS

We will need theological creativity. We'll need it because the coming climate crisis will present challenges that, akin to McCord Adams's characterization of horrendous evils, "boggle the mind," "crash in," and "shatter" our abilities to make meaning, to organize our world, or to make it comprehensible.[12]

Even now, climate-induced immigration, ocean acidification, fires, flooding, and political unrest threaten to overwhelm our resources—political, social, and emotional.[13] Our thoughts grope forward into questions that are simultaneously historically unprecedented and intimate. Which species will survive extinction rates that rival the dinosaurs (and what does it mean that we are the asteroid)? Who and how many of our own will make it through the bottleneck? How can we address the grossly unequal distribution of blame, responsibility, and suffering spread across every region of the planet? What will happen to me and to my loved ones, now and in the future?

No matter the nature of circumstances—historically unprecedented, or mundane—our patterns of meaning-making are complex. We weave together multiple strands from scientific, personal, experiential, psychological, philosophical, creative aesthetic, and spiritual narratives. Add to this the complexity of this crisis and the fact that it will unfold over generations, and it becomes clear: there are no single narratives, no unified world views, no universal, or planet-wide solutions out there—nor will there be—to the myriad complex, culturally specific movements of adaptation and mitigation that need to be undertaken.

Our work will take place at the intersection of lived reality and inherited ethics, rituals, and symbols. Our responses to climate change now and in the future will require overlapping, multiple, and creative efforts arising independently and creatively borrowed, synergistic at times, and at other times at odds. It is at the sites of climate chaos that these creative efforts will take place. There, as we negotiate multiple and often competing claims, we will find new ways of keeping compassion central to the story of what it means to be human.

---

12. McCord Adams, "Introduction," in *Wrestling for Blessing*, 6–26.

13. For worst case scenarios, see Wallace-Wells, "When Will the Planet Be Too Hot?"

This approach resonates with contemporary ethicists who suggest that, given the complexities of climate change, our moral imagination will develop in real-time, in the thick of it all. Willis Jenkins, for instance, argues that it is the work of responding to problems—with imperfect concepts, and in the midst of imperfect communities operating within multiple overlapping narratives—that will, "fire the moral imagination, improve our concepts and make communities more competent to meet their challenges."[14] Underlying this approach is a pragmatic view of morality as learned in bodies, carried by practices, and formed into repertoires that teach us how to see and solve problems.[15]

McCord Adams worked out a similar view as part of her response to horrendous evils. Her solution to horror-defeat lifts up what is particular to Christian cultural meaning-making, emphasizing the metaphysical size gap between creatures and God, thus, taking God out of the calculus of human-scale responsibility. At the same, she emphasizes God as Incarnate and Crucified, intimately present in our bodies and to our sufferings and the fact that Christians have life-giving stories and presence to bring to horrendous evils. Engaging the particularity of this Christian confession and working it out in real time in our bodies through liturgy offers space to engage in meaning-making capable of defeating horrors.[16]

Perhaps, then, the question about how to claim God in the face of climate change is best thought of as a series of questions that go something like this: What claims regarding the being of God can we bring to the sites of climate chaos that will help us see and solve problems with equity and compassion? In the ongoing work of mitigation and adaptation, with our imperfect communities and multiple narratives, in what ways will we call on the power of transforming love? How will the crises of climate create new incarnations of stories, liturgies, and theologies? What aspects of loving divine presence might we bring to our work at levees, legislatures, board rooms, immigration camps? In these embodied, site-specific contexts, what new creative expression will we bring to the strands of our own lived spiritual tradition?

We will need to draw from multiple spiritual traditions to speak love to loss, fear and doubt, and to urge ourselves and our fellow humans

---

14. Jenkins, *The Future of Ethics*, 4.

15. Jenkins, *The Future of Ethics*, 10. As Richard Rohr puts it, "You don't think yourself into a new way of living, you live yourself into a new way of thinking." Rohr, "A New Way of Thinking," *Center for Action and Contemplation*.

16. McCord Adams, *Horrendous Evils*.

towards greater compassion. Many others, from a wide range of traditions, have begun the work of imagining the spiritual implications of climate change and articulating ethical responses.[17] For McCord Adams, it was the particularities of the Christian tradition that go the distance necessary in transforming our thinking and living in the world. Thinking alongside her, I turn now to the strands of Christian identity from which her sermons suggest we might draw.

3. "A LIFE FOR A LIFE!"[18]

In her unpublished sermons, McCord Adams leans heavily into a favorite theme: the metaphysical gap between God's being and ours.[19] No surprise to her students! Here, instead of training our gaze on how the gap works to recalibrate responses to evil, these sermons explore its implications for relationships between humans in a world of limited resources.

Her focus is on the claim, fleshed out in biblical narratives and philosophical insights, that God's being is self-sustaining, and ours is not. She argues that rooted in the Being of a self-sustaining God, covenant and cross offer meaning-making narratives that both diagnose the root of our problems as humans on this Earth and offer life-giving alternatives. In contrast to the tribe-protecting, hoarding instincts of our animal inheritance on the one hand and the minimalist obligations that mark the self of the liberal state on the other, McCord Adams positions biblical covenant living, and the liturgies that help us work it under our skin, as presenting a Creation-sustaining alternative invitation: humans as "embedded in webs of overlapping networks" bound to "one another, to nature, and to God."[20]

"A Life for a Life!," the title of one of the unpublished sermons, simultaneously names the central challenge for our species and its biblical antidotes. As personal animals, humans, like all other animals, are not self-sustaining. We "literally can't eat without devouring and destroying other life to conserve our own."[21] This is true not just of our consumption of "cows and carrots"; we extend and amplify consumption in the richer

---

17. See, for instance, the range in Moore and Nelson, *Moral Ground*.
18. McCord Adams, "A Life for a Life!" (unpublished).
19. See n5 above.
20. McCord Adams, "Ignorance" (unpublished).
21. McCord Adams, "A Life for a Life!" (unpublished).

pockets of the developed world, gobbling up excess food, fuel, and goods that in turn "devour" and "destroy" the land and bodies of people across the planet with both fast-moving and "slow violence."[22]

As personal animals, "belief in Darwinian struggle" is part of nature, perhaps even partly written in our genes.[23] Scarcity drives us to see the world in terms of an us-versus-them contest, which in turn produces a combination of entitlement and hoarding. Animal instincts insist that "we are entitled to necessities that sustain our life . . . but the necessities of life are in short supply." Our evolutionary history, paired with privilege, power, and cultural evolution, teach that we, "our kind, our country, our race, our class matters most, that others count for less." We come to feel "entitled to the necessities that sustain our life, and to the self-defense to preserve our life."[24]

Because animal life by nature is not and cannot be self-sustaining, "the logical conclusion," McCord Adams notes, "is the demand that 'us and ours' be the unifying principle of the universe, the organizing principle that presses everything and everyone else into service to meet our needs."[25] Animal logic leads us to reason that we can't afford to treat every human being as a person with rights and interests. Down through the centuries, empire and nation-state deliver the necessary goods to their members, glossing over the inequity of resource distribution within and justifying violence to bodies within and without, using the narratives of civic religion which featured gods like "mascots, genies in a bottle who exist to grant our wishes and promote our aims!"[26]

Ironically, we have arrived in the present mess via a crucial blindness. Forgetting we are a species among other species, we have built civilizations on the illusion of limitlessness, imagining an unending frontier of extraction for our use.[27] Gathering momentum in the age of global colonization, and reaching warp speed in the historically unprecedented energy-gobbling age of fossil fuels in the twentieth century, we have in fact proceeded as if our resources were not scarce.[28] The illusion of

22. Nixon, *Slow Violence*.
23. McCord Adams, "A Life for a Life!" (unpublished).
24. McCord Adams, "A Life for a Life!" (unpublished).
25. McCord Adams, "Resurrecting the Cosmos" (online).
26. McCord Adams, "Resurrecting the Cosmos" (online).
27. Richards, *The Unending Frontier*.
28. Burke, "The Big Story," 44–45.

infinite material abundance in the last two centuries has yielded an intensification of earlier cultural pathology: an addiction to limitless material consumption as the measure of happiness.[29] Our culture and institutions have been driven by the competition-hoarding-entitlement logic of our animal inheritance, and simultaneously, by a denial of the fact that we are an animal species living in a world of limited resources.

Animal instincts for hoarding and entitlement, paired with the illusion of limitlessness and the technologies that allow us to meet our desires, have produced the current threshold moment: climate change is only one of multiple tipping points we have pushed in the planetary systems that keep us alive and ticking.[30] Scarcity, real and felt, and the resulting political chaos and hardening of us-versus-them boundaries is likely to reactivate instincts embedded in our animal nature at newly vicious levels. Is there an alternative?

4. "GOD IS A CENTER THAT WILL HOLD, BECAUSE DIVINE LIFE IS SELF-SUSTAINING"[31]

Marilyn McCord Adams argues that the nature of God's being, interpreted and appropriated through theology and ritual, can fundamentally change the animal calculus. Our species and our planet are finite. God's being, in contrast, is of an entirely different kind: self-sustaining life. McCord Adams writes, "God is life, life that is self-sustaining, life that does not depend on the existence or the destruction of anything else. God keeps on being and doing without needing to gobble up anything else."[32]

But wait, there's more! God's being is not simply self-sustaining. Neo-Platonizing strands suggest that the divine being, as the highest good, is maximally self-diffusive—superabundant, overflowing goodness. Biblical and Franciscan strands concur, adding that God is also Supreme Love, suggesting that the being of God also must therefore be inherently relational, for it is the nature of love to flow forth into others.[33] As the fountain

---

29. Berry, "Faustian Economics."
30. Folke, "Respecting Planetary Boundaries," 19.
31. McCord Adams, "Resurrecting the Cosmos" (online).
32. McCord Adams, "Resurrecting the Cosmos" (online).
33. McCord Adams, *Horrendous Evils*, 140–42; McCord Adams, "Introduction," in *Wrestling for Blessing*, 6–26. See St. Bonaventure's elaboration, *Commentary on the First Book of Sentences*, dist. 27, p. 1, a. un., q., and "Introduction"; and St. Bonaventure, *Bonaventure*.

fullness of Goodness and Love, God can't help but pour Godself, freely but necessarily, into consubstantial, coequal, coeternal others, Creation, the first Incarnation. Christ, as the medium and exemplar "before all things" is "the one in whom all things hold together" (cf. Col 1:17). Christian meaning-making revolves around a center that will hold: God's being as self-sustaining, superabundant, maximally self-diffusing Love.

How does claiming the self-sustaining, self-diffusive being of God help us face the scarcity of real resources, conflict between groups, violence towards bodies at the borders of "us and them?" How does sinking into the abundance of God's being experientially in liturgy, meditation, and prayer change our instinctual responses in a limited world?

McCord Adams argues that it is by drawing on a God as self-sustaining, abundant Life and Goodness that we find the blueprint and the personal and communal resources we need to rewire our responses to scarcity and re-order our body-politics into just communities. We are called to see and live into a divinely-animated cosmos where every creature is held and belongs: "God calls us to experience the whole universe as a society, a body-politic held together and animated by God, its *esprit de corps*." Further, and crucially, "God is the One, *the only One*, Who can underwrite this project."[34] Nothing else is big enough; nothing else self-sustains. It is precisely by trading in the currency of the spirit that we begin to bend the ways of this world towards wholeness and justice.

The consequences of listening only to the scarcity and competition-driven instincts of our animal inheritance are clear and not pretty. As she argues, "if we keep on living like smart animals, driven by red-in-tooth-and-claw, dog-eat-dog competition . . . we can expect the world to go as before: rape of environment with devil-may-care abandon." The Bible's diagnosis is explicit: "making human life the center of all things is life-wrecking, life-devouring, life-destroying."[35]

---

34. McCord Adams, "Resurrecting the Cosmos" (online).
35. McCord Adams, "Terrifying Truths" and "Glorious Challenge!" (unpublished).

5. "EVEN A LITTLE TASTE OF WHO AND WHAT GOD IS RE-SIZES EVERYTHING"[36]

Living into the claim that God is a center that holds and that there is enough of God to go around shifts our gaze, disrupts our habits, and counteracts our animal-competition logic in multiple ways.

To begin, if God's self-sustaining being animates and sustains the cosmos, we can see each and all as belonging, connected by divinely-sustained tissue, held together by a spirit Big Enough for all parts. Humans are "planted" in material creation, McCord Adams argues, "organically connected with the rest of the world."[37] The invitation is to live out our identity as a member of the body-politic of a "cosmos-wide project" that features God's being as the "animating principle, the organizing force of creation, of human personality, and of harmonious society."[38] All beings around us carry the imprint of divine ordering, and thus are part of a body-politic of divine nature.[39]

Belonging to a divine body-politic presents an alternative vision of the self, and thus, of the obligations of belonging. The ideology of the liberal state, in contrast, presents the myth of human beings "first and foremost as individuals . . . atoms or islands . . . self-contained integrities . . . subjects of basic rights, and constrained by minimalist obligations, by a social contract to live and let live."[40] We inhabit nation-state identity and divine cosmos-member identity simultaneously, but the latter calls for core allegiance. This is tricky. We need training, daily and weekly reminders in mind and body, to "naturalize" into divine-centered-cosmos citizenship. Traditions of sacrifice and covenant are divinely designed to deliver just the reminders we need!

The logic of sacrifice turns our animal inheritance on its head, moving us away from competition and entitlement and towards gratitude. As McCord Adams points out, when Jesus speaks of a new covenant in His blood, "he is not thinking of Darwinian struggle in which only the fittest survive. Jesus's mind is shaped by Torah-training. He is seeing His death as a covenant sacrifice. The logic of sacrifice is different. God is the source of life and its only reliable sustainer. All life belongs to God. We

36. McCord Adams, "Terrifying Truths" and "Glorious Challenge!" (unpublished).
37. McCord Adams, "Interconnection" (unpublished).
38. McCord Adams, "Resurrecting the Cosmos" (online).
39. McCord Adams, "Resurrecting the Cosmos" (online).
40. McCord Adams, "Interconnection" (unpublished).

are entitled neither to life nor to the means of its preservation. We receive life—its beginning, continuing, and multiplying—as a gift.[41] Recognition of the logic of sacrifice reinforces the gift-quality of life itself: "We are meant to receive life, not as a thing to be grasped, but as a gift from a Boundless Source."[42]

Reminders of the gift quality of life loosen our grip on entitlement and hoarding, thus opening us to the alternative: courteous consumption. Because our animal nature is deeply embedded, we need to work out courtesy in our bodies, as a "civilizing" process operates with different rules than natural human or animal kingdoms. McCord Adams writes: "Because courtesy does not come naturally to human beings, God works hard to civilize us into harmonious living. God prescribes liturgies in which we 'act out' the fundamental truths of our existence. . . . Eating and drinking sacrificial foods reminds us how we are entitled neither to life nor to the necessities of life, but receive both as gifts from a Boundless Source."[43]

When Christians gather to eat and drink, we remind ourselves that "we live by Jesus's life, a life freely returned to God,"[44] and we work out in our bodies a stance of gratitude instead of entitlement. Covenant living is divine answer to the dilemmas we face as beings who are not self-sustaining. She writes, "Because God knows that material life cannot be naturally self-sustaining, God cut a covenant, setting out a lifestyle of courteous consumption: human beings will be generously provided for so long as they honor God as the source of life and respect life in other creatures."[45]

God's being as abundant, self-sustaining Love shows up most fully, and perhaps most counter-intuitively, to our animal logic in the body of Christ on the cross. Without the claim that Christ's being shares in the self-sustaining Being of God, we gaze on the death of a finite body. Holding the superabundance of God's Being in mind, we see wounds and death held in ever larger circles of Love and Life. We can lean into the places of suffering, death, and loss in this finite world precisely because in and through them we can see, taste, and feel a Love that is bigger, stronger, and able to hold and transform them. Christ's wounded body,

---

41. McCord Adams, "Crucifixion" (unpublished).
42. McCord Adams, "Resurrecting the Cosmos" (online).
43. McCord Adams, "Resurrecting the Cosmos" (online).
44. McCord Adams, "Interconnection" (unpublished).
45. McCord Adams, "Interconnection" (unpublished).

our own and other wounded bodies, and the wounded body of our Earth, are held in a Love that is Enough. The purpose is not to bless wounds in themselves and the powers that create them, but instead to draw close, to see them as part of a larger whole, and to experience them transformed.

6. "TRUTH TO TELL, GODHEAD CANNOT HELP BEING REALLY PRESENT"[46]

Rooting ourselves in the limitless abundance of God's self-diffusing Love helps expand definitions of self and community, making it clear why community is life-giving for all species, and how it works. Boundaries, borders, and carrying capacities of self, community, and nation-state are revised; instead of hard fast walls, we are invited to see border regions as frontiers of meeting difference and expanding our circles of belonging. How does this work?

The idea of God as the self-sustaining principle of all creation switches up competition logic so that instead of defending "me and mine" we see that each and all are a slice of a single, finite pie, held by a being of infinite Love. This shift allows us to sink into the parts of our evolutionary inheritance that prioritize connection, sacrifice, altruism. When we live or work alongside others, we get close enough to feel love, connection, and gratitude in real time, all of which we are also wired to seek given our animal nature. Community shortens the feedback loop on the positive returns of our own gift-giving and sacrifice.

As we work out in our bodies the knowledge that there is enough Love for all, we become more motivated to share finite resources. This body-knowing helps us to advocate for making the distribution of scarce resources more equitable and just. Interconnection and interdependence help to defeat the illusions of separateness and self-sufficiency and urge us ever further towards practices of courteous consumption. We can be courteous consumers—sharing parts of the "real" world finite pie—because the Being of God is enough for our souls, psyches, and hearts.

Fed by the "enoughness" of God, we are primed to extend courteous consumption to those we perceive as outside our inner circle. The self-sustaining nature of God's being provides the Whole from which we can re-imagine boundaries, borders, and carrying-capacities, all of which will be crucial work in negotiating climate chaos with compassion. As

---

46. McCord Adams, "Omnibus Benediction" (online).

our spirits draw on a limitless source of Love in prayer, meditation, and liturgy, we find our bodies and brains have more capacity to move away from biological fight or flight.[47] We create space in mind and heart to include those who lie beyond the borders of our own identity.

Knowing in our bodies that we live within the boundless Love of God can allow us to be curious and receptive, rather than threatened and reactive, towards others. We can think of the boundaries of self and community not as walls, but instead as horizons to populate with the voices and experiences of others.[48] Drawing on God's limitlessness Love weekly, practicing courteous consumption in community, allows us to expand our carrying capacity, supporting and urging us to go beyond the limited receptive capacities of ego, self, nation. Being of God as self-diffusing, inherently relational Trinity works as an imaginative model for self and other, encouraging us to include those outside our small conceptions of self and community.[49]

6. "STUMPED-BY-NOTHING IS GOD'S NAME"[50]

Our mammalian hearts and minds will be stretched in historically unprecedented ways by the crises of climate change. There has perhaps never been a better time to discover anew the resiliency of the human spirit. Many fear that the crisis is too much for the moral and spiritual capacity of our species. Some argue we need to make an "evolutionary leap" to develop care-instincts for future generations, the land, and other species in order to navigate the territory ahead.[51] Others suggest it is time to leave behind the God of the Judeo-Christian tradition: too much hubris; too anthropocentric; too implicated in the systems that have caused the harm.[52]

McCord Adams urges us to lean in to this God more fully. The problem is not the God of this tradition, but the appropriation of this God as

---

47. See, for instance, the research collected at University of California Berkeley, "Greater Good Science Center."

48. Ó'Tuama, "Belonging Creates and Undoes Us," See also Ó'Tuama, *In the Shelter*.

49. Rohr with Morrell, *The Divine Dance*.

50. McCord Adams, "Curse and Promise," in *Wrestling for Blessing*, 59.

51. Roberts, "Why Climate Change Doesn't Spark Moral Outrage." Naomi Klein makes a compelling argument for moral action using the language of leap: The Leap Manifesto, "The Leap Manifesto."

52. Terry Tempest Williams articulates this beautifully and compellingly in "Gods among Us."

a genie of blessing for the projects of nation-state, empire, and wealth-production. In McCord Adams's reading, biblical traditions of sacrifice and covenant arose precisely to address, with grit and precision, the fact that is at the root of this climate crisis, a fact we have been simultaneously blind to and driven by: that we are a species among species, not self-sustaining, devouring others in a world of scarce resources. In place of mindsets of entitlement and hoarding, God establishes traditions of sacrifice and covenant. Frequent, embodied practice encourages the very dispositions we most need: gratitude and courteous consumption.

God's being as self-sustaining Life undergirds it all. Leaning deeply into God's ceaselessly flowing, superabundant Love allows us to access compassion, which is also part of our animal inheritance. With practice and reinforcement, we learn to extend compassion to those beyond the borders of self, tribe, nation, and species. When we experience boundless love ourselves, we are better able to assuage fears, to speak hope to loss and despair, and to witness the transforming power of love. God invites us to engage in compassion work as part of a much larger project: citizenship in a divine-centered, divine-sustained cosmos where all are interconnected and all belong. In McCord Adams's mind, the path towards the "evolutionary leap" we most need was laid down long ago. Our task is to lean into this inheritance and reinterpret it again and again, courageously and creatively.

This is not to suggest that we bring the substance of faith claims to bear on secular climate work. Particularly, Christian identity is nurtured in Christian community with stories, symbols, and feasts that feed our minds, hearts, and souls so that we have enough for ourselves and others. In turn, our work at the multiple sites of climate mitigation and adaptation gives new energy to our theological imaginations, spurring creativity in liturgies, sermons, songs. The result of this interchange of spirit work and climate work is more than simply new directions in theological imagination. The kind of citizenship we are naturalized into shapes how we advocate for distribution of resources in the real world, how we respond to instances of violence of "us versus them," and how we intervene in conversations about boundaries and borders.

Superabundant, self-sustaining Goodness and Love is big enough for even the worst of the climate crises to come. Drawing on God's Being is what will allow us to keep compassion part of the vocabulary of what it means to be human in the years ahead. As McCord Adams reminds us in her work on horrendous evils, there is no problem, no wound, no horror too big for this God. When the crises of climate change threaten to overwhelm us, we can remember what Marilyn says: "Stumped-by-Nothing is God's name."[53]

---

53. Adams, "Curse and Promise," in *Wrestling for Blessing*, 59.

8

Scotus on Common Natures

JT Paasch

Marilyn McCord Adams had a stock of informal phrases she used to talk about scholastic thought. For example, many will remember how she talked about "hunks of matter" (she preferred "hunks" to "chunks"), or how she talked about material substances "here below" (i.e., in the Aristotelian sublunar world), or how she questioned whether some particular object had enough "causal oomph" to do the theoretical job it was postulated to do.

Her musings were challenging and thought provoking too. I have never stopped thinking about something she said about Scotus. She wondered if, deep down, Scotus thought God is best characterized by unlimited productivity. And indeed, Scotus did see in God a spectacular amount of productivity. (Think of the production of the Son and Spirit, God's thoughts, the creation of the universe, and so on.)

In a similar vein, when speaking about how Scotus understood common natures, McCord Adams would sometimes say that natures "really want to share themselves, but here below they are too limited, so they have to settle for copying themselves." But, she would point out, the divine nature can (and does) share itself completely in the production of the Son and Spirit.

In what follows, I would like to take up McCord Adams's suggestion and present an interpretation of Scotus that sees the divine nature as a single and undivided entity but sees sublunar common natures as copyable tropes. This interpretation of Scotus's ontology has some attractive features. Philosophically, it takes a theory of Scotus whose details can often feel quite obscure, and it makes a lot of sense out of it. But there are also ethical and theological implications that can come out of this too, which I think are deeply amenable to McCord Adams's own theological vision.

1. THE PLAN

The view I want to present runs as follows. As Scotus sees it, the most perfect kind of production that could ever be realized is the kind where the nature of the producer is shared in its entirety with the product, without being divided. In the Godhead, this happens in the production of the Son and Spirit. So divine production is the highest expression of productivity that could possibly be manifested.

Here below, in the sublunar world, Scotus believes creatures are too weak to share their natures through production. All they can do is make (exactly or at least sufficiently similar) copies of their natures. And this means that, for Scotus, sublunar natures are tropes rather than immanent universals, and in particular they can be copied.

However, Scotus believes that each material substance is a completely unique singleton, which cannot be copied. Each human, each tree, each stick, and each stone—each of these are utterly unique and cannot be duplicated in their entirety. If scientists could clone me, for example, they would get another human being, but they would not get another *me*.

How can that be, if all of my nature-tropes can be copied? To explain this, Scotus proposes that we each have another type of trope in us that is special. This trope, which we nowadays call a haecceity, is a completely unique singleton. It cannot be copied. Hence, although all of my nature-tropes can be copied, my haecceity cannot, and that is why there cannot ever be another copy of me in my entirety.

This particular view is articulated in a rather clear and direct way in Scotus's *Ordinatio*, and that is the text I will attend to in what follows.[1]

---

1. I will refer to Duns Scotus's *Ordinatio* as "Ord," and I will use the text from the Vatican Edition (Civitas Vaticana: Typis Polyglottis Vaticanis, 1950–), referenced as "Vat.," with volume, page, and line number. Translations are mine, but I will cross-reference the English translation in Spade, *Five Texts*, 57–113.

Scotus has more to say about natures elsewhere (for instance in the *Lectura* and the *Reportatio*). But I will not address those texts, for reasons of space.

I will not discuss every aspect of the view I ascribe to Scotus, since some of these points are well known. For example, I will not discuss Scotus's view that the Son's and Spirit's productions are nature-sharing productions.[2] I take that as a given.

Nor will I discuss the literature on this topic, since it is accessible in standard places. The references cited in, say, the relevant *Stanford Encyclopedia of Philosophy* articles serve as perfectly good resources for this.[3]

Instead, I will focus my attention on the claim that Scotus believes sublunar natures are copyable tropes. For that, I turn to Scotus's discussion of common natures in the *Ordinatio*. After that, I will turn to some of the potential ethical and theological implications of this view.

2. WHAT IS SCOTUS REALLY ASKING ABOUT?

In *Ordinatio* 2.3.1.1, when Scotus turns to the question of common natures, he asks right up front: why are material substances individual or singular?[4] By "material substances," Scotus means paradigmatic Aristotelian substances—sticks, stones, living organisms, and the like. But what does he mean by "individual" or "singular?"

On the face of it, we might think Scotus means *merely* that material substances are non-universal particulars—i.e., discrete, often spatially separated, enumerable items. I can point to one and say, "there's one," I can point to another and say, "there's two," and so on.

However, to speak of discrete particulars in this fashion is not precise enough. The reason is that we can draw a distinction between particulars that can be copied and particulars that cannot.

Let us say that a discrete item can be copied if it is possible for there to be one or more exactly (or sufficiently) similar replicas of it. To draw on D. C. Williams's famous analogy, think of a candy supplier that sells sticks for lollipops. The supplier can of course produce many replicas of

---

2. For example, see Cross, *Duns Scotus on God*, ch. 13; Paasch, *Divine Production*, ch. 5.

3. For instance, see Cross, "Medieval Theories of Haecceity."

4. Ord., 2.3.1.1 (Vat. 7:391.9–10; Spade, 57): "primo quaerendum est de distinctione individuali in substantiis materialibus."

that lollipop stick.[5] We might formulate the point like this (where I use the word "particular" in the technical sense, i.e., a non-universal particular):

> (1) For any particular x, x can be copied iff (if and only if) it is possible that there be another particular y such that (i) y is not the numerically same as x, and (ii) y is exactly (or sufficiently) similar to x.

By contrast, let us say that a particular is a singleton if it cannot be copied: it is so unique that there cannot, and never will be, any other particular like it.

> (2) For any particular x, x is a singleton iff x cannot be copied.

This is a crucial distinction. We can talk about Scotus's views on "individuation" until we are blue in the face, but unless we specify (1) or (2), we will not be stating in precise terms what we think Scotus means.

So which type does Scotus think material substances are: (1) or (2)? Does Scotus believe material substances can be copied, or is each substance an uncopyable singleton?

Scotus gives a clear answer. He explains that, when he talks about individuals or singulars, he is thinking of items that cannot be divided into "subjective parts," which is just a fancy scholastic way of saying there cannot be other instances of them:

> Among entities, there is something that is indivisible into subjective parts; this is [the sort of entity] for which it is formally repugnant to it that it be divided into others, each of which is [an instance of] it.[6]

That matches (2), not (1), for to say there cannot be other instances of a thing means at the very least that it cannot be copied.

Scotus zeros in on this point. He takes it that material substances are singletons in this very sense, and his central question is *why* can material substances not be copied? As he puts it:

---

5. Williams, "On the Elements of Being: I," 3–18; Williams, "On the Elements of Being: II," 171–92.

6. Ord., 2.3.1.2n48 (Vat. 7:413.4–6; Spade, 69): "in entibus est aliquid indivisibile in partes subiectivas, hoc est 'cui formaliter repugnat dividi in plura quorum quodlibet sit ipsum.'" See also Ord., 2.3.1.4n76 (Vat. 7:426–27; Spade, 76), and Ord., 2.3.1.5–6n165 (Vat. 7:473; Spade, 100).

> It is incompatible with an individual [i.e., a material substance] that it be divided into subjective parts, and the cause of that incompatibility is what is sought.[7]

Lest there be any doubt that he is interested in (2) rather than (1), Scotus goes on. Taking a cue from the way we talk about singletons, he explains that when we want to refer to a specific individual, we often use a demonstrative pronoun, as when we say "*this* particular thing" or "*that* particular thing." And Scotus explicitly restricts his query to the singletons picked out by such expressions:

> First I explain what I mean by "individuation," or "numerical oneness," or "singularity." Certainly not the generic oneness by which any member of a species is said to be one in number, but rather the oneness that is designated [by expressions] such as "this [particular thing]" . . . [and] the cause is asked not of singularity in general, but of the singularity that is especially designated by [the demonstrative] "this," as in "this particular [thing]."[8]

This is a significant and helpful passage. Note first that Scotus says he is *not* asking about the generic sense in which every member of a species is one thing. So right away we can see that Scotus is not asking merely about how material substances are particulars. He is asking something more specific.

Note second that, at the beginning of this passage, Scotus *identifies* "individuation," "numerical oneness," and "singularity"—that is, he sees these terms as synonyms. This is important. Whatever *we* might think these terms mean, Scotus himself uses them to talk *only* about singletons. For Scotus:

> (3) For any particular *x*, (i) *x* is "singular" iff *x* is a singleton, (ii) *x* is "numerically one" iff *x* is a singleton, and (iii) *x* is "individuated" iff *x* is a singleton.

So, when Scotus says material substances are "individual" or "singular," he does not mean that each is merely a particular. His claim is much

---

7. Ord., 2.3.1.4n76 (Vat. 7:427.1–3; Spade, 76): "individuum incompossibile est dividi in partes subiectivas et quaeritur ratio illius incompossibilitatis."

8. Ord., 2.3.1.4n76 (Vat. 7:426.18—427.1; 427.5–7; Spade, 76): "primo expono quid intelligo per individuation sive unitatem numeralem sive singularitatem. Non quidem unitatem indeterminate (qua quidlibet in specie, dicitur esse unum numero), see unitatem signatam (ut 'haec') . . . quaeritur causa non singularitatis in commune sed 'huius' singularitatis in special, signatae, scilicet ut est 'haec' determinate."

stronger. He is saying that each is a singleton. Each person, each tree, each stick, and each stone—each is totally unique. They cannot be copied.

(4) For any material substance x, x is a singleton.

As far as I know, Scotus does not explicitly defend this claim. He simply takes it as a given. Nevertheless, it is a sensible enough position to take. As I noted earlier, the intuition seems to be that, if scientists could clone me (for instance), they would not get another me. Rather, it seems like they would get another human being. That person might look and act exactly like me, but it would not be another me. It would be another human being.

3. COMMON NATURES

In this text from the *Ordinatio*, Scotus will eventually put forward his own explanation of (4): he will say that material substances are singletons because each has a special trope (a haecceity) which is itself a singleton. However, before he gets to this conclusion, he considers a number of other candidate theories, each of which attempts to explain (4).

The first theory he considers (and ultimately rejects) is important, because in rejecting it, Scotus reveals his own view that sublunar natures are copyable tropes. The theory in question claims that each material substance is, as Scotus puts it, "individual or singular from itself—that is, from its nature."[9]

Since Scotus uses the term "individual" or "singular" to mean "singleton" (see (3) above), the question Scotus is asking here is this: is it possible that material substances are singletons through and through, even down to their natures?[10] To be more precise, the view on offer holds something like this:

(5) For any material substance x, the nature N of x is a singleton.

Notice what this entails. If (5) were correct, no two natures would ever be alike. Each would be completely unique. That is, (5) would entail this:

(6) For any material substances x and y, the nature N_1 of x and the nature N_2 of y are not exactly (or sufficiently) similar.

9. Ord., 2.3.1.1nn5–28 (Vat. 7:393–402; Spade, 58–63).
10. Ord., 2.3.1.1 (Vat. 7:391.14—392.2; Spade, 57): "utrum substantia materialis ex se sive ex natura sua sit individua vel singularis."

So, Scotus is not wondering merely if the nature in each material substance is a particular. Rather, he is wondering if the nature in each material substance is itself a unique singleton.

Scotus rejects this view—i.e., he rejects (5) and (6). As he sees it, things of the same kind must have natures that are exactly (or sufficiently) similar. If each and every material substance were so dissimilar through and through, it would be hard to explain how and why we perceive so many regularities in nature.

Consider natural reproduction. Even if nobody were around to see it, Scotus thinks it obvious that cows would still beget cows, elms would beget elms, and so on. But since that would continue even if there were no minds to perceive it, Scotus concludes that we cannot be inventing (with our minds) the similarities that we seem to perceive between parents and their offspring. Those similarities must be real.[11]

And what about biological classification? If individuals really had nothing in common, we would have no reason to group anything into species.[12] Any concept we might form that classifies, say, all humans together would be a fiction, because there wouldn't be anything grouping them together in reality. As Scotus put it:

> [If material substances were so distinct], it would follow that the mind could no more abstract something common from Socrates and Plato than from Socrates and a line, and any general [concept] would be a pure fiction of the mind.[13]

Scotus also highlights that we sometimes cannot distinguish objects that are too much alike. For example, if there were two indistinguishable

---

11. Ord., 2.3.1.1n28 (Vat. 7:401.20—402.3; Spade, 63): "Nullo existente intellectu ignis generaret ignem . . . et aliqua unitas realis esset 'generantis ad genitum' secundum formam, propter quam esset generatio univoca. Intellectus enim considerans non facit generationem esse univocam, sed congnoscit eam esse univocam."

12. Scotus makes this point by talking about numerical unity, but remember that by "numerical unity," he means the utter uniqueness of a singleton. Hence, Ord., 2.3.1.1n23 (Vat. 7:400:18–21; Spade, 62): "si omnis unitas realis est numeralis [= unica], ergo omnis diversitas realis est numeralis [= unica]. Sed consequens est falsum, quia omnis diversitas numeralis in quantum numeralis [= unica], est aequalis,—et ita omnia essent aeque distincta [singularia monodica]."

13. Ord., 2.3.1.1n23 (Vat. 7:400.21—401.2; Spade, 62): "[si omnia essent aeque distincta] tunc sequitur quod non plus posset intellectus a Socrate et Platone abstrahere aliquid commune, quam a Socrate et linea, et esset quodlibet universale purum figmentum intellectus."

white spheres (located in some indistinguishable way), we could not tell them apart:

> If features commonly perceived by the senses are discarded (such as differences in place and position), and if two [equally] sized objects entirely similar and equal in whiteness were put in simultaneous existence by divine power, sight would not be able to discern that there are *two* white objects there.[14]

But how could that be if they were not actually similar? If the spheres were radically unique singletons, with no similarities, then surely we could not "confuse" them in this way.[15]

At a general level, Scotus thinks we simply could not perform many of the empirical observations that we do perform. We measure things by standards that apply to more than one thing, but how could that be if everything in the world were utterly dissimilar?[16] We regularly identify things as being the same, similar, or equal, but surely that would not be possible if there were no real basis for such comparisons.[17]

For Scotus, the world just cannot be made up of radically disparate singleton natures, as (6) claims. Rather, members of the same species must have genuinely similar natures. Scotus's view is thus this:

> (7) For any members x and y of a natural kind K, the nature N_1 of x and the nature N_2 of y are exactly (or sufficiently) similar.

---

14. Ord., 2.3.1.1n21 (Vat. 7:399.19—400.3; Spade, 61–62): "si circumscribantur omnia sensibilia communia (puta diversitas loci vel situs), et si ponerentur duo quanta simul esse per potentiam divinam, quae etiam essent omnino similia et aequalia in albedine,—visus non distingueret ibi esse duo alba."

15. Ord., 2.3.1.1n21 (Vat. 7:400.3–5; Spade, 62): "si tamen cognosceret alterum illorum in quantum est unum unitate numerali, cognosceret ipsum in quantum est unum distinctum unitate numerali!" More generally, Ord., 2.3.1.1n21 (Vat. 7:399.13–17; Spade, 61): "potentia cognoscens obiectum . . . cognoscit ipsum in quantum est distinctum a quolibet quod non est unam hac unitate,—sed sensus non cognoscit obiectum in quantum est distinctum a quolibet quod non est unam illa unitate numerali."

16. Ord., 2.3.1.1nn11–15 (Vat. 7:396–97; Spade, 59–60).

17. Ord., 2.3.1.1n18 (Vat. 7:398.13–17; Spade, 61): "idem, simile et aequale fundantur super 'unum', ita quod licet similitudo habeat pro fundamento rem de genere qualitatis talis, tamen relatio non est realis nisi habat fundamentum reale et rationem proximam fundandi realem; igitur unitas quae requiritur in fundamento relationis similitudinis, est realis."

4. NOT UNIVERSALS

If members of the same species have common (i.e., exactly similar) natures, could we propose that those natures are immanent universals?

Scotus knows someone might want to take this stance, for he points it out himself in the form of an objection. He explains that someone (not favorable to immanent universals) might object to the view that natures are "common" if that involves postulating that there are real universals in material substances:

> But against this [viz. the view that natures are "common"], there seem to be two objections. One is it seems to postulate that a universal is some real entity in the thing.[18]

Scotus rejects this possibility. As far as he is concerned, there are no real universals. There can be concepts that are universal in nature, but nothing outside the mind can be like that.

To be more precise, Scotus thinks the mark of a genuine universal is that we can identify it with each particular instance of it. As Scotus likes to put it, we can say "this is this," where the first "this" refers to the instance in question, and the second "this" refers to the universal.

> An actual universal is that which ... can itself, one and the same thing, be directly ascribed to each individual [exemplifying it] ... by a predication saying "this is this."[19]

Of course, this will apply to each and every instance, so all instances of a universal will simultaneously be identical to that one universal. Hence, Scotus could define universals along these lines:

> (8) For any nature N, N is a universal iff for any x and y that exemplify N, (i) the instance of N in x (call it N_1) is identical to N, and (ii) the instance of N in y (call it N_2) is identical to N.

But that, Scotus maintains, is only possible in the realm of concepts. I can have a concept that genuinely applies to many instances, but there cannot

---

18. Ord., 2.3.1.1n35 (Vat. 7:405.3–4; Spade, 65): "Sed contra istud [viz., opinionem quod naturae sunt universales], videntur esse duae obiectiones: Una, quia videtur ponere universale esse aliquid reale in re."

19. Ord., 2.3.1.1n37 (Vat. 7:406.11, 12–13; 407.2–3; Spade, 65): "universale in actu est illud quod ... ipsum idem est in potentia proxima ut dicatur de quolibet supposito ... praedicatione dicente 'hoc est hoc.'"

be some item in the world, outside the mind, that can be identified with each instance of it in that way. As Scotus puts it:

> Nothing ... in reality is such that ... it can be said of each instance that "each is it." This is only possible for an object [of thought] ... actively being considered by the mind. For insofar as it is conceptualized, it has the numerical oneness of an object [of thought], according to which it is applicable to every [relevant] singular by saying "this is this."[20]

According to Scotus then, common natures are not universals, for as he sees it, there simply are no real universals. Concepts can be universal, but not anything outside the mind.

If extant universals are impossible, then the opposite must hold. That is to say, if each instance of a nature cannot be numerically identical with others of the same type, then they must be numerically distinct. So Scotus must hold this:

> (9) For any material substances x and y of the same kind K, the nature N_1 in x and the nature N_2 in y are numerically distinct.

And that equates to a trope theory. If each nature is a discrete particular, then each nature is a trope.

> (10) For any extant nature N, N is a trope.

By using the label "trope," I do not mean to import any unnecessary philosophical baggage here. Some philosophers feel the label "trope" brings along with it unhelpful assumptions.[21] I mean to use the term only in the most minimal sense: something particular, as opposed to something immanently universal.

5. NATURES ARE COPYABLE

If natures are tropes rather than immanent universals, then how exactly can they be "common" to all members of a species? According to Scotus, the answer is that they are copyable.

---

20. Ord., 2.3.1.1n37 (Vat. 7:406.15—407.1, 5–9; Spade, 65–66): "Nihil enim ... in re est tale quod ... potest dici de quolibet inferior, quod 'quodlibet est ipsum'; hoc enim solum est possibile de obiecto ... actu considerato ab intellectu,—quod quidem 'ut intellectum' habet unitatem etiam numeralem obiecti, secundum quam ipsum idem est praedicabile de omni singulari, dicendo quod 'hoc est hoc.'"

21. See, for instance, Heil, *From an Ontological Point of View*, 126–28, 138.

He points out that even though each material substance is itself a singleton (and so cannot be copied), this does not imply that its nature cannot be copied into another singleton:

> In an extramental thing, where its nature is [found along] with [the unique] singularity [of the thing itself], the nature in itself is not restricted to [that unique] singularity.... [I]t is not repugnant to it to be [copied in another thing] without being bound [by the unique singularity of the first thing].[22]

To use an example that Marilyn herself often mentioned: although Beulah the cow is a unique singleton, that does not mean she cannot make a copy of her bovine nature when she produces offspring.

What makes a nature copyable? Scotus proposes that the reason natures are copyable is that they have no internal restrictions on being copied. If we could pry open a nature and look inside, we would find nothing that requires it to be copied zero times (= a singleton), or one or more times (= a copyable trope). Scotus puts it like this:

> There is nothing in a nature that requires it to be "one" [thing] by numerical oneness [= a singleton], nor is there anything in it that requires it to be "many" [= a copyable trope] by a manyness opposite to that oneness.[23]

Nor would we find inside the nature anything that requires it to be conceptualized in someone's mind (= a universal concept), or even that it be instantiated in the world (= a particular or trope):

> Neither is [there anything in] a nature [which requires that it be] actually "universal" in the way in which something is universal as an object of thought, nor is [there anything in a nature which requires that] it be a [real, extant] "particular" [in the world].[24]

There is just nothing inside a nature that says it has to be conceptualized, or that it has to be copied any particular number of times in the world. We can put the point like this:

---

22. Ord., 2.3.1.1n34 (Vat. 7:404.6–8, 10; Spade, 64): "in re extra [intellectu], ubi natura est cum singularitate, non est illa natura de se determinata ad singularitatem ... non repugnat sibi esse sine illo contrahente [singularitate illa]."

23. Ord., 2.3.1.1n31 (Vat. 7:403.2–3; Spade, 63): "[natura] non est 'ex se una' unitate numerali, nec 'plures' pluralitate opposita illi unitati."

24. Ord., 2.3.1.1n31 (Vat. 7:403.3–5; Spade, 63): "nec [natura] 'universalis' actu est (eo modo scilicet quo aliquid est universale ut est obiectum intellectus), nec est 'particularis' de se."

(11) For any nature *N*, *N* has no intrinsic feature *F* which requires (i) that *N* be represented in the mind by a concept, nor (ii) that there be any particular number of copies of *N* in the world.

For Scotus, this is precisely what makes natures copyable. Because they have no internal restrictions on being copied, it is possible for them to be copied. Indeed, to put it the other way around, one might say it would be *impossible* to make copies of natures if they had some internal or intrinsic feature that were *incompatible* with being copied. Hence, we can say:

(12) For any particular *x*, *x* is copyable iff no intrinsic feature *F* of *x* is incompatible with *x* getting copied.

Note that these are modal claims: they are claims about what is possible and what is impossible. But the idea is straightforward enough. For instance, we might point out that Scotus believes God is all powerful, meaning God can do anything except bring about a contradiction. So for any particular item in the world, God could certainly produce another copy of it, unless there were something intrinsic to it that would make copying it contradictory. And Scotus's point here would be that there is in fact nothing intrinsic to a nature-trope that makes it contradictory for it to be copied.

6. TROPES AND UNIVERSALS

If we do not distinguish between (1) and (2), it is easy to misunderstand what Scotus is saying about a number of the points discussed above. Consider the following.

I noted above that Scotus rejects the view that a common nature is "individual or singular from itself—that is, from its nature."[25] I pointed out that this is the view that natures are singletons—each nature is radically unique—and this is clear because, by his own admission, Scotus uses the terms "individual" or "singular" to refer to singletons (see (3) above).

However, suppose we forget this. Suppose we see the word "individual" or "singular" and think it refers to mere particulars (e.g., copyable tropes). Since Scotus goes on to reject the view that natures are not "individual" or "singular" in this way, we would conclude that Scotus rejects the notion that natures are particulars. That is, we might think Scotus holds this:

25. Ord., 2.3.1.1nn5–28 (Vat. 7:393–402; Spade, 58–63).

(13) For any nature *N*, *N* is not a particular.

And then, we could easily conclude that Scotus believes natures must therefore be *universals*, at least in some sense. That is, we might think Scotus believes this:

(14) For any nature *N*, *N* is a universal.

This would be a serious misunderstanding. For one thing, it simply cannot be right, because it directly contradicts Scotus's explicit claim that there are no universals (see (9) above). But also, we would be ignoring Scotus's own claim (in (3) above) that when he uses the terms "individual" or "singular," he is speaking only about singletons, not mere particulars.

The view Scotus is rejecting is not the view that natures are mere particulars, but rather the view that each individual's nature is radically unique. Scotus does believe that sublunar natures are common to all members of their species, but only in the sense that all members have a copy of the relevant nature-trope.

7. NO DIMINISHED BEINGS

There is a second point where a failure to distinguish between (1) and (2) can lead to an incorrect interpretation of Scotus's position. As I noted above, Scotus says sublunar natures are neither one or many, nor universal or particular. I pointed out that Scotus uses this to explain what it means to be copyable: something is copyable if it has no intrinsic features that restrict it to being a singleton, multiplied, or conceptualized in the mind (see (11) above).

However, it can be easy to think that Scotus is saying that *there are* natures which are neither one or many, particular or universal. In other words, it can be easy to think that Scotus is proposing that natures can have a special, "pure" state of existence which is somehow in between (or perhaps underneath) the one and the many, the particular and the universal. We might attempt to characterize such a view along these lines:

(15) For any nature *N*, *N* has a special state of existence such that (i) *N* is not a single discrete item, (ii) *N* is not many discrete items, and (iii) *N* is not a universal item.

But this too seems like it would be a serious misunderstanding. For one thing, it seems incoherent. How can anything be neither one nor many? If it exists at all, then surely there is at least one of it, namely itself.

Also, what would natures in this "pure" state of existence be like? Would they be ghostly or shadowy sorts of things? And where, exactly, would they exist? In the corner of the room? It seems very hard to imagine such things.

Most importantly, (15) cannot be right because Scotus explicitly denies it: natures, he says, never exist without satisfying (i), (ii), or (iii).[26] In Scotus's ontology, there are no such shadowy natures. There are just particular tropes in the world, or representations of them in someone's mind. The view that Scotus holds is thus this:

> (16) For any nature *N*, *N* is either (i) a particular trope in reality, or (ii) represented by a concept in someone's mind.

When Scotus says natures are not "of themselves" one or many, particular or universal, he is not making a *positive* claim by proposing that there is some special entity that is neither one or many, nor particular or universal. Rather, he is making a *negative* claim by proposing simply that natures lack any internal restrictions to be one or the other.[27]

8. LESS THAN NUMERICAL ONENESS

There is a final point where a failure to distinguish between (1) and (2) can lead to misunderstandings. Scotus notoriously claims that natures have a "real oneness" which is "less than a numerical oneness."[28] What does this mean?

To say something has "oneness" is an abstract way of saying it is *one* thing—a discrete, enumerable item (a particular). And from (3) above, it is clear that "numerical oneness" is a label Scotus uses for singletons: it involves not just being one thing, it involves being the *only* one.

---

26. Ord., 2.3.1.1n32 (Vat. 7:403.6; Spade, 63): "enim [natura] numquam sit realiter sine aliquo istorum [viz., singularitate vel pluralitate in numero, sive universalitate in conceptu vel particularitate in realitate]."

27. Giorgio Pini highlights the negative character of Scotus's claims too, in "Scotus on Universals."

28. See for instance Ord., 2.3.1.1n8 (Vat. 7:395.1–4; Spade, 59).

So, what Scotus means to say (and does say) is that a nature is one thing (it is a particular trope), but it is not the one and only unique one of its kind (it is not a singleton):

> Apart from any operation of the mind, there is some real oneness in the thing [i.e., in a nature] that is less than numerical oneness, i.e., [it has less than] the oneness proper to a singular [= a singleton].[29]

So long as we are careful to distinguish between (1) and (2), and so long as we are careful to remember (via (3) above) that by "numerical oneness" Scotus means the complete uniqueness that a singleton has, then the claim that a nature has *less* than numerical oneness is straightforward. It simply means that a nature is not completely unique, because there can be many copies of it.

However, if we do not keep the above distinctions in mind, we might head down a very different path of interpretation. If we forget that "numerical oneness" refers to the oneness (uniqueness) of a singleton and instead think it refers to the oneness of mere particulars (copyable tropes), then the claim gets read as saying that a nature has less oneness than a *particular*. In other words, we might end up ascribing to Scotus this view:

> (17) For any nature N, N has less individuality than a particular.

But this cannot be right. For one thing, Scotus does not use "numerical oneness" to refer to particulars. He uses it for singletons, as already noted. But also, what could an item be like if it were less than an individual? Again, would it be some shadowy, ghost-like entity? Scotus rejects the existence of such things (see (16)).

Despite the obscurity of the phrase "a real oneness that is less than numerical," Scotus simply means to say with it that natures are copyable tropes—they are particular, but each is not completely unique, because there can be many copies.

---

29. Ord., 2.3.1.1n30 (Vat. 7:402.11–12; Spade, 63): "aliqua est unitas in re realis absque omni operatione intellectus, minor unitate numerali sive unitate propria singularis."

9. HAECCETIES

In the narrow portion of the *Ordinatio* text that I discussed here, Scotus has not shown why each material substance is a unique singleton. What he has shown is that the uniqueness of each material substance does not derive from its nature, because its nature is not itself utterly unique. But, as I noted at the outset, this is precisely the place where it comes out clearly that Scotus thinks natures are copyable tropes.

In the rest of his *Ordinatio* discussion on this topic, Scotus goes on to consider a number of other theories that attempt to explain why each material substance is a unique singleton. For example, he considers whether material substances are unique because they are composed from distinct hunks of matter.

In the end, Scotus rejects all such theories. He finds that each such theory fails to provide an explanation as to why material substances are so utterly unique. So, he feels compelled to postulate a very special kind of trope in each material substance—namely, an uncopyable trope (a haecceity).

This ties back to McCord Adams's original point. Natures really like to share themselves. In God, the divine nature does get shared, in its entirety, but here below, sublunar natures have to settle for copying themselves. When parents reproduce, they produce in their offspring a copy of their relevant nature-trope(s).

This explains why members of the same species are the same in kind. But the haecceity explains why a clone of me would be another human being rather than another me—the clone would have copies of my nature-tropes but not my haecceity.

10. ETHICAL IMPLICATIONS

Why should we care about Scotus's ontology of copyable tropes, haecceities, and singletons? What difference does it make to our lives?

Well, one reason it matters is historical and philosophical accuracy. Marilyn McCord Adams was one of the world's foremost experts on medieval philosophy. Her publications in the area are extensive.[30] Even

---

30. Some of her most-cited works are the following: *William Ockham*, 2 vols., which runs well over a thousand pages, took fourteen years to complete, and was done on a typewriter; "Universals in the Early Fourteenth Century"; "Ockham on Identity and Distinction"; "Did Ockham Know of Material and Strict Implication?"; "Ockham's

though it goes without saying, it is worth pointing out that McCord Adams *cared* about getting the past right. In the preface to the 1989 printing of her two volume study of William Ockham, she says that her aim in that book was to give the non-political works of Ockham "an accurate reading," and to "meet his writings in philosophy and theology as he intended them to be met: philosopher-to-philosopher." But the "historian of philosophy, like any fair-minded discussion partner, must listen hard to what the other philosopher is saying, and enter into his/her point of view."[31] McCord Adams believed it was important first and foremost to get our *history* correct, and to treat it *philosophically*.

The interpretation of Scotus's ontology that I presented above satisfies both requirements. It is historically sensitive. It stays close to the text, and it takes Scotus's own words about singularity seriously. At the same time, it is philosophically illuminating. This part of Scotus's thought can feel obscure, and even unintelligible. The view I presented above takes the demand to be philosophically intelligible seriously, delivering a clear picture of how Scotus understands the metaphysical structure of individuals.

Yet even beyond its merits for the historian of philosophy, I want to suggest that Scotus's ontology can have some interesting ethical implications. In particular, I want to suggest that it can serve as a straightforward foundation for theories of human (and non-human) dignity, irreplaceability, and value.

In the *Groundwork for the Metaphysics of Morals*, Kant famously claims that whatever has a price can be replaced, whereas whatever has dignity cannot, and human beings have dignity. The implication is that each human is irreplaceable, and maybe also the implication is that each human is infinitely valuable. For Kant, the reason that humans have such dignity is that they alone are self-governing moral agents.[32]

Theory of Natural Signification"; "Ockham's Nominalism and Unreal Entities"; "What Does Ockham Mean by 'Supposition'?"; and "Was Ockham a Humean about Efficient Causality?" She made important contributions to philosophical theology too. For instance, see her *What Sort of Human Nature?*; "The Resurrection of the Body according to Three Medieval Aristotelians"; "The Immaculate Conception of the Blessed Virgin Mary"; "The Metaphysics of the Incarnation"; "The Metaphysics of the Trinity"; and *Some Later Medieval Theories of the Eucharist*.

31. McCord Adams, *William Ockham*, ix.

32. "In the kingdom of ends, everything has either a *price* or *dignity*. What has a *price* can be replaced with something else, as its *equivalent*. By contrast, whatever is exalted above all price and hence admits of no equivalent has *dignity*. Whatever relates to general human inclinations and needs has a *market price*. . . . But what constitutes

Perhaps being irreplaceable and being infinitely valuable come to the same thing, or perhaps not, depending on how you want to interpret Kant. You might think they are orthogonal: an infinitely valuable item can be replaced by another equally infinitely valuable item, while a relatively valueless item (a family photograph, say) can be irreplaceable. Alternatively, you might think that to be infinitely valuable is to be beyond any actually payable price, and that therefore makes it irreplaceable.

However you want to read it, twentieth and twenty-first-century discussions of ethics and human rights often put these Kantian ideas front and center. It seems commonplace to find it asserted that each and every human being has some sort of immeasurable dignity, that each and every human being is irreplaceable, and so on.

A metaphysician might wonder: what grounds the irreplaceability of a person, and gives them such infinite value? On which features of the world (and the persons inhabiting it) are such claims based?

Linda Zagzebski proposes that the exalted value of humans is based on their rational natures, while their irreplaceability is based on their personhood. According to Zagzebski, each person is utterly unique, and this uniqueness is grounded in the irreducibly first-personal consciousness that every human has. In particular, each person has a stream of conscious states which are so unique that the likelihood of anyone else having the same stream of conscious states is so vanishingly low that it is effectively impossible. Part of the reason for this (says Zagzebski) is because we can reflect on our own states in numerous ways, and also that our states depend on interactions with other people, objects, and environments.[33]

If Zagzebski is right, then replicating anyone's conscious history would be effectively impossible. In order for anyone to have the same stream of conscious states that I have, they'd not only have to have the

---

the condition under which alone something can be an end in itself does not merely have a relative worth or price; rather, it has an inner worth, or *dignity*. Now morality is the only condition under which a rational being can be an end in itself. . . . Thus morality, and humanity insofar as it is capable of morality, is the only thing that has dignity" (434); "*Autonomy* is thus the ground of the dignity of human nature, and of every rational nature" (436). Kant, *Groundwork for the Metaphysics of Morals*, using the standard Akademie edition's pagination.

33. See Zagzebski, "The Dignity of Persons"; Zagzebski, "The Uniqueness of Persons." Zagzebski bases part of her reasoning on a distinction between an individual human nature-instance, on the one hand, and the human person, on the other. Zagzebski traces this distinction through the Christian tradition. McCord Adams examines some of the metaphysical issues that underlie this distinction in scholastic philosophy in "What's Metaphysically Special about Supposits?"

same stream of base states that I have, they'd also need to interact with all the same people, objects, and environments that I do, and they'd have to reflect on all of them in exactly the same ways that I do, in exactly the same order.

However, it is worth pointing out that although it may be extremely improbable that anyone's conscious history be replicated, it does not seem to be a logical impossibility. And if we suppose for the sake of argument that someone's conscious history does get replicated, then it is not clear that Zagzebski's account of a person's irreplaceability has the resources to deliver a satisfactory analysis.

For the sake of argument, let us imagine a scenario where conscious histories are replicated. Take our universe, and call it U. Let us suppose there is a parallel universe U^*, qualitatively twin to ours. Every molecule, every person, and every event in U—each one is replicated in U^*. Even every U-person's conscious history gets replicated in U^*.

Now suppose that in our universe U, a certain Harold and June love each other very much, and as far as they know, they have lived a happy life together for the last fifty years. Of course, in U^*, Harold* and June* have twin experiences. But, unbeknownst to each couple, powerful agents decided to meddle in these two universes, and twenty years ago, they silently swapped Harold and Harold*, without either of the Harolds or either of the Junes noticing.

Suppose now that someone informs June that her Harold was swapped for a twin from a parallel universe. What should June feel at this point? Should she feel that she has just discovered that someone has done an injustice to her, by taking her precious Harold away from her? (A parallel question could be asked of June*.) Or, should it not matter to her, since she's carried on with qualitatively identical conscious experiences?

My intuitions tell me that June would feel that someone very special to her has been taken away from her. If my intuition is right, then what sort of analysis could Zagzebski's account give to explain why that is so?

If Scotus is right that no matter how many copyable tropes two individuals share they will always be different singletons because they have distinct haecceities, then we have a ready answer to the question. June has been wronged, because indeed the two Harolds are different individuals, no matter how qualitatively alike they are, even in terms of their conscious histories. If Scotus is right, we could explain why June has been wronged: it is because *her* Harold has been taken away from her.

Scotus's ontology of created individuals can thus serve in a straightforward way as a ground for questions about the uniqueness of human beings. For we need only point to the fact that each person is a singleton to explain why they cannot be replaced. You can replicate all of their copyable tropes, but you can never replicate their haecceity.

One can go further. One could say that, according to Scotus's ontology, *every* created individual is a singleton, and thus one could propose that *every* created individual is irreplaceable. One could then have a rather high view of the irreplaceability of *all* creatures, and not just of human beings.

Another aspect of human experience is that we develop deep emotional attachments to particular individuals (be they human or non-human), and we cannot migrate or transfer those attachments to other individuals. Let us call these "intimate singleton attachments."

Scotus's ontology offers a straightforward explanation of this too. We can develop various kinds of intimate emotional attachments to things, based in part on the various copyable tropes they possess. But there will always be a particular individual with whom we are developing such intimate emotional attachments. It explains why we develop intimate singleton attachments to particular people in our lives, or to that one special dog. It even explains why we can develop singleton attachments to, say, that elm tree in the back yard, or the Blue Jay that visits the feeder every morning.

What Scotus's view offers is a straightforward basis for theories of human (and non-human) irreplaceability and dignity. A Scotist does not need to look for self-governing moral agents, nor do they need to look for features of human experience that are improbable to replicate. For the Scotist, every creature is a singleton, and hence irreplaceable in their very constitution.

11. THEOLOGICAL IMPLICATIONS

To close, I want to make one final point. This particular interpretation of Scotus's ontology, along with the ethical implications I sketched a moment ago, are quite amenable to McCord Adams's own theological vision.

An idea that is fundamental to McCord Adams's theological thought is something she called the "metaphysical size gap." To explain the idea, McCord Adams sometimes quoted Monty Python: "God is very, very big, and we are very, very small."[34] In other words, God is infinitely and intensively perfect, while we are metaphysically puny in comparison.

McCord Adams took the idea of a metaphysical size gap directly from the medieval writers she read and studied so often. And rightly so. It is indeed a fundamental idea in Bonaventure, Scotus, Julian of Norwich, and many others.[35]

As McCord Adams sees it, the metaphysical size gap is significant because it has striking ethical and theological implications regarding (among other things) how we should understand the relationship between God and creatures, and between creatures and creatures.[36]

One of the things the size gap entails is that God freely *chose* to create creatures. McCord Adams takes this point from Scotus, who believed that creatures are finite goods, and this provides a reason for everybody to love them. However, Scotus also believes that such reasons are not compelling but defeasible.[37] Consequently, to put it as McCord Adams does, Scotus "reckons that, because finite goods furnish only defeasible reasons to love them, God has no compelling reason to create anything."[38] That God actually *did* create what he did is sheer grace.

This means that God *decided* to create a world where God could treat us with respect, care, and kindness. And as McCord Adams sees it, this puts the relationship between God and creatures at the center of theologically significant meaning-making activities.[39]

---

34. McCord Adams, "The Metaphysical Size Gap," 129. Marilyn was explicit that the metaphysical size gap is fundamental to good theology on p. 132: "My point is not that the metaphysical size gap is *sufficient* for true and wholesome philosophical theology, but that it is *necessary*. My purpose is to commend (what I shall—perhaps contentiously—call) a 'mainstream medieval' interpretation of it and to press my case for its systematic importance with examples from medieval thought."

35. See McCord Adams, "Metaphysical Size Gap," 130–31; McCord Adams, *Horrendous Evils*, 139–41.

36. McCord Adams, "Metaphysical Size Gap," 137: "The personified metaphysical size gap is a great theological idea because it focuses a distinctive and—I would say—true cosmological picture. Equally impressive and of no less moment is the range of soteriological consequences to which it is thought to give rise"; McCord Adams, "Metaphysical Size Gap," 138: "The personified metaphysical size gap is a great theological idea because it shows divine and created agency not to be in competition."

37. McCord Adams, "Metaphysical Size Gap," 131, 138.

38. McCord Adams, "Metaphysical Size Gap," 138.

39. McCord Adams, "Metaphysical Size Gap," 144: "The personified metaphysical size gap guarantees that God has no obligations to us or any other mere creatures. But the Bible's God is personal and—for reason's of God's own—cares about personal

Moreover, the size gap entails not only that *God* gets to choose to love humans, it also entails that *humans* get to choose to love both God and creatures. McCord Adams puts this in terms of courtesy: God treats us with courtesy, and we get to choose to treat each other with courtesy as well.[40] For McCord Adams, this is indeed a crucial part of what it means for humans to "claim God."

But this ties back to singletons. If courtesy is one of the primary dispositional stances that we should take toward others, then one could argue that our courteous action toward others would not be guided solely by general "laws" that we might apply indiscriminately to all members of a species. Rather, our courteous action toward others would be directed uniquely at each particular individual that we want to treat courteously. In other words, when we act courteously, we will tend to focus on the *singletons* of creation, and through courteous care, we will tend to develop the kind of intimate singleton attachments that undergird the variety of loving relationships that Marilyn McCord Adams believes stand at the heart of theologically significant meaning-making activities.

---

creatures so much as to make divine-human relations the center of positive meaning in our lives."

40. McCord Adams, "Courtesy, Human and Divine," 159: "The metaphysical size gap is our key to courtesy. . . . Boundless goodness is the heart of reality. . . . Because the heart of reality is three-personal, boundless goodness is love, given and received among Father, Son, and Holy Spirit, and poured out and to produce and maintain, to (ful)fill and enfold all creation"; McCord Adams, "Courtesy, Human and Divine," 161: "Certainly, the metaphysical size gap convinces us that all creatures are 'little,' indeed, metaphysically miniscule, in relation to God. To call them all 'brother' and 'sister' implies a band of friends coming together to help one another strive toward a common goal."

9

Queering Worship

RUTHANNA B. HOOKE

MARILYN MCCORD ADAMS AND I both arrived in the Fall of 1993 at Yale Divinity School, she as Professor of Historical Theology, and I as a first-year Master of Divinity student. My first encounter with her was attending her inaugural lecture, an intricate and rigorous discussion of Anselm's *Cur Deus Homo*. Many of us students were completely lost during this lecture; hence we dubbed her, in our frustration and embarrassment (because we wanted to think of ourselves as smart), the "Dreaded Anselm Woman." Then, much to our surprise, she turned up at the first meeting of the LGBT student group, of which I was a member, and announced that she was available to work with any student who wanted to study queer theology with her. We were shocked and even more befuddled than we were at her lecture. How could this frighteningly intelligent historical theologian who was steeped in the arcana of Anselm broadcast herself as studying and teaching queer theology? Most of us were not even using the word "queer" in those days. It seemed like an incongruous marriage of two contradictory impulses; yet it was this marriage that made Marilyn so formidable and so beloved by those of us who counted ourselves misfits and needed a champion to prove, with devastating brilliance and invincible courage, that there was a place for us within the Christian faith and tradition. A few weeks later, when she preached at YDS's Coming

Out Day service, and described coming out as a lifelong process for all of us, straight and queer, we dubbed her, in our admiration and love, the "Blessed Anselm Woman," and so she remained.

In preparing this essay, I had the blessing of unearthing a trove of Marilyn McCord Adams's liturgical writings from services that she created with her students at Yale Divinity School over twenty years ago. As one of the students involved in these liturgies, I took for granted the vibrancy, edginess, and visceral nature of her liturgical writing and sermons. Now, after overseeing chapel worship at an Episcopal seminary for the past several years, I recognize how far ahead of her time, and of our time, McCord Adams was in what she created. More even than when she wrote them, her beautiful, searing words stand for me as an example of what liturgy can be and do. The Appendix to this paper provides a flavor of these writings, set alongside the parallel eucharistic language from the *Book of Common Prayer* of the Episcopal Church, making it clear how venturesome and bold McCord Adams's liturgical writing is. McCord Adams's reworking of the *sursum corda*, the well-known words at the beginning of the Great Thanksgiving of the Eucharistic Prayer, offers one example of how she invigorated liturgical language. The original words are:

> *Celebrant*: The Lord be with you.
> *People*: And also with you.
> *Celebrant*: Lift up your hearts.
> *People*: We lift them to the Lord.
> *Celebrant*: Let us give thanks to the Lord our God.
> *People*: It is right to give him thanks and praise.

McCord Adams rewrote them thus:

> *Celebrant*: Our God is here.
> *Congregation*: Holy Spirit is with us.
> *Celebrant*: Unlock the doors of your hearts.
> *Congregation*: We open them to God and to one another.
> *Celebrant*: We have come to meet God, our Friend and our Lover.
> *Congregation*: It is good to love God, now and always.

In this essay I will draw a few principles from what McCord Adams was doing in these writings and suggest how we can use these principles to guide our own liturgical creations today. To begin with, I will explore the theological commitments that underlie McCord Adams's willingness to experiment with liturgy in the bold way that she did. Her warrant for playing with the forms and words of liturgy is rooted in her convictions concerning the nature of the church and the purposes of liturgy itself.

1. THEOLOGICAL COMMITMENTS: THE CHURCH AS HUMAN AND DIVINE

McCord Adams's liturgical writings used the basic structure of the Eucharistic *ordo*, or deep liturgical structure, but she rewrote the words in her own vivid and iconoclastic language. In doing this, McCord Adams was operating within the possibilities provided by the *Book of Common Prayer*, and thus within her own Episcopal tradition, since the *BCP* provides the option for the writing of Eucharistic Prayers.[1] McCord Adams's choice to exercise this option, and to re-write liturgies in the edgy way that she did, was based on deep theological commitments. She tended to view Christian tradition from the margins, and thus developed a hermeneutic that privileged the working of the Holy Spirit rather than the settled mores of the church. For instance, in urging the church to rethink its sexual mores and taboos, she turns not to the passages in Scripture that deal with homosexuality in particular, but rather to the stories in Acts 10–15 about the early church needing to rethink its position on Gentile inclusion. Here she argues that the taboo against Gentile inclusion is "challenged by experience," such that eventually the church "'learns from the Spirit' and changes its policies."[2] Her hermeneutic for interpreting Scripture and tradition is decisively shaped by an honoring of human experience, as well as by a sense that the Spirit is a "hurricane" that "permit[s] the old order to unravel, indeed huff[s] and puff[s] it down."[3]

This privileging of human experience is in keeping with Anglican understandings of the mutual balancing of sources of authority for theology and Christian life: the proverbial Anglican "three-legged stool" calls for the interplay of Scripture, tradition, and reason as sources of authority, and often a fourth "leg" of the stool, that of experience, is added to this list of sources. For McCord Adams, though, the movement of the Spirit and the "challenge" posed by human experience usually count as more important than settled tradition. She argues that this is in keeping with

---

1. See "An Order for Celebrating the Holy Eucharist," in Episcopal Church, *Book of Common Prayer*, 400–405.
2. McCord Adams, "Hurricane Spirit," 130.
3. McCord Adams, "Hurricane Spirit," 141.

understandings of the authority in the Episcopal Church, which rejects the "strong argument from tradition," which holds that if tradition never allowed a practice (such as the ordination of women or LGBT+ persons), then it cannot be allowed.[4] Instead, the Episcopal Church distinguishes between the doctrinal norms set forth in the historic creeds of the church and ethical norms, which can and do evolve over time. These norms need to develop because humans "are not very skilled at social organization . . . we have a poor understanding of how what we do as a group of individuals gives rise to group propensities and dynamics that we neither aim for nor anticipate. Good intentions regularly spawn systemic evils that are deeply rooted and take on a life of their own."[5] She rejects a strong argument from tradition because she is keenly aware of the capacity of tradition to enshrine and perpetuate these pernicious patterns of social organization. The privileging of the Spirit and of experience over against church tradition is buttressed by her reading of Scripture, since "the general drift of the Bible is that God does not set the divine seal of approval on any merely human social system."[6] This "general drift" of the Bible also means that Scripture itself, while a "primary authority for Christian faith and practice," is not infallible, since Scripture, like tradition, bears the marks of the systemic evils of the cultures in which it was formed.[7]

This critique of human patterns of social organization underlies McCord Adams's ecclesiology, which distinguishes sharply between the divine and human dimensions of the church, reflecting her keen sense of the goodness of God over against the fallibility and brokenness of human systems, including the church. God's realm is "utopic: perfectly integrating the good of individuals and the good of the whole, it is comprehensive in a way no human society can be."[8] As divine, the church participates in this utopic realm of God; the church is organized by God and united under the direction of Christ its head, such that its unity and harmony are not in doubt, because God guarantees them. However, the church as human is subject to the human limitations present in modes of social organization, and to the systemic evils that arise from these fallible modes of social organization. Since the church cannot escape fallibility, its vocation

---

4. McCord Adams, "The Ordination of Women," 65.
5. McCord Adams, "Shaking the Foundations," 714.
6. McCord Adams, "Hurricane Spirit," 132.
7. McCord Adams, "The Ordination of Women," 69.
8. McCord Adams, "Hurricane Spirit," 132.

"is not to boast of being 'holier than thou,' all the while claiming divine sanction for its institutional policies . . . rather, the church is summoned to vigilance, to institutional circumspection which is ever on the lookout to identify the systemic evils to which it gives rise."[9] Since human institutions, including the church, will always be plagued by systemic evils, the temptation is to submit to the *status quo*. However, McCord Adams insists that the church's calling is exactly the opposite: "to discern where evils are ripe for uprooting and to take the lead in eradicating them."[10]

McCord Adams's ecclesiology, distinguishing rigorously between the divine and the human dimensions of the church, leads to what might be termed a "hermeneutic of suspicion" toward the church as an institution, and toward its traditions and policies. However, on the other hand, McCord Adams consistently summons the church to claim its divine calling, to uproot systemic evils in its own practices, and to create spaces in which human flourishing can take place. For instance, one of the systemic evils to which humans are prone is the tendency to organize social life around various taboos, walling off behaviors that are seen as disruptive, or excluding those who do not fit certain norms. For McCord Adams, the taboo mentality is "untheological," in that it is based in fear, it oversimplifies human complexity, and it is a sacralizing of merely human patterns of organization. In response to such destructive patterns of social organization, the church needs to be a place that resists and overturns the taboos that limit human well-being, even though as a human institution it may want to cling to them: "the church is always called to trust the Spirit and dare to bring what is feared, said, and done in the dark 'out of the closet' and up to full consciousness, into the intimacy of the Spirit's classroom, for rational and prayerful examination."[11] The church ideally should be a taboo-free zone in which those aspects of our lives which have been hidden or rendered inarticulate because of the taboo mentality can be brought to light and prayerfully explored.

As an extension of this understanding of the church, McCord Adams conceives of her role as priest and liturgical leader in unconventional ways, which also undergird the freedom and edginess of her liturgical creations and her preaching. Her rejection of the "strong argument from tradition" leads her to question the hierarchies of ministry within the

---

9. McCord Adams, "Shaking the Foundations," 714.
10. McCord Adams, "Shaking the Foundations," 714.
11. McCord Adams, "Hurricane Spirit," 134.

church. She defends the more recent understanding of the Episcopal Church that baptism is the "principal holy order," as that is when the gift of the Holy Spirit is given to the believer, and it is this indwelling Spirit that is necessary for the existence of the church. Thus, "instead of putting bishops at the apex, priests a little lower, deacons lower still, with the laity at the base, the priesthood of all believers should top the pyramid, while the ministries of deacons, priests, and bishops should be derivative and so descend from that as variations on a theme."[12] McCord Adams even questions whether the three-fold ministry of bishops, priests, and deacons is an historical artifact that may have outlived its usefulness, serving to obscure the primary ministry of all of the baptized. To be a minister is to be commissioned by Christ to act in Christ's name, and the ontological basis of this commission is to be a friend and partner of the indwelling God. This friendship and partnership is universally given to Christians, and thus "there is no ontological deficit that would prevent any and all Christians from functioning in any and all liturgical functions now assumed by ordained clergy," including presiding at the Eucharist or laying on hands at ordinations.[13] The logical conclusion of this argument is McCord Adams's daring promotion of "the episcopacy of all believers."[14] This understanding of ministry leads her to a fluid doctrine of the priesthood, fueling her sense that her role as a priest is to empower the ministry of others, especially those with less power in society and in the institutional church. This questioning of established clerical hierarchies also funds her willingness to play with liturgy, using her power as priest to invert and unsettle established liturgical forms.

2. THE PURPOSES OF LITURGY: REVOLUTIONARY ENCOUNTER WITH GOD

These ecclesiological and theological convictions provide the warrant for McCord Adams's bold rewriting of traditional liturgies. She felt free to rewrite the church's liturgies because for her these were traditional forms that did not need to be treated as sacrosanct, but instead could be transformed. She claimed license to play with what tradition had created, since tradition partook of systemic evils as well as of divine inspiration; she felt

---

12. McCord Adams, "The Ordination of Women," 71.
13. McCord Adams, "The Episcopacy of All Believers," 24.
14. McCord Adams, "The Episcopacy of All Believers," 9.

free to challenge the church's human forms in order to help it fulfill its identity as divine.

Not only does McCord Adams's warrant for liturgical re-creation stem from her ecclesiology, but her motivation for such re-creation likewise comes from a conviction that the liturgies of the church need to manifest clearly the identity and vocation of the church. Liturgy is fundamentally where the church proclaims and realizes its identity; it declares in liturgy both what it is and what it aims to become. If the church's essential vocation is to root out social evils and to reclaim its identity as the body of Christ and its allegiance to his kingdom, then the liturgies of the church must proclaim and further that calling. The church's liturgies do this, McCord Adams argues, by presenting participants with a conflict between competing world orders, between human social organizations with their systemic evils, on one hand, and the realm of God, on the other. We come to worship marked by social evils such as racism and sexism, but we come to affirm our allegiance to Jesus Christ, in contradiction to identities shaped by these evils:

> We take the initiative to enter the cultic drama where we know in advance (whether or not we consciously think of it every time) that we will be confronted with Jesus' embodiment of social aims that contradict the deep structures of our everyday world. We eucharistic participants thus set ourselves up to have our contradictory allegiances exposed, to be confronted with the choice between our conventional selves and who Jesus says we are and who we should become.[15]

Liturgy has the task of highlighting this conflict, bringing participants to this confrontation and to the decision to claim their primary belonging, which is to Christ.

Liturgy achieves this confrontation by creating a familiar enough frame to allow participants' defenses to come down, so that the encounter with the holy that we both desire and fear can take place; the ritual structures of cultic drama "aim to domesticate just enough to keep close encounters [with the Holy] beneficial, without flattening the force of their transforming power."[16] Cultic drama can bring down our defenses in one of two ways: either by "gentle coaxing and subtle seduction," an indirect approach that woos us toward transformation, or by a "frontal

---

15. McCord Adams, "Eucharistic Drama," 209.
16. McCord Adams, "Eucharistic Drama," 213.

assault . . . [that] crashes through our defenses." The "frontal assault" was the approach that Jesus used, confronting the powers that be directly and aggressively, enacting "the apocalyptic invasion of the one who comes in the name of the Lord."[17] Both approaches have their risks; the former risks leaving the *status quo* intact, and the latter risks provoking a violent reaction to reject the direct challenge. The latter result is what Jesus experienced, in the forces of the *status quo* that united to silence and kill him. However, Christian cultic drama, as essentially comic, brings a happy ending out of this tragedy, in God's raising Jesus from the dead.

The church's cultic drama releases energy for transformation, but McCord Adams cautions that if this energy is not harnessed, it can turn into a neurotic obsession with liturgy as an end in itself. Likewise, if we participate in liturgy but do not accept its invitation to transformation, we act out our ambivalent response by a fixation on liturgical details, a fixation that ultimately has a deadly effect on liturgy itself: "our refusal of transformation energizes a vicious cycle of seeking and refusing the very thing that would make us whole," a refusal that will make participants sick and the liturgy distorted.[18] The liturgy, instead of provoking transformation, can instead display the fallibility of the church as a human institution, devoted to reinforcing social taboos, buttressing the *status quo*, and making honest exploration of the messiness of human existence impossible. She scathingly describes public worship as all too often

> a place for pardoning picadilloes, offering and accepting polite apologies, above all for pretending that everything was all right. Sunday services were scenes where failure and loss were scarcely acknowledged, and even death was advertised as a blessing. The message was strong and effective: people with real problems should take them elsewhere; they should definitely not disturb the peace of "organized religion" and its conventional god.[19]

All too often, liturgies reinforce the systemic evils found in fallible human modes of social organization, keep taboos firmly in place, and gloss over the messiness of human existence that prompts the desire to encounter the Holy One and to be transformed.

In response to these failures of liturgy, McCord Adams's writings and liturgical experiments aim to realize the capacity of liturgy to

---

17. McCord Adams, "Eucharistic Drama," 219.
18. McCord Adams, "Eucharistic Drama," 217.
19. McCord Adams, *Wrestling for Blessing*, 11.

provoke transformation and even revolution. Both by "gentle seduction" and "frontal assault," she aims to take down worshippers' defenses, so that they can meet the holy and reaffirm their primary allegiance to Christ and his realm, over against all forms of human social organization that seek to define them. Her writings enlist liturgy in the church's task of rooting out systemic evils, purifying itself of its human nature so as to manifest more completely its divine nature as the body of Christ. Her writings aim to make Christian liturgies into sites that instead of reinforcing social norms and their attendant taboos can be places of resistance, taboo-free zones that promote human well-being and especially the healing of those most hurt by taboos.

3. ENCOUNTER WITH THE HOLY: HORROR-DEFEAT AND QUEER AUTHENTICITY

For liturgy to achieve its purpose of creating an encounter with the God whom we both long for and fear, liturgy needs to allow for a confrontation with the reality of horrors, as that which most deeply threatens our sense of God's goodness and our willingness to encounter and be transformed by God. McCord Adams wrestled vigorously with questions of theodicy—why humans were created to be so vulnerable to horrors, and who God would have to be, and what God would have to do, to make good on all of this suffering. As she struggled with these questions, she relied heavily—in her academic work, and in her personal life and priestly ministry—on Christian worship, and especially on the Eucharist, as the event in which horrors are confronted, and in which God's defeat of horrors in all three Stages is enacted and manifested. As McCord Adams observes in *Christ and Horrors*, for horror-defeat it is not enough to know that God is with us in horrors (Stage I); we somehow have to appropriate and understand this (Stage II). Liturgy is a place where this happens; it needs to manifest, to enact, in some way, the drama of overcoming horrors that is happening in Stage I, so we can feel and appropriate it; this appropriation constitutes Stage II of horror-defeat. Liturgy also needs to signal toward Stage III horror-defeat, to invite worshippers into a proleptic taste of that stage at which humans are no longer vulnerable to horrors.

In order for Christian liturgy to enact God's proleptic defeat of horrors, it needs above all to be a space of honesty. One of the major themes of her sermons, McCord Adams says, is the necessity of "utter candor" in wrestling with God. Liturgy should be a place where those in the grip of horrors can cry out to God in despair and outrage: "The suffering and compromised will not be able to believe that blessing is theirs without imitating Job, dropping the masks of liturgical politeness, with all the pain and fear and rage 'telling it like it is,' confronting God with how bad it seems from our human point of view."[20] Her liturgical writings speak with this honesty: "With those who befriended and fed you, who argued with You and touched You, who got angry with You and saw Your face, who ran away from you only to meet You on their path, we praise you."[21] When the bread and wine are offered to be consecrated, McCord Adams writes:

> We set the table with gifts from our world, this bread and this wine, and we offer to you our closets, our fears, and all that binds us, our brothers and sisters who live and die with AIDS, the harms we have suffered and the grief we have caused. By your Holy Spirit may they become for us the bread of life and cup of salvation, Your Body and Blood, that we may love as your Body in the world.[22]

Liturgy becomes the site where, instead of tidily packaging and discounting suffering, worshippers can be ruthlessly honest about it. What is striking here is that not only are the elements of bread and wine offered as Christ's body, but all the worshippers are also offered, and *in particular* their sufferings and losses. All of *this* becomes Christ's body. This incorporation into Christ's body is a step toward claiming an allegiance to him that contradicts and overcomes our fealty to socially constructed identities that are constricting and even death-dealing.

Inasmuch as horrors are person-destroying, "engulf[ing] the positive value of [the participant's] life and penetrat[ing] into his/her meaning-making structures seemingly to defeat and degrade his/her value as a person,"[23] affirmation of our authentic personhood is closely connected to the defeat of horrors. For liturgy to be a site in which horrors are faced and proleptically overcome, liturgy needs to allow space for honesty not only about horrors, but also about who we are more broadly. But for

20. McCord Adams, *Wrestling for Blessing*, 23.

21. McCord Adams, "Eucharistic Prayer for Coming Out Day Liturgy." A version of this Eucharistic Prayer was published as "Eucharistic Prayer for the Powerless, the Oppressed, the Unusual." Adapted from a Eucharistic Prayer in Morley, *All Desires Known*, 46.

22. McCord Adams, "Prayer for Coming Out Day."

23. McCord Adams, *Christ and Horrors*, 33.

McCord Adams, who we are is fundamentally queer: "because God loves variety, God created, calls each of us to live into our own queerness."[24] There is a Christological basis for our queerness, since, to quote McCord Adams, "Jesus Christ is queer." He is queer by virtue of his two natures, human and divine, making him the consummate "boundary smudger and category-straddler."[25] For this reason, while the Gospels give a wealth of images for Christ—Son of Man, Son of God, Messiah, etc., Jesus "squeezes under [them] only to misfit, overlap, superimpose, contradict each and all of them, because the reality of Jesus is so much more than any of them can say."[26] Moreover, God in God's own triune being is queer—a gay love triangle, as McCord Adams sometimes described the Godhead.

If we are made in the image of Christ, and in the image of the triune God, then we are all a lot queerer than we might suppose. As McCord Adams notes, "queerness is not just about gender and sexual orientation. It's about refusing to be a copy of a copy, a slogan, or a cliché."[27] McCord Adams, who described herself as a "woman who's barged her way into two or three male professions, who's misfitted every category ever offered her," insists that coming out is a life-long process for each of us, not just for LGBTQ persons. Queerness, then, is another way of talking about authenticity, about showing up as the people we truly are. "Why be normal when you can be interesting?," McCord Adams demands.[28]

Christians are called to grow into the full stature of Christ, which means to grow into our full queerness, and this happens paradigmatically in liturgy. As liturgical theologian Don Saliers put it, "worship is participation in God's very life."[29] By participation in the liturgy, we are incorporated into Christ, becoming ever more like him. To use the language of Pierre Bourdieu, liturgies form us over time in a *habitus*, a distinctively Christian identity and way of life. In the Eucharist, we both eat and become the Body of Christ, and thus are formed in a *habitus* that ever more closely resembles Christ's image. As McCord Adams puts it, liturgies are "identity-conferring dramas."[30] If the identity conferred upon us in lit-

---

24. McCord Adams, *Wrestling for Blessing*, 125.
25. McCord Adams, "Prologue to Celebration of the Holy Eucharist."
26. McCord Adams, *Wrestling for Blessing*, 124.
27. McCord Adams, *Wrestling for Blessing*, 124.
28. McCord Adams, *Wrestling for Blessing*, 126.
29. Saliers, *Worship as Theology*, 48.
30. McCord Adams, *Wrestling for Blessing*, 20.

urgy is that of Christ's body, as we are fashioned in his image, then this means that liturgy ought to form us in a *habitus* that is ever more queer.

Liturgies therefore need to be "taboo-free zones" where our queerness can be made manifest, where the full variety that God creates and loves can be on glorious display. In a Eucharistic Prayer that McCord Adams wrote for a Coming Out Day liturgy, she wrote: "Remember Your holy family, and especially this community, . . . women and men learning to value variety, gay and lesbian persons giving birth to new identities, church-damaged, excluded and unusual people, seeking the power of Your kiss, and the strength of your love."[31] Creating space for this unabashed display of humanity in all its diversity is one of the ways that liturgy fulfills the call of the church to resist societal norms that constrain expressions of selfhood, and to root out the systemic evils of homophobia, sexism, and racism.

4. WELCOMING QUEER BODIES

If liturgies are to be places of queerness, taboo-free zones, then they need to be places where queer bodies—meaning all bodies—can be welcomed. Given the church's very mixed record in its treatment of bodies, hospitality to bodies in the liturgy is by no means given. And yet, as McCord Adams insists in *Christ and Horrors*, the very power of the Eucharist rests on its being an embodied event. We need to meet Christ in the Eucharist, body to body, not only because we ourselves are embodied and know in and through our bodies, but also because it is in our bodies that we are vulnerable to horrors, and so we need to know Christ as one who takes these horrors into his own body and so offers healing to our bodies.[32] Expressing this in one of her Eucharistic prayers, McCord Adams writes: "We remember your death for us, Your friends. We shout your resurrection, our bold new life. Come, sweet Jesus, embrace us face-to-face."[33] These words summon us to worship God in and through our bodies.

To use a distinction employed by Ola Sigurdson in *Heavenly Bodies*, I suspect that McCord Adams has in mind here not the classical body, which is autonomous and delimited, but what Sigurdson calls "the grotesque body," the body that is open, permeable, unfinished, excessive. In

---

31. McCord Adams, "Prayer for Coming Out Day."
32. McCord Adams, *Christ and Horrors*, 299.
33. McCord Adams, "Prayer for Coming Out Day."

the grotesque body suffering and horrors are evident, but so is openness to transcendence.[34] For Sigurdson, the grotesque body is closely connected to the erotic body, and I am struck by how erotic McCord Adams's liturgical writings are. Queerness may not be only about sexuality, but it is at least about that. So McCord Adams, in making space for queerness, for the body, for a space free of taboos, brought the erotic into liturgy as well. We hear that in her words about seeking the power of Jesus' kiss, longing for his face-to-face embrace, in her version of the *sursum corda*, in which we seek God as Friend and Lover.

The governing principle in all of McCord Adams's work in liturgy is that the liturgy does not need to be cleaned up or made pretty, nor should it be. In espousing a strong doctrine of Christ's real presence in the Eucharist, in *Christ and Horrors*, McCord Adams describes the importance of eating the real body of Christ, making him the target "we bite and chomp and tear with the teeth, returning horrors for horrors to God."[35] Only this shocking understanding of the Eucharist, experienced viscerally, allows us to feel that God really has taken on the burden of the horrors we experience. For McCord Adams, liturgy in general ought to be untidy, disruptive, raw, and her liturgical writings express this. In a liturgy for the feast day of St. Francis, in which themes of the demolition and rebuilding of the church were central, she wrote, "When You condemned Herod's temple to destruction, all the Babels of human fear and greed, we wrecked the temple of Your Body, slashed and ripped It top to bottom, desolating sacrilege where splendor was before."[36]

This is the kind of language one simply does not usually find in liturgies (see appendix of parallels to the *Book of Common Prayer* at end of this chapter), and it calls us to consider how far we are from offering such liturgies in our churches. McCord Adams herself felt that in general we are quite far, hence her critique of liturgies that merely reinforce the *status quo* and leave restrictive and cruel taboos unspoken and unchallenged. Speaking for McCord Adams's own Episcopal Church, in which I am a priest and seminary professor, I agree with her assessment. Too often liturgies are events where our real sufferings are papered over with a polite façade. They are not places of honesty or authenticity. They are not moments where true lament, the true cost of horrors, can be spoken.

---

34. Sigurdson, *Heavenly Bodies*, 583.
35. McCord Adams, *Christ and Horrors*, 309.
36. McCord Adams, "Eucharistic Prayer for St. Francis Day Liturgy."

They are not rituals where our bodies, all of them queer in one way or another, are really welcomed. Instead, too often they feel like heavily censored spaces, spaces in which we repeat familiar scripts that form us in a *habitus* that cuts us down to size, feels like a Procrustean bed, teaches us to hide the scandal of who we really are, and thus prevents us from experiencing the scandal of who Christ really is. They are spaces in which bodies are still an embarrassment and need to be hidden. The grotesque body must be prettied up, the erotic body checked at the door. Given the church's record of suspicion of and discomfort with the body, there is often a sense that anything that foregrounds the body in worship is suspect taboo. Bodies misfit many Christian liturgies, and this is one of the ways in which liturgy fails its purpose to confront us with the choice of God's realm in contradiction to socially constructed norms that constrict our full personhood.

To address these failures of liturgy, we ought to embrace a principle that McCord Adams espoused, which is that the liturgical traditions we have inherited are not fragile. Rather, they are sturdy. Just as God is strong enough to take our Job-like railing against God about the horrors we have endured, the tradition can take our messing with it, coloring outside the lines (to use a favorite phrase of Marilyn's), even treading the edges of blasphemy so as to speak the truths of horror and queerness. We are not going to break our liturgical traditions by doing this; in fact, we may discover a life in them that sometimes seems to have almost ebbed away. As Gordon Lathrop observes, liturgy is alive when the old symbols are broken open to speak something new, at once transforming, destroying, and saving the old words.[37] This breaking and remaking of molds is what McCord Adams's liturgical work does and invites us to do.

A place to start is with our liturgical language. "We need images that root down into the core of our being and network out through the fabric of our experience," says McCord Adams, and urges us not to get locked into a narrow range of images for God, but to strive for an "experimental juxtaposition of a variety of images."[38] So McCord Adams took it as her responsibility not to simply repeat the words of the *Book of Common Prayer*, but to write her own Eucharistic prayers (a practice allowed but not often done), seeking fresh language for liturgy, as in the St. Francis Day Eucharistic Prayer, where she riffs on the theme of building and demolition:

---

37. Lathrop, *Holy Things*, 23.
38. McCord Adams, *Wrestling for Blessing*, 17.

> Seized by fear, we grabbed for space, vandalized your house, knocked down walls to occupy rooms designed for others. . . . [W]e boarded up windows to darken your image. We locked you in a closet, out of sight, out of mind, out of our way in our desperate quest for MORE. Convinced that all was ours, but unable to afford the upkeep, we brought down the house of Your creation into this state of disrepair.[39]

These are words that wake us from our liturgical slumber and invite us to encounter God afresh.

We also need to consider whether there is space for bodies in our liturgies. Are bodies welcome there? Can they dance, sing, lament, rage and cry, express desire? And which bodies are allowed to lead the assembly? At one memorable liturgy McCord Adams led at Yale Divinity School for the Feast of the Immaculate Conception, she invited two Roman Catholic women to lead the service and gave them her cope to wear—the garment that signals priestly leadership in a particularly ostentatious way. As a misfit herself, she made space for others who "misfitted" the qualifications for liturgical leadership. In this liturgical moment, McCord Adams bore witness not only to her fluid sense of ordained ministry, but also to the necessity of liturgy to manifest the revolutionary realm of God. As the cope passed from one woman to the other, their bodies were blessed. No longer were these bodies illegitimate for liturgical leaders; instead, these bodies were just what God had called to this task, no matter what the institution might say. It was, as McCord Adams would say, a "moment in the kingdom," a moment that heralded Stage III horror-defeat, when we are brought to an eschatological state of full flourishing beyond horrendous evil.

It was Marilyn's gift to me, and to many, to bless us in this way—to celebrate and welcome our souls and bodies, in all of their queer variety. She gave us language to name horrors and their defeat, and in particular, to draw us into liturgies that put all of this in the hands of God. In such liturgical interventions Marilyn enacted a bodily knowledge of God and drew those who worshipped with her into such embodied and authentic knowledge. She demonstrated that liturgy is an event in which God can be encountered honestly, a site of transforming truthfulness about the wonder and horror of the human condition, but in that very honesty also a place where God can be claimed as active in overcoming these horrors. Liturgy can fulfill its purpose of provoking confrontation between our

---

39. McCord Adams, "Eucharistic Prayer for St. Francis Day Liturgy."

conventional selves and the selves we long to be as members of the body of Christ. Most importantly, the authenticity of such liturgies allows worshippers not only to claim God but to know in their bodies and souls that God claims them. In order for liturgy to be such a container for grace, to sustain us in times of profound suffering as well as joy, and to move us toward the eschatological *telos* of the church in God's realm, we would do well to follow and further Marilyn's vision, and to continue to offer the gift of honest, queer, revolutionary liturgy.

APPENDIX

Liturgical Language Parallels

Book of Common Prayer, 1979	Marilyn McCord Adams
Sursum Corda	*Sursum Corda*
Celebrant: The Lord be with you.	*Celebrant:* Our God is here.
Congregation: And also with you.	*Congregation:* Holy Spirit is with us.
Celebrant: Lift up your hearts.	*Celebrant:* Unlock the doors of your hearts.
Congregation: We lift them up to the Lord.	*Congregation:* We open them to God and to one another.
Celebrant: Let us give thanks to the Lord our God.	*Celebrant:* We have come to meet God, our Friend and our Lover.
Congregation: It is right to give God thanks and praise.	*Congregation:* It is good to love God, now and always.[40]
Proper Preface	*Proper Preface*
Therefore we praise you, joining our voices with angels and archangels and with all the company of heaven . . .	With those who befriended and fed you, who argued with You and touched You, who got angry with You and saw Your face, who ran away from You only to meet You on their path, we praise you . . .[41]

---

40. McCord Adams, "Eucharistic Prayer for Coming Out Day Liturgy."
41. McCord Adams, "Eucharistic Prayer for Coming Out Day Liturgy."

Book of Common Prayer, 1979	Marilyn McCord Adams
Oblation and Epiclesis	*Oblation and Epiclesis*
And we offer our sacrifice of praise and thanksgiving to you, O Lord of all; presenting to you, from your creation, this bread and this wine. We pray you, gracious God, to send your Holy Spirit upon these gifts that they may be the sacrament of the Body of Christ, and his Blood of the new Covenant.	We set the table with gifts from our world, this bread and this wine, and we offer to you our closets, our fears, and all that binds us, our brothers and sisters who live and die with AIDS, the harms we have suffered and the grief we have caused. By your Holy Spirit may they become for us the bread of life and cup of salvation, Your Body and Blood, that we may love as your Body in the world.[42]
Intercessions	*Intercessions*
Remember, Lord, your one holy catholic and apostolic church, redeemed by the blood of your Christ. Reveal its unity, guard its faith, and preserve it in peace.	Remember Your holy family, and especially this community, . . . women and men learning to value variety, gay and lesbian persons giving birth to new identities, church-damaged, excluded and unusual people, seeking the power of Your kiss, and the strength of your love.[43]
Memorial Acclamation	*Memorial Acclamation*
We remember your death. We proclaim your resurrection. We await your coming in glory.	We remember your death for us, Your friends. We shout your resurrection, our bold new life. Come, sweet Jesus, embrace us face-to-face.[44]
Great Thanksgiving	*Great Thanksgiving*
We turned against you and betrayed your trust, and we turned against one another.	When You condemned Herod's temple to destruction, all the Babels of human fear and greed, we wrecked the temple of Your Body, slashed and ripped It top to bottom, desolating sacrilege where splendor was before.[45]

42. McCord Adams, "Eucharistic Prayer for Coming Out Day Liturgy."
43. McCord Adams, "Eucharistic Prayer for Coming Out Day Liturgy."
44. McCord Adams, "Eucharistic Prayer for Coming Out Day Liturgy."
45. McCord Adams, "Eucharistic Prayer for the Feast of St. Francis."

Book of Common Prayer, 1979	Marilyn McCord Adams
Great Thanksgiving	*Great Thanksgiving*
We failed to honor your image in one another and in ourselves; we would not see the goodness of the world around us; and so we violated your creation, abused one another, and rejected your love.	Seized by fear, we grabbed for space, vandalized your house, knocked down walls to occupy rooms designed for others . . . we boarded up windows to darken your image. We locked you in a closet, out of sight, out of mind, out of our way in our desperate quest for MORE. Convinced that all was ours, but unable to afford the upkeep, we brought down the house of Your creation into this state of disrepair.[46]
Great Thanksgiving—the Incarnation	*Great Thanksgiving—the Incarnation*
You, in your mercy, sent Jesus Christ, your only and eternal Son, to live and die as one of us, to reconcile us to you . . . He stretched out his arms upon the cross and offered himself, a perfect sacrifice for the whole world.	At the right time, You sent Christ our Teacher, to set Wisdom's table among us. But we preferred 'fast food' to gourmet indigestion. We couldn't cope with subtlety, crucified Truth with lies.[47]

---

46. McCord Adams, "Prayer for the Feast of St. Francis."
47. McCord Adams, "Eucharistic Prayer."

PART III

Knowing God

10

Why There Wasn't, and How There Can Be, a Latin Social Trinity

Scott M. Williams

When Marilyn McCord Adams was the canon at Christ Church College at Oxford University, I was a graduate student at Oriel College studying scholastic theology. I went to Oxford University in order to study under Richard Cross on the topic of John Duns Scotus on the Trinity. But by the time I arrived at Oxford, Cross had just published his *Duns Scotus on God* that covered just about everything I would have written about Duns Scotus. I needed an alternate route and I decided to work on Henry of Ghent on the Trinity. I took several seminars on scholastic philosophy and theology from McCord Adams (and some were co-taught with Cecilia Trifogli) and learned a great deal about scholasticism, philosophy, and theology. In studying Henry of Ghent, I became fascinated and frustrated with him; but McCord Adams expressed more frustration than fascination with Henry because of his verbosity (compared to Duns Scotus or William Ockham). After years of reading and thinking about Henry, I understand him better than I did back then. I think McCord Adams would have liked to read what I have written in this chapter because it clarifies some things that we were not certain about. She helped make me zealous for scholastic philosophy and theology, and so, I write this chapter for her.

* * *

Marilyn McCord Adams was interested in the Trinity for its own sake, and in how it figures into Christology, soteriology, and theodicy. We see these overlapping interests in her book *Christ and Horrors: The Coherence of Christology*. In a section of the book titled "Maximally well-organized lover!" she takes a cue from Duns Scotus regarding the Trinity and friendship.

> Scotus' account begins with glory, the glory of the Divine self-love and of the Trinitarian friendship circle. It continues with God's predestining rational creatures to glory-first and foremost, the soul of Christ, and secondarily other human souls and angels of which Christ is the head. It proceeds to the provision of those things which are for the sake of their glory—hypostatic union, graces and spiritual endowments—and then on to other suitables that will make it all possible. Thus, Scotus' analysis clearly asserts that the soul of Christ is made for God's sake, for the sake of widening the Trinitarian friendship circle; that the soul of Christ is God's first end in creation; and the other created co-lovers and the whole material cosmos are made for Christ's sake.[1]

In this chapter I want to focus on what it might mean to speak of the "Trinitarian friendship circle." There are at least two ways to consider this friendship circle. One way is to consider the Trinity in itself, which is what theologians call the "immanent Trinity." If we consider a "Trinitarian friendship circle" with regard to the immanent Trinity, then we would be talking about whether before the creation of the world, the three divine persons were in some sense "co-lovers." Another way is to consider the Trinity in relation to creatures, which is what theologians call the "economic Trinity." The latter includes discussion of God the Son's incarnation, and the work of the Holy Spirit among creatures. In what follows, I am interested in exploring what some medieval theologians, whom McCord Adams wrote so much about, had to say about this Trinitarian friendship circle with regard to the immanent Trinity. This is speculative stuff. Some theologians might object that this kind of speculation is unwarranted. They would contend that (e.g.,) the ecumenical councils were mostly focused on the Trinity with regard to creation. At most, we find in Nicaea I (325 CE) the claim that God the Father and God the Son are of the same essence ("homoousia"). This doesn't signal anything specific

---

1. McCord Adams, *Christ and Horrors*, 182.

regarding whether God the Father and God the Son each have their own act of loving the divine essence (or another divine person) in eternity past. This sort of view is what is today sometimes called Social Trinitarianism, according to which we should count the number of divine acts of knowing and loving according to the number of divine persons. On this Social Model of the Trinity, the Father loves the divine essence, the Son loves the divine essence, and the Holy Spirit loves the divine essence, and none of these acts of loving are numerically the same acts of loving the divine essence. There are three acts of loving, one by each divine person. (I should mention here that I reject this Social Model of the Trinity.)

The way that McCord Adams presents Scotus here might (wrongly) suggest that Scotus might be interpreted as a Social Trinitarian, in the sense I described above. I think it would be wrong to interpret Scotus as a Social Trinitarian because of his account of the numerical unity of the divine essence and the divine persons' sharing numerically the same ("essential") acts of understanding and willing.[2] But I do think McCord Adams is right that there may be some sense in which the divine persons are co-lovers and friends (even apart from any consideration of divine persons' relation(s) to created things). One motivation (among others) to suppose that the divine persons are (eternally) co-lovers and friends is that each divine person is (believed to be) omniscient. If a divine person is omniscient, then that divine person knows which divine person that they are and that they love another divine person. Surely God the Father knows that they are God the Father (and not God the Holy Spirit). Likewise, God the Son knows that they are God the Son (and not God the Father), and God the Holy Spirit knows that they are God the Holy Spirit (and not God the Father).[3] Philosophers distinguish third-person thoughts and first-person thoughts. It's one thing for me to know *that* Scott M. Williams speaks American English, and it's another thing for me to know *that* I speak American English. Philosophers classify the former as *de re* propositional knowledge (propositional knowledge about things), and the latter as *de se* propositional knowledge (propositional knowledge about oneself). If each divine person truly is omniscient and one thing a divine person could know is which divine person that they are and who they love, then it is reasonable to suppose that each divine person knows which divine person that they are. It's at least possible, if

2. For discussion and references, see Cross, *Duns Scotus on God*, 223–29.

3. For discussion of gendered language and the Trinity, see Harrison, "The Trinity and Feminism."

not plausible, that each divine person has *de se* propositional knowledge. If each divine person has *de se* propositional knowledge, then it would be good to have a model or account for how this might be so. And, if each divine person has *de se* propositional knowledge, then each divine person would know that they themself love another divine person. (God the Father would know that they love God the Son, etc.)

A systematic theologian today might suppose that speculation about the divine persons' *de se* propositional knowledge is warranted because it is consistent with what is thought to be a Greek Social Model of the Trinity. After all, systematic theologians today are usually taught that there is an important difference between ancient Greek Trinitarian theology and Latin Trinitarian theology. Roughly, the former is said to be consistent with a Social Model of the Trinity (as described above), and the latter is said to be inconsistent with a Social Model of the Trinity (as described above). If we thought this proposed difference were historically correct, then we might suppose that a Greek Social Trinitarianism can address (or be used to address) the issue of how it might be that the divine persons have *de se* propositional knowledge. Moreover, if one believed this historical characterization between Greek and Latin Trinitarian theology, then one might suppose that a Latin Non-Social Model of the Trinity does not (and could not be used to address) how it might be that the divine persons have *de se* propositional knowledge. But this proposed difference between ancient Greek and Latin Trinitarian theologies is false. Michel Barnes and Richard Cross have persuasively argued that Greek Trinitarian theology, as found in Cappadocian theologians like Gregory of Nazianzus and Gregory of Nyssa, is not a Social Trinitarianism,[4] but rather is more akin to what has been labeled Latin Trinitarianism.[5]

Moreover, I have shown (in a forthcoming paper)[6] that the Sixth Ecumenical Council (Constantinople III, 680–681 CE) has the most detailed Trinitarian theology among the first seven ecumenical councils, and what it says about the Trinity puts a relevant constraint on the sort of account of the divine persons' *de se* propositional knowledge that a Christian theologian might propose. I argue that Constantinople III explicitly *rejects* that very claim that is essential to Social Models of the immanent Trinity, namely, it rejects the claim that we should count the

---

4. Barnes, "De Régnon Reconsidered."
5. Cross, "Two Models of the Trinity?"
6. Williams, "Discovery." For a summary of my findings, see Williams, "Gregory of Nyssa."

number of (e.g.,) powers, thoughts, and volitions according to the number of divine *persons*. Regarding McCord Adams's statement about the divine persons being "co-lovers" and "friends," what this means is that an account for what would make her statement about the Trinity to be true can't be a Social Model of the Trinity (as described above). Some other account for what might make this statement true will be needed, if one aims to be consistent with Conciliar Trinitarianism.

Constantinople III affirmed that we should count the number of divine powers, thoughts, and volitions according to the number of divine *natures*, and not according to the number of divine persons. The council affirms that given that there is just one singular divine essence or nature, it follows that the divine persons share numerically the same powers, thoughts, and volitions. Constantinople III used this counting rule (that is, count the number of, e.g., powers and volitions according to the number of natures, and *not* according to the number of persons) to justify its assertion that in Christ there are two will-powers (the shared singular divine will, and a human will). Most of the authoritative passages used to affirm this counting rule were from Greek authors (e.g., Cyril of Alexandria, Gregory of Nazianzus, and Gregory of Nyssa), and a very small minority were from Latin authors (e.g., Augustine is quoted just once). Constantinople III asserted that numerical unity of the divine persons' (shared) will-power, and (shared) volitions, should be endorsed, and any model of the immanent Trinity that is incompatible with this counting rule should be rejected. It turns out, then, that what is today called "Greek Social Trinitarianism" is precisely what was rejected by Constantinople III, on the basis of Greek authorities; and what is today called "Latin Trinitarianism" is consistent with the pronouncements of Constantinople III. So, if an account is to be given of how it might be that the divine persons are "co-lovers" and "friends," then Christian theologians (who wish to be consistent with Conciliar Trinitarianism) may do well to consider what has been called a Latin Model of the Trinity.

I wish to explore what some medieval Latin theologians whom Marilyn McCord Adams wrote so much about—namely, Augustine, Thomas Aquinas, Henry of Ghent, and John Duns Scotus—had to say about the divine persons' loving one another. As we will see, these medieval Latin theologians agree that there is some truth to claiming that the divine persons love one another, but the details of their answers reveal that they are far from what a Social Model of the Trinity would say about the divine persons' mutual love.

In what follows, I give a brief history of different interpretations of Augustine's claim that the Father and Son love themselves by the Holy Spirit. This history supports my contention that a majority report among scholastics has it that the Holy Spirit, as a divine person, is not a unique object of an act of love, nor is any other divine person a unique object of an act of love. What the divine person's love is their shared divine essence. This is what can be called a reductive interpretation of Augustine's statement. A minority position, held by Henry of Ghent, is that the Holy Spirit (as the Holy Spirit) makes it the case that the divine persons love that they love the divine essence. Henry is distinctive in defending an interpretation according to which the Holy Spirit, as a specific divine person, uniquely contributes something to a certain act of loving that is shared by all divine persons. I believe Henry's claim that a specific divine person can contribute something unique to an intellectual act or an act of will that can be used in the development of a "Latin" Model of the Trinity that accounts for the divine persons' *de se* propositional knowledge. That is, a "Latin Social" Model of the Trinity offers an account of how it could be that, e.g., God the Father can be aware of the proposition that I know that I love God the Son. Nonetheless, Henry himself does not develop a view in which a divine person has *de se* propositional knowledge. So far as I am aware, no scholastic teaches that a divine person makes use of "I" for self-reference (apart from, e.g., the Incarnation) or *de se* propositional knowledge.

If one wanted to develop McCord Adams's contention that the divine persons are mutual friends, then if we look at what Henry of Ghent has done then we can develop his insights into what I have labeled a "Latin Social" Model of the Trinity. While there are likely several ways that Henry's moves can be developed into a Latin Social Model of the Trinity, I will summarize one way it could be done, that is, the way I have done it.

1. "WHETHER THE FATHER AND SON LOVE THEMSELVES BY THE HOLY SPIRIT?"

In *On the Trinity*, book 6, chapter 5, Augustine discusses the Holy Spirit in relation to the Father and Son.

> Therefore the Holy Spirit also consists in the same unity and equality of substance. For whether the Holy Spirit is unity of both, or holiness or love, whether [the Holy Spirit] is the unity because love, and love because holiness, it is clear that [the Holy

> Spirit] is not one of the two [i.e., Father and Son], since [the Holy Spirit] is that by which each are joined, by which the begotten is loved by the one who begets him and in turn loves the begetter. Thus "They keep unity of the Spirit in the bond of peace (cf. Eph. 4:3)," not in virtue of participation but of their essence, not by gift of some superior but by their own gift. . . . So the Holy Spirit is something common to Father and Son, whatever it is, or is the very communion, consubstantial, and coeternal. Call this friendship, if it helps, but it is more aptly called love. And this too is substance because God is substance, and "God is love," as it is written (cf. 1 John 4: 8, 16). But just as it is substance together with the Father and Son, so is it great together and good together and holy together and whatever else is said in relation to them, because with God it is not a different thing to be and to be great or good, etc., as we have shown above. . . . And therefore there are not more than three; one loving him who is from him, and one loving him from whom he is, and love itself. If this is not anything, how is it that "God is love?" If it is not substance, how is it that God is substance?[7]

Augustine is trying to work out the distinctions between divine persons. The Father generates the Son; the Son is generated by the Father; and the Holy Spirit is somehow the love by which the Father loves the Son, and the Son loves the Father. The Father's act of love is directed at the Son, and the Son's act of love is directed at the Father. There are two different objects of love. It is important to point out that elsewhere in *On the Trinity*, Augustine denies this, e.g., the Father loves by means of the Holy Spirit. Augustine asserts that each divine person, in themselves, knows and loves.[8] Nevertheless, Augustine's discussion from the passage above was taken up in Peter Lombard's *Sentences*, and so, scholastic theologians discussed the claim that the Holy Spirit is that by which the Father loves the Son, and that by which the Son loves the Father.

Peter Lombard quotes most of the passage that I have quoted above in *Sentences* book 1, distinction 32.[9] He considers several ways to interpret the claim that the Father loves the Son by the Holy Spirit and the Son loves the Father by the Holy Spirit, and he rules out some options.

---

7. Augustine, *On the Trinity*, 209–10. I have modified parts of the translation: Augustine, *De Trinitate*, 235 (lines 1–9), 235 (line 16), 236 (line 33).

8. For references and discussion, cf. Williams, "Augustine," 39–40.

9. Cf. Lombard, *Textus Magistri Sententiarum*, 1122–23. Also, cf. Lombard, *The Sentences, Book 1*, 180.

Lombard reports Augustine's claim that, e.g., "to be" and "to be good" are the same thing in God, and he worries about someone who might contend that "to love" is the same thing as "to be" in God. If the Holy Spirit just is "love," then it would follow that the Father exists by virtue of the Holy Spirit. But that is false. So, somehow the Father loves the Son by the Holy Spirit, but the Father's mere existence is not at issue here. Another interpretation is that the Father *per se* does not love the Son (and vice versa), but the Father loves the Son only by someone else, namely the Holy Spirit. Lombard denies this; instead, we should say that the Father *per se* loves the Son by the Holy Spirit, and vice versa.

Thomas Aquinas discusses the question, "Whether the Father and the Son love themselves by the Holy Spirit?" (*Utrum Pater et Filius diligant se Spiritu Sancto?*) in *Summa Theologiae* I, q. 37, art. 2. He considers several reactions to this question. Some theologians simply denied that the statement in any sense is true. I call this an *eliminative* interpretation. Others invoked the distinction between divine "essential acts" and "notional acts." "Essential acts" include operations (doings, not productions) that are shared by all divine persons because all divine persons share numerically the same divine essence. Essential acts include acts of understanding and acts of loving. "Notional acts" are productions (not doings) and are not shared by all divine persons. The Father produces the Son by intellectually producing the Son, who is the Word; and, the Father and Son produce the Holy Spirit by voluntarily producing the Holy Spirit, who is Love. So, in this interpretation, e.g., the Father and Son love themselves [*se*] by an essential act of loving. The term "love" is appropriated to the Holy Spirit, but it is not unique to the Holy Spirit. We can *say* that, e.g., the Father loves by the Holy Spirit, but technically the Father loves by the divine essence that is shared with the Holy Spirit. I call this is a *strong reductive* interpretation.

A third interpretation stipulates that the phrase "by the Holy Spirit" should be interpreted as a formal *cause*. (A formal cause of something explains why something is the kind of thing that it is. For example, a human substantial form (the human soul) explains why a human being is human, as opposed to any other kind of thing.) So, in this interpretation, the Holy Spirit is the formal cause of the Father and Son's love for themselves. I call this a *non-reductive* interpretation. Note that this interpretation has it that the Holy Spirit as such contributes to the content of a divine act of loving. The Holy Spirit, as such, explains why such a divine act is an acting of loving. The fourth interpretation stipulates that the phrase "by the Holy Spirit" should be interpreted as a formal *effect*. In short, the Holy Spirit is the end term or product of a productive act of love (that is not a doing). The Holy Spirit is the (eternal) result of an internal divine production. Aquinas gives the example: A tree produces flowers. The flowers themselves are not the act of "flowering" but the result of a productive act. Likewise, the Holy Spirit is the result or product from a productive act (that is not itself an act of loving in the sense of a doing). I call this a *weak reductive* interpretation. Aquinas endorses this last interpretation because it allows him to hold that all divine persons love themselves by virtue of the shared divine essence (which is the formal cause of the act of loving). Their acts of loving are essential acts (operations, not productions). Since they are essential acts, numerically the same acts of loving are shared by all divine persons. Furthermore, Aquinas can avoid the eliminativist position by interpreting Augustine's statement as implying that the Holy Spirit, who is called Love, is the result of a productive act.

Having briefly surveyed (1) the eliminative interpretation, (2) the strong reductive interpretation, (3) the non-reductive interpretation, and (4) the weak reductive interpretation, we can connect them to the question of whether a divine person, (e.g., the Holy Spirit), contributes any content to the divine persons' operations (doings). (1), (2), and (4) each imply the denial of the Holy Spirit contributing any unique content to the divine persons' act of loving themselves and each other. By contrast, (3) the non-reductive interpretation implies that the Holy Spirit as the Holy Spirit contributes unique content to the divine persons' act of loving themselves. For, in this interpretation the Holy Spirit is the unique formal cause of the divine persons' mutual love; the divine essence as such is not the unique formal cause of the divine persons' mutual love, as is the case with other interpretations. Moreover, this non-reductive interpretation violates Aquinas's general distinction between essential acts and notional acts. Essential acts, acts of understanding and loving, are formally caused by the divine essence as such; essential acts are not formally caused by any specific divine person. For Aquinas, a divine person has all divine operations because of the divine essence, and not because of a certain divine person. But the non-reductive interpretation implies that there is an essential act of loving, i.e., an operation shared by all divine persons, that is formally caused by the Holy Spirit as such and not by the divine essence as such.

Duns Scotus engages with some of the same interpretations that Aquinas does, including Aquinas's interpretation, and more or less endorses an interpretation much like Aquinas's own interpretation.[10] He distinguishes essential acts and notional acts; the formal cause of the divine persons' act of loving themselves is the divine will. Duns Scotus holds that the phrase "love themselves by the Holy Spirit" from the sentence "the Father and Son love themselves by the Holy Spirit" should be interpreted as an essential act of loving that connotes the notional act that is the internal voluntary (and necessary) production of the Holy Spirit. Basically, the statement is really about the divine persons' act of loving themselves (which is an essential act) and it implies the act productive of the Holy Spirit because this productive act is also from the divine will.

Furthermore, Duns Scotus raises an important interpretive question about the term "themselves" (*se*). He distinguishes two interpretations of the term "themselves." One interpretation is that "the Father loves the Son by the Holy Spirit, and, the Son loves the Father by the Holy Spirit." The other interpretation is that "the Father loves the Father by the Holy Spirit, and, the Son loves the Son by the Holy Spirit." He concedes that both interpretations are acceptable because each is compatible with his position on the Father and Son's internal production of the Holy Spirit. The production of the Holy Spirit is relevant because Scotus holds that the statement "the Father and Son love themselves by the Holy Spirit" connotes the voluntary (and necessary) production of the Holy Spirit.

For Scotus, the principle that is productive of the Son is the divine memory, and, the principle that is productive of the Holy Spirit is the divine will.[11] Scotus holds that the Father's generating the Son by the divine memory implies that the Son has everything in the divine essence, including the divine will. Scotus concedes that there are two who produce the Holy Spirit by the singular divine will, but denies that the Son adds anything to this principle. Scotus says the Father and Son are in concord with regard to the production of the Holy Spirit, but their being in concord does not contribute anything to the principle that is productive of the Holy Spirit.

Returning to the issue at hand, Scotus claims that what the Father loves in loving himself is the divine essence, and likewise for the Son and Holy Spirit. Each divine person loves the divine essence by virtue of the divine will. Since each divine person is really the same as the divine

---

10. Duns Scotus, *Ordinatio* 1, d. 32, q. 1–2, n. 34. In the following edition, abbreviated subsequently as "Vatican," vol. 6, edited by C. Balić, OFM, et alii (Vatican: Typis Polyglottis Vaticanis, 1963), 238.

11. For references and discussion, cf. Cross, *Duns Scotus on God*, 131–43.

essence, it follows that, e.g., the Father's loving themself is equivalent to the Father loving the divine essence.[12] Given this, it seems that each divine person does not use "I" to make self-reference. For all divine acts of understanding are essential acts, that is, they are shared by all divine persons. The Father's act of loving "themself" is numerically the same act as the Son's loving "themself." Consequently, in Duns Scotus's model, there is no *de se* propositional knowledge involved (or required) for divine persons to love themselves and each other. Each divine person loves their shared, singular, divine essence.

Still, Richard Cross discusses one passage of Scotus's where he has it that Christ refers to himself by using "I." The referent of "I" is the "suppposit of the Word" [= second person of the Trinity] and not his human nature as such. Cross comments saying,

> One puzzling feature: Scotus believes that divine persons are capable of making self-reference (using the word "I"). I do not know how he would integrate this claim (evidently correct, giving Scotus's interpretation of the text under discussion in the passage just cited (cf. John 10:18)) given his claims about the persons' shared mental contents, though there clearly are strategies that could be used.[13]

I think the easiest way for Scotus to "integrate this claim" would be to point out that Jesus's statement ("I lay down my soul by myself," which is from John 10:18) itself is a created thing, as opposed to something grounded in the eternal divine essence. He *made* the statement at a certain time and place. (As McCord Adams suggests in the quotation at the beginning of this chapter, Jesus expands the Trinitarian friendship circle. What we learn about this expansion from John 10:18 is the uniqueness of Christ's soul and Christ's mission in expanding the Trinitarian friendship circle.) Given this, it seems that Jesus refers to himself by a statement that he makes, which the other divine persons do not make. The statement is not a divine "essential act" shared by all divine persons. If this is correct, then Scotus could say that Jesus's self-reference is explained in part by his Incarnation. Given this, it does not follow that Scotus must revise his

---

12. Cf. Duns Scotus, *Quod.* 8, n. 6 (pp. 205–6): "The intellect of the three is the same, and the will [of the three is the same], and consequently entirely the same act of understanding is there, and of will, and the same object." Translation is from Cross, *Duns Scotus on God*, 223.

13. Cross, *Duns Scotus on God*, 224n2.

model of the Trinity such that a divine person can make self-reference by using "I" in the case of their essential acts.

Thus, despite his discussion of "I" in the context of the Incarnation, it seems that Scotus (like Thomas Aquinas) does not give resources for the development of a model of the Trinity that can account for how it could be that the divine persons have *de se* propositional knowledge in relation to their mutual love. If the divine persons are "co-lovers" and "friends," and we go with Duns Scotus's account of the divine persons' mutual love, then we have an account that does not include *de se* propositional knowledge. Instead, we have an account for how the divine persons' share numerically the same act of loving their shared, singular, divine essence.

2. HENRY OF GHENT: A PROTO LATIN SOCIAL TRINITARIAN?

Unlike Aquinas and Duns Scotus, I believe that Henry's Trinitarian theology could be developed in Latin Social direction. What I mean by a Latin Social Model of the Trinity is a model that is consistent with Conciliar Trinitarianism and articulates how it might be that each divine person has *de se* propositional knowledge. When connected with the divine persons' mutual love, the Latin Social Model will articulate how it might be that each divine person knows that they themself love another divine person (e.g., God the Father knows that they themself love God the Son, and God the Son knows that they themself love God the Father). Now, as I see it, what Henry of Ghent says about the divine persons' mutual love could be taken in a Latin Social direction because Henry accepts that a divine person, as this specific divine person, contributes content to the divine persons' thought and volition. So, in this account, a specific divine person is the formal cause of some act (i.e., an operation/doing something) that is shared by the divine persons. In what follows I survey what Henry says about the Holy Spirit's unique (unshared) contribution to an act of loving (that is, an operation) that is shared by each and every divine person. (For Henry, there is a parallel story to be told about God the Son's unique (unshared) contribution to a specific intellectual operation that is shared by each and every divine person.)[14]

Henry of Ghent asks the question, "Whether the Holy Spirit is the love by which the Father and Son love themselves and others?" (*Utrum*

---

14. For discussion and references, see Williams, "Augustine," 58–63.

Spiritus Sanctus sit amor quo Pater et Filius diligunt se et alia?)[15] in *Summa Quaestionum Ordinariarum* [= *SQO*] 61, question 7. Notice that whereas Aquinas asked "whether the Father and Son love themselves by the Holy Spirit," Henry adds "and others." This is not an insignificant addition but its significance is clear only after we understand his reply. (The upshot is that for Henry, the Holy Spirit is the formal cause by which God the Father, God the Son, and God the Holy Spirit love that God the Father, God the Son, and God the Holy Spirit love the divine essence. Each divine person, along with the singular shared divine essence, is included in the object of this second-order act of love.)

Henry structures his reply in two parts. First, he surveys his predecessors and then he gives his own reply. Second, his own reply requires further explanation because it assumes Henry's overall account of the Trinity. Whereas several of Henry's predecessors focused on how to interpret the ablative phrase "by the Holy Spirit," Henry finds this insufficient, given his own Trinitarian theology. He revises the statement to read, "The Father loves by a love who is the Holy Spirit." He contends that we should take "loves by a love" as the key phrase to interpret.[16] By taking the ablative phrase "by a love" with the verb "loves," Henry has a way to interpret the statement that fits with his Trinitarian theology so that the statement comes out true. To understand the sense or senses in which this statement is true, we need to grasp the outlines of Henry's Trinitarian theology.

First, whereas Duns Scotus holds that the Son, who is the divine Word, is produced from the divine memory, Henry claims that the Son is generated from the divine intelligence. The basic difference, roughly, is that the former holds that the Father produces the Son from something like *habitual* knowledge, and the latter holds that the Father produces the Son from something like *occurrent* knowledge. For Henry, the Word images the Father's (explanatorily prior) act of knowing the divine essence. The Father knows the divine essence. But if the Father is to know this act of knowing the divine essence, the Father needs the divine Word who images (represents) the Father's act of knowing the divine essence.[17] For, the divine Word is the formal cause by which the divine persons know their knowing the divine essence. The Word contributes the content of

---

15. Henry of Ghent, *Summa (Quaestiones Ordinariae)* art. 61, q. 7 (p. 199). References to the *Summa* are as follows: for art. 47–52, see vol. 30; for art. 60–62, see vol. 33.

16. Cf. Henry of Ghent, *Summa (Quaestiones Ordinariae)* art. 61, q. 7 (p. 207, lines 204–8, 210).

17. For references and discussion, see Williams, "Augustine," 57–65.

the divine persons' second-order (essential) *shared* act of knowing that the Father, Son, and Holy Spirit know the divine essence. That is to say, God the Father knows that the Father, Son, and Holy Spirit know the divine essence; God the Son knows that the Father, Son, and Holy Spirit know the divine essence; and, God the Holy Spirit knows that the Father, Son, and Holy Spirit know the divine essence. So, the Word, as such, is uniquely responsible (so to speak) for the divine persons' shared act of knowing that they know the divine essence. This is *de re* propositional knowledge according to which the divine persons know the singular shared act of knowing the divine essence. But it is not *de se* propositional knowledge, given that it is not the case that a divine person knows which divine person that they are. Nonetheless, Henry maintains that the divine Word is the formal cause by which each and every divine person knows the shared act of knowing the divine essence.

Second, there is a parallel difference between Duns Scotus and Henry regarding the production of the Holy Spirit. For Duns Scotus, the Holy Spirit is produced from the divine will and this production does not itself require an occurrent act of loving the divine essence. For Henry of Ghent, the production of the Holy Spirit requires an (explanatorily) prior act of loving the divine essence. Moreover, the Holy Spirit is produced from the divine will by two who are in concord in voluntarily producing the Holy Spirit. (This is one of Henry's arguments for the *filioque* clause—that the Holy Spirit proceeds from the Father *and the Son*.) The fact that there are two who voluntarily produce the Holy Spirit is crucial for Henry (unlike for Duns Scotus). Given this, Henry argues that the Holy Spirit should be called "Zeal" (which is parallel to claiming that God the Son should be called the divine "Word." It is noteworthy that—so far as I know—Henry invents this name for the Holy Spirit because he needs a name that is apt for the Holy Spirit that parallels God the Son's name, "Word." He chooses the name "Zeal" because he thinks it most relevant for what he wishes to ascribe to the Holy Spirit.) Just as the Word directs a second-order (essential) act of knowing toward a prior act of knowing the divine essence, so the Holy Spirit directs a second-order (essential) act of loving toward a prior act of loving the divine essence.[18] The Holy Spirit is the formal cause by which each and every divine person loves that they love the divine essence. That is to say, God the Father loves that the Father, Son, and Holy Spirit love the divine essence; God the

---

18. Cf. Henry of Ghent, *Summa (Quaestiones Ordinariae)* art. 61, q. 7, ad 1 (pp. 210–11).

Son loves that the Father, Son, and Holy Spirit loves the divine essence; and, God the Holy Spirit loves that the Father, Son, and Holy Spirit love the divine essence. So, the Holy Spirit, as such, is partly responsible (so to speak) for all divine persons' loving that they love the divine essence.

With this outline of Henry's Trinitarian theology in mind, we can understand Henry's interpretation of the statement that "the Father loves by a love who is the Holy Spirit." Henry reports three ways to interpret the verb "loves," and endorses the second and third ways. First, the verb "loves" denotes an essential act that is an operation (a doing), and which is a "simple act" of loving the divine essence. "Simple act" denotes a first-order act that is explanatorily prior to a second-order act. (For example, I can love my daughter. This is a first-order act. I can also love that I love my daughter. This is a second-order act.) On this interpretation, the statement is false, because (on Henry's view) the Holy Spirit makes it the case that the divine persons have a second-order act of love, but does not make it the case that the divine persons have a first-order act of love.[19]

Second, the verb "loves" denotes a different essential act of loving, that is, the persons' act of loving their loving the divine essence. Here, "loves" is interpreted to mean second-order loving. Henry asserts that the statement is true on this interpretation. Third, Henry interprets "love by the Holy Spirit" to denote the Holy Spirit's "act of inflaming" (*actu flagrandi*) the shared divine will such that the Holy Spirit directs the second-order act of loving such that it has the object it has.[20] "Inflaming" is Henry's term for the Holy Spirit's contributing the content of all the persons' essential act of loving that they love the divine essence. (In other words, for Henry, if there were no Holy Spirit, then, e.g., the Father and Son would not love that they love the divine essence.) Henry asserts that the statement is also true on this interpretation.

What we find in Henry is the claim that the Son or Word uniquely contributes to the content of a shared act of knowing, and the Holy Spirit or Zeal uniquely contributes to the content of a shared act of loving. It is important to notice that Henry maintains that a specific divine person, and no other divine person, makes a unique and specific contribution to some shared divine act. While this contribution is not *de se* propositional knowledge, Henry is proposing a *non-reductive interpretation* of

19. Cf. Henry of Ghent, *Summa (Quaestiones Ordinariae)* art. 61, q. 7, ad 1 (p. 213, lines 351–58).

20. Cf. Henry of Ghent, *Summa (Quaestiones Ordinariae)* art. 61, q. 7, ad 1 (p. 209, lines 242–46).

Augustine's statement about the Holy Spirit's being the love between the Father and the Son. This non-reductive interpretation is supported by the following passage from *Summa Questiones Ordinariae* 61, 7:

> And so, in this there is a great diversity to be noted on the part of those who are said to understand by the Word and are not the Word [i.e., the Father and Holy Spirit], and on the part of the one who is the Word itself, and likewise on the part of those who are said to love by a love who is the Holy Spirit, and are not [the Holy Spirit] [i.e., the Father and the Son], and on the part of the one who is itself the Holy Spirit.[21]

In *SQO* art. 49, q. 8, Henry asks, "Whether the beatitude of God presupposes the production of the persons?" and answers in the affirmative. For Henry, not only are the produced divine persons, Word (Son) and Zeal (Holy Spirit), required for the beatitude of all divine persons but also for the beatitude of all created persons. Henry's suggestion that the divine Word and Zeal expand (so to speak) the divine persons' knowledge and love fits nicely with McCord Adams's claim that the Trinitarian friendship circle expands when more persons are included!

> For the perfect basis of the known truth is in the Word, and the perfect basis of the loved good is in the produced Love [i.e., Zeal], so that an intellectual operation in the three persons is not perfected without the Word, since by the same Word the intellect of the three persons is perfected, although [the Word] proceeds from just one person [i.e., the Father]. And it is similar for proceeding Love [i.e., Zeal] in regard to an operation of the will, as was held above. Similarly, the intellectual operation of some creature is not perfected without the Word, nor an operation of the will without proceeding Love [i.e., Zeal], just as it ought to be declared when talking about the beatitude of a creature, so that all intellects—created and uncreated—are not perfected except in the produced divine Word, and likewise neither is the operation of the will [perfected] except in the produced divine Love [i.e., Zeal]—so that the beatitude of God and of the saints are completed in one and the same thing.[22]

---

21. Henry of Ghent, *Summa (Quaestiones Ordinariae)* art. 61, q. 7 (p. 214, lines 386–90). Translation is by me.

22. Henry of Ghent, *Summa (Quaestiones Ordinariae)* art. 49, q. 8 (p. 172, lines 70–173, 81). Translation is by me.

It is important to be clear that Henry is not positing a Social Trinitarianism as described above. The Son and Holy Spirit are required for all persons' beatitude because they are required for directing second-order acts to their object(s). The divine Word directs a second-order thought and the divine Zeal directs a second-order volition. We do not find in Henry any discussion of the divine persons' using "I" to make a self-reference (that is, *de se* propositional knowledge). If Social Trinitarianism requires that divine persons, independently of creatures, can make self-reference, then neither Thomas Aquinas, Duns Scotus, nor Henry of Ghent are Social Trinitarians. Moreover, their commitment to the divine persons' operations (thoughts and volitions) being essential acts or shared acts mitigates against the development of a full-blown Social Trinitarianism according to which each divine person requires their own incommunicable mental powers or incommunicable mental acts or both.[23] Nevertheless, Henry's claim that one divine person (God the Son/Word) contributes to the content of a shared act of knowing and another divine person (God the Holy Spirit/Zeal) contributes to the content of a shared act of loving, is one step toward the development of a Latin Social Model of the Trinity. The reason that this is so is that *de se* propositional knowledge requires that a specific person contributes to the content of an act of thought. For example, if I say, "I like coffee," then the "I" refers to me, Scott Williams. But if you say the same sentence, then the "I" refers to you. What is so interesting about Henry's Trinitarian theology, with regard to supposing that the divine persons have *de se* propositional knowledge, is that he claims that a specific divine person is uniquely required for the divine persons to know a specific fact (that is, the Word is required for the divine persons' knowing their knowing the divine essence), and another specific divine person is uniquely required for the divine persons to love a specific fact (that is, the Zeal is required for the divine persons' loving their loving the divine essence). Consequently, if one were to develop a Latin Model of the Trinity so that it accounts for how it can be the case that each divine person might have *de se* propositional knowledge, then one might retrospectively label Henry of Ghent a proto Latin Social Trinitarian.

---

23. Cf. Williams, "Unity of Action," 339.

3. A LATIN SOCIAL MODEL OF THE TRINITY

In my discussion of Duns Scotus I mentioned Richard Cross's suggestion that there might be several strategies that Duns Scotus could have used to develop his model of the Trinity into some sort of social model of the Trinity. While I am not sure how Duns Scotus might do this, given that he seems to deny that a divine person as such functions as a formal cause or basis for the content of a divine thought or volition, it seems that Henry of Ghent could have developed his model of the Trinity to give an account for how it might be that each divine person has *de se* propositional knowledge, and how each divine person might know that they (singular pronoun) love another divine person, and *vice versa*. Attempting to make this development is very challenging, but over the last few years I have developed Henry's model of the Trinity in a social direction.[24]

The challenge is in giving an account of how it is that the divine persons share numerically the same acts of intellect and acts of will, nonetheless, each can have *de se* propositional knowledge. This would mean that there is some divine intellectual act by which, e.g., God the Son knows that they are God the Son, *and* God the Father and God the Holy Spirit share numerically the same intellectual act as God the Son. The apparent problem is that if, e.g., God the Father also has numerically the same intellectual act as God the Son, in this example, then God the Father would know that they are God the Son. But, since the Father and Son are not the same person, it would follow that the Father has a false belief (they'd believe that they, God the Father, are God the Son). But the Father doesn't have false beliefs. Consequently, God the Father doesn't share with God the Son the intellectual act of knowing that they (God the Father) are God the Son. So, either (i) the divine persons do not share numerically the same intellectual acts and God the Son has their own (unshared) act of knowing that they are God the Son, or, (ii) the divine persons do not have *de se* propositional knowledge (even if they have *de re* propositional knowledge about themselves—that is, a third-person thought about oneself). Option (i) is what a Social Model of the Trinity would contend for, and option (ii) is what many Latin Models of the Trinity would contend for.

But a Latin Social Model of the Trinity denies that this disjunction between (i) and (ii) is exhaustive because there is a third option. This

---

24. Williams, "Indexicals and the Trinity"; Williams, "Unity of Action," esp. 325, 329–30.

third option says that once we get more detailed about the philosophy of language and the ontology of thought (what is a thought?) then we can give an account of the Trinity such that the divine persons share numerically the same acts of intellect and acts of will (this is what makes this a *Latin* Social Model that is consistent with Conciliar Trinitarianism), and in some cases each divine person can be aware of a different proposition, including different *de se* propositions (this is what makes this a Latin *Social* Model that is consistent with Conciliar Trinitarianism). In what follows I summarize the basics of my Latin Social Model of the Trinity.

According to this Latin Social Model of the Trinity, the divine persons are not identical because of their incommunicable (unshareable) attributes. (Only God the Father is unbegotten and begets; only God the Son is begotten (and became incarnate); and, only God the Holy Spirit proceeds from the Father (and Son).) Nonetheless, the divine persons share *numerically* the same divine essence, nature, powers, intellectual operations, and volitions. Ascribing a "thought" to the divine persons needs to be clarified (to a certain extent). In my view, what it means to claim that a divine person has a thought is that a divine person uses some mental sentence and in using it that person is aware of something; they are aware of some proposition. So, to claim that God the Father is aware that the Father is divine needs to be explained by saying that God the Father uses a mental token of "I am divine," and in using it, the Father is aware that the Father is divine. My positing mental sentences (which are analogous to written sentences or spoken sentences because they have semantic content and syntax) is what is central to this Latin Social Model. (Originally, I introduced an example of Bilbo Baggins's conversation with Gandalf the Grey in order to illustrate how numerically the same use of one sentence ("Good morning!") in different contexts (said to Gandalf, by Bilbo, at a certain time, and at a certain place) can mean different things at the same time.)[25] I claim that the divine persons share numerically the same use of a mental sentence because they share numerically the same divine nature and power(s). So, the divine persons share numerically the same use of a mental sentence, "I am divine." God the Father's using it entails that the Father is aware that the Father is divine. God the Son's using it entails that the Son is aware that the Son is divine. God the Holy Spirit's using it entails that the Holy Spirit is divine. The divine persons

---

25. See Williams, "Indexicals and the Trinity," 82–83; Williams, "In Defense of a Latin Social Trinity," 113–14.

share numerically the same use of a mental sentence, but in this example, each is aware of a different *de se* proposition.

We can understand how this is possible once we consider the nature of a (mental) sentence like, "I am the divine Father."[26] The referent of the pronoun "I" depends on who uses it. Since there are three divine persons who use it, there are three referents. The Father's using "I" entails that the Father is aware of something about themself; the Son's using "I" entails that the Son is aware of something about themself; and the Holy Spirit's using "I" entails that the Holy Spirit is aware of something about themself. Moreover, the copula ("am") can be used to express different relations. Philosophers distinguish the "is" of identity (e.g., "Clark Kent *is* Superman"), the "is" of predication (e.g., "Beulah *is* a cow"), and the "is" of numerical sameness without identity (e.g., "This statue of David *is* (numerically the same thing as) this marble (without being identical to this marble)"). Lastly, the meaning of the predicate term, "the divine Father," depends on the meaning of "I am." Since the divine persons do not have false beliefs (given their omniscience), they don't believe false propositions. So, in the case of God the Father using "I am the divine Father," the Father is aware of the *de se* proposition *that* they (the Father) are identical to the divine Father. In the case of God the Son using "I am the divine Father," the Son is aware of the *de se* proposition *that* they (the Son) are numerically the same divinity as the Father without being identical to the Father. In the case of God the Holy Spirit using "I am the divine Father," the Spirit is aware of the *de se* proposition *that* they (the Holy Spirit) are numerically the same divinity as the Father without being identical to the Father. The divine persons share numerically the same act of using "I am the divine Father," but each is aware of a different *de se* proposition. This is the case because pronouns like "I" get their referent from the context of their use (who uses it?), and the copula ("am") can be used to express different relations (even at the same time, as the example from Bilbo Baggins suggests).

By contrast, in cases that do not involve *de se* propositions, the divine persons' shared use of a mental sentence entails that they are aware of the same proposition. For example, the divine persons using a mental sentence "the divine essence is infinite," entails that they are aware of the same proposition *that* the divine essence is infinite. It is only in cases involving *de se* propositions that the divine persons are aware of different

---

26. For detailed discussion, see Williams, "Indexicals and the Trinity," 83–88.

propositions through their numerically the same use of a mental sentence. (There are important clarifying questions and objections that have been raised against this model, and I have answered them elsewhere. Here, I only wish to outline the distinctive features of this model of the Trinity.)[27] All of this implies that the divine persons cannot even possibly disagree with each other in their thoughts (or in their volitions). The necessary unity of the divine persons' action(s) is accounted for by this Latin Social Model of the Trinity.

There are at least four motivations for developing (and wishing for) a Latin Social Model of the Trinity. First, if Christianity is to be somehow continuous with *Jewish monotheism*, then an account of the Trinity should say how it is that the divine persons cannot even possibly be in conflict or disagreement; allowing for the mere possibility of conflict between the divine persons would smack of polytheism, and not of monotheism. Second, *Conciliar Trinitarianism* claims that there is just one God, and not three Gods, and, Constantinople III made explicit that the number of, e.g., divine power(s) and volition(s) is according to the number of divine natures and not according to the number of divine persons. What this meant is that the divine persons share numerically the same divine will and numerically the same divine volitions. If God the Father wills to make this particular world, then God the Son and God the Holy Spirit share numerically the same act of willing to make this world (and vice versa). Constantinople III clarified that the divine persons' unity of action is *numerical* unity of action (and not merely co-specific unity of action whereby the divine persons typically will the same things, but don't share numerically the same act of willing what they will). In effect, Constantinople III rules out most social models of the Trinity. Third, arguments for God's existence typically aim for a conclusion that there is just one ultimate source for all created existing things, and not three numerically distinct ultimate sources that just so happen to agree on creating this particular world. Fourth, if the divine persons are omniscient (they know everything that could be known), then we should say that each divine person knows which divine person that they are. So, we need a Latin Social Model in order to say how all these claims about the Trinity may fit together.

---

27. William Hasker has raised several objections against my Latin Social Model of the Trinity, and I have responded in detail. See Hasker, "Can a Latin Trinity Be Social?"; Williams, "In Defense of a Latin Social Trinity"; Hasker, "Is the Latin Social Trinity Defensible?"; Williams, "Gregory of Nyssa."

The Latin Social Model of the Trinity borrows from Henry the claim that a divine person, e.g., God the Son as such, can be a unique formal cause of some shared divine intellectual act. (I have also borrowed from Henry's discussion of divine powers in my Latin Social Model).[28] But I have replaced Henry's stipulation that the Word and Zeal contribute the content of certain second-order acts with (among other things) the stipulation that each divine person contributes the content and reference of the divine person's use of "I."

One of Marilyn McCord Adams's research projects was to investigate the extent to which medieval Christian theologians revised Aristotelian logic, physics, and/or metaphysics in order to give a coherent account of some Christian doctrines (e.g., Incarnation, Trinity, and Christ's real presence in the Eucharist).[29] While some of her work was limited to historical investigation, McCord Adams's work on the problem of evil borrowed insights from Christian theology—especially medieval Christian theologians—and she used them in her development of her response to the problem of evil.[30] Her work in historical theology and constructive work that uses her knowledge of historical theology are profound, clear, and admirable. She has been an exemplar in showing us how to work through the medieval scholastics, both for the sake of historical knowledge and for the sake of developing theories that are needed today. Following her lead, in this chapter I surveyed some historical theology (ancient and medieval), and attempted to show how it might be useful for developing a Latin Social Model of the Trinity. But even more, by articulating a Latin Social Model of the Trinity, we can understand a little bit more what it might mean to speak of the Trinitarian friendship circle and how it expands to include others. By having a little better understanding of the Trinitarian friendship circle, we can speak with more clarity and confidence about how others can come to be "co-lovers" and "friends" with (not just) God, but also with each of the Trinitarian persons.

---

28. Williams, "Unity of Action," 329–30.

29. See McCord Adams, *William Ockham*; McCord Adams, "Chalcedonian Christology"; McCord Adams, "The Metaphysics of the Trinity"; McCord Adams, "What's Metaphysically Special about Supposits?"; McCord Adams, "The Metaphysics of the Incarnation"; McCord Adams, *Some Later Medieval Theories of the Eucharist*.

30. See McCord Adams, *Horrendous Evils*, 80–85; McCord Adams, *Christ and Horrors*, 108–43, 234–41.

11

God as the Form of the Intellect
or, Beatific Union in Thomas Aquinas and Giles of Rome, with a Concluding Christological Postscript Wherein Is Proposed a Novel Account of Uncreated Grace

RICHARD CROSS

IN HIS EARLY SENTENCES commentary, Aquinas borrows an idea from Averroes to try to explain the nature of the unity between God and the saints in heaven: God becomes in some sense the *form* of the saint's intellect, and this unity in turn explains the presence of the divine essence as an object of human cognition.[1] On the face of it, this claim raises a number of problems for Aquinas. One is rather general, connected to Aquinas's view that God is immutable: how can it be the case that God is united to the intellect *antecedent* to any created change in the intellect (e.g., the beginning of an intellectual operation that has God as its object)?[2] After all, God is already fully present in the universe, and on

---

1. Aquinas, *Scriptum super Sententiis* [= *In sent.*] IV, d. 49, q. 2, a. 1 c; see too *In sent.* IV, q. 2, a. 1, c. A version of the first two parts of this paper was delivered at the "Aquinas and the Arabs" meeting in Mexico City, August 2018.

2. For divine immutability, see Aquinas, *Summa Theologiae* [*ST*] I, q. 9, art. 1; I, q.

the face of it cannot simply intensify his presence sporadically.³ (I shall label this the "presence worry.") Another one is philosophical: Aquinas holds that cognitive acts are the actualization of intelligible species.⁴ Now, God's presence in the intellect is supposed to replace the intelligible species in the case of beatific cognition, and this seems to suggest—apparently absurdly—that an act of beatific cognition is simply an actualization of God. (I shall label this the "psychological worry.") And a third is more specifically theological: it seems to violate Aquinas's claim that God cannot enter into composition with anything.⁵ (I shall label this the "composition worry.")

Indeed, in relation to the first of these (the immutability worry), it is worth recalling that theories of union with God generally fall into two discrete types: those that explain union in terms of some kind of activity directed to God as its immediate object—typically, cognitive or appetitive activity—and those that suppose union to be immediate, antecedent to any activity. Clearly, if, first, we suppose, with Aquinas, that God's immediate presence replaces the intelligible species, we will likewise suppose that union with God is immediate, antecedent to any cognitive or appetitive act. But, secondly, Aquinas also seems to hold the conflicting view that it is our cognitive vision of the divine essence that explains union with the divine. On this second reading, Aquinas is an activity-theorist, explaining union in terms of activity. Is Aquinas just confused? Or is the standard two-type analysis of beatific union somehow misleading? At any rate, if Aquinas is an immediate-union theorist, his account is clearly vulnerable to the third problem raised in the first paragraph (the composition worry).

In what follows, I explore these issues, and—by examining in turn the accounts in the early *Sentences* commentary and the late *Summa Theologiae*—argue that Aquinas never managed to resolve these problems satisfactorily, and may not even have noticed them. I then present an account closely related to that of Aquinas—Giles of Rome's—which shows

---

14, art. 15 ad 1.

3. For divine omnipresence, see Aquinas, *ST* I, q. 8.

4. "An intelligible species is sometimes in the intellect . . . according to the final completion of the act: and then [the intellect] actually understands. Sometimes it exists in a way intermediate between potency and act, and then the intellect is said to be in habit. And in this manner the intellect conserves species, even when it does not actually understand." Aquinas, *ST* I, q. 79, a. 6 ad 1.

5. See, e.g., Aquinas, *ST* I, q. 3, a. 8.

more sensitivity to at least the first two of these problems (the presence worry and the psychological worry) than Aquinas's own account does. (Aquinas, unlike Giles, does indeed briefly consider the third problem, the composition worry.) But this cluster of issues crops up later in a very unexpected context—seventeenth-century Thomistic Christology—and I conclude by discussing an author whose reflections tend to moderate the severity of Aquinas's denial of divine composition in both Christological and mystical contexts. My aim is to make a proposal, inspired by Thomist and Thomistic Christology, but going much beyond what Aquinas and his followers ever contemplated, to show how immediate union with the divine might be possible.

1. THOMAS AQUINAS

The relevant text from the *Sentences* commentary has long interested commentators as an instance of Aquinas's enthusiastic borrowing of an idea in Averroes that was thought to lead, at least in its unmitigated form, to theologically heterodox conclusions: the theory of the unicity of the intellect.[6] Part of this theory—the part relevant for Aquinas's account of beatific union—consists in the claim that human cognition of the one immaterial shared intellect consists in that substance's becoming a *form* of the human cognizer.[7] Aquinas borrows the theory, replacing the shared intellect with God: what it is for humans to cognize God directly is for God to become a form of the intellect:

> Since in every cognition it is necessary that there is some form by which a thing is known or seen, the form by which the intellect is perfected for seeing separate substances . . . is the separate substance itself, which is joined to our intellect as a form, so that it is both what is seen and that by which it is seen.[8]

The idea is that cognition of an object requires that the object is in some sense united to the intellect. In standard cases, this union is achieved by

---

6. The text and surrounding issues have been quite well served in the literature. See Taylor, "Arabic/Islamic Philosophy; also Black, "*Cognoscere Per Impressionem*," 31–34; Brenet, "Vision béatifique"; Krause, "Albert and Aquinas on the Ultimate End of Humans."

7. Aquinas refers to book 3 of Averroes's *Long Commentary on De anima*; see Taylor, "Arabic/Islamic Philosophy," 537.

8. Aquinas, *In sent*. IV, d. 49, q. 2, a. 1 c.

means of the form of the object, "a likeness (*similitudo*) of the same specific kind . . . existing in the intellect," which "is the principle of cognition . . . according to the kind in which it communicates with the external thing."[9] In the divine case, the divine essence itself performs this role directly: it is not only "what is seen," but also "that by which it is seen," the "principle of cognition."[10] On this view, Aquinas is an immediate-union theorist, and the relevant cognitive act follows from the union automatically.

Aquinas attempts to deal with the composition worry by noting that it is not literally the case that the divine essence is a form of the intellect, just as it is not literally the case that an external object of cognition is the form of the intellect:

> It should not be understood that the divine essence is as it were a true form of our intellect, or that from [the divine essence] and our intellect there is made something unqualifiedly one, as is the case in natural objects, from matter and form. Rather, the relation (*proportio*) is analogous to the relation of form to matter. . . . For just as from the natural form (by which something has existence) and matter there is made one being unqualifiedly, so from the form by which the intellect understands and the intellect itself there is made one thing in cognizing (*in intelligendo*).[11]

What we make of this, I suppose, depends on what it is to be "one thing in cognizing." Typically, this is the relation that obtains between the intellect and an object *as represented*. But, obviously, not so in the beatific case.

The account in the *Summa* has some distinct shifts in emphasis. For one thing, while he still maintains the view that "the essence of God is made to be the intelligible form of the intellect,"[12] Aquinas drops the reference to Averroes, whom he has clearly come to regard with more suspicion. And he seems equivocal on the question of the immediacy of union with the divine. On the one hand, as we have just seen, he keeps the language of God's being the "intelligible form of the intellect," and he maintains that "the divine essence is united to the created intellect as something actually cognized, making the intellect actual through himself"[13] (where "making the intellect actual" means "making the in-

---

9. Aquinas, *In sent.* IV, d. 49, q. 2, a. 1 c.
10. Aquinas, *In sent.* IV, d. 49, q. 2, a. 1 c
11. Aquinas, *In sent.* IV, d. 49, q. 2, a. 1 c.
12. Aquinas, *ST* I, q. 12, a. 5 c.
13. Aquinas, *ST* I, q. 12, a. 2 c ad 3.

tellect actually cognize something"). But this latter claim seems at best ambiguous on the question of what explains what—operation explaining presence, or *vice versa*. And on the other hand, Aquinas in the *Summa* sometimes simply identifies beatific union with the act of cognizing: beatitude is "union with the uncreated good,"[14] and is identified as an "operation": specifically the act of cognizing.[15] Obviously, if Aquinas shifts from accepting an immediate-union theory to an activity theory, he has some kind of reply to the first worry raised in my very first paragraph: what unites God to the created intellect is God's being the object of a created cognitive act. Furthermore, an activity theorist likewise need have no worries of a compositional kind: for God to be the form of the intellect is just for God to be the object of a cognitive act. And, indeed, the *Summa* account has no discussion of the composition problem that plays such a significant role in the *Sentences* account.

Neither discussion has a convincing account of the relation between God, as principle of the relevant cognitive act, and the act itself. The problem—the psychological worry—is that a cognitive act is just an actualized species, and (it seems) no created act could be an actualization of the divine essence. Indeed, the situation is more complex still in the later text, since Aquinas comes to build another component into his cognitive theory. He maintains not only that a cognitive act is the actualization of a species, but also that this actualization involves the production of some further entity, known as a mental word:

> That which the intellect forms, in conceiving, is the word. But the intellect itself, as it is in act by the intelligible species, is considered absolutely. And likewise understanding (*intelligere*), which is related to the intellect in act as existence is to being in act [is considered absolutely]. For understanding does not signify an act passing out of the intellect, but remaining in the intellect. Therefore, when it is said that the word is knowledge (*notitia*), knowledge is not understood to be an act or habit of the cognizing intellect, but for the thing that the intellect conceives when it cognizes.[16]

The idea is that neither the intellect nor its act of understanding involves the production of anything external to the intellect (each is "considered

---

14. Aquinas, *ST* I-II, q. 3, a. 3 c.

15. Aquinas, *ST* I-II, q. 3 a. 2 ad 3. For discussion of this, see my "Deification in Aquinas."

16. Aquinas, *ST* I, q. 34, a. 1 ad 2.

absolutely," as Aquinas puts it). But an act of understanding does indeed involve the production of something internal to the intellect, and the produced word is quite literally the "thing conceived" in understanding, neither a habit (the species) nor an act (the production of the word). We learn elsewhere that the mental word is what is "signified by a definition."[17] I do not know whether this item is supposed to be something real, situated in one of Aristotle's categories, or something simply intentional. And in any case it is not at all clear how this notion could fit in to a picture in which God plays the role of the intelligible species relative to the production of a concept of God in the creaturely mind: not least since such a concept will certainly be some kind of mental representation, and it is a keystone in the whole Thomist edifice, early and late, that there can be no mental representation of God: that is the whole reason why God himself, not some kind of species, has to be something like a form of the intellect.

2. GILES OF ROME

Aquinas's account, it seems to me, as it stands raises more problems than it answers. Giles of Rome was aware of the difficulties and set himself to sorting at least some of them out. Giles's task is made easier for him than it was for Aquinas because he does not believe that a cognitive act is the actualization of a species, and thus does not have to confront the psychological problem that Aquinas's theory of cognition raises in this context.

Giles agrees with Aquinas that in standard cases—those in which the object of cognition is not immediately present to the intellect—a species is required for cognition. But as he sees it the role of the species is causal, substituting for the causal activity that would have been played by the object in causing an act of cognition:

> A species is required to supply the role of the object, for since the object is not present supplying to the mind that it can cause an intellection of itself in the mind, for this reason the species is there, in place of the object, from which species flows intellection and knowledge (*notitia*) in the mind. . . . The object or the thing itself cannot be present to the intellect and cause in it an intellection of itself; for this reason there is required there a species which supplies the presence of the object, and though which this kind of intellection is caused.[18]

17. Aquinas, *Summa contra Gentiles* I, c. 53, n. 443.
18. Giles, *Quodlibeta* [= *Quod.*] V, q. 9 (fol. 59va).

In contrast to Aquinas's view of the matter, the species's role here is purely causal (efficiently causal); the act's *content* is provided by what is formed by the mental act—that is to say, the mental word:

> Just as a species is required to supply the role of the object . . . so there is required a word, so that, since a thing not present to the intellect in such a way that its nature can be seen in itself, for this reason there is formed a word, so that the nature of the thing can be seen in the word, as in a mirror.[19]

Again, it is not clear to me whether or not the mental word is simply the content of the act, or rather something real, located in Aristotle's categories. But either way, it certainly includes the act's content: "The word of the mind . . . is the definition [of a thing] conceived in the mind."[20]

In the case of the beatific vision, there is neither species nor word: God as object is immediately present, and thus can cause cognition of God; and this cognition in turn does not need to produce a mental word since the act's content is derived directly from the object itself:

> Since the divine essence is present to the intellect, it follows that, just as we do not need another species through which the intellection is caused (but rather the divine essence, existing in itself and present to the intellect, causes an intellection of itself in the intellect itself), so in that blessed vision there will not be formed a word really distinct from the divine essence, but the divine essence, existing as present to the intellect, will be seen in itself.[21] . . . If it is asked, how the blessed find God in themselves, I reply that they do not find God in a word that really differs from the divine essence, but they find the divine essence in itself.[22]

The idea is that what it is for God to be present to the intellect is for that intellect to have a cognitive act that has God as its object. And this act has the content it does in virtue of its having its object really present to it.

This solves at a stroke both of Aquinas's first two difficulties, the presence worry and the psychological worry. On the first, there is a real change in the creature that explains God's presence: the cognitive act, caused by God:

---

19. Giles, *Quod.* V, q. 9 (fol. 59va).
20. Giles, *Quod.* V, q. 9 (fol. 59rb).
21. Giles, *Quod.* V, q. 9 (fol. 59va).
22. Giles, *Quod.* V, q. 9 (fol. 60ra).

> Just as God is said to be somewhere because he begins to be somewhere where he was not, not by a change in God, but by a change made in us, so God is said to be conceived, apprehended, and formed in us, not by a change made in God, but by a change in us. For when the open vision (by which we apprehend and find God, and see the beauteous one) begins to be in us, then the divine essence is said to be in us in the ways just mentioned, and to have in some way the notion of a word.[23]

On the second, Giles abandons the pair of claims that make Aquinas's view so puzzling: first, that a cognitive act is an actualized species, and secondly that this actualized species produces a mental word. The species has a merely causal role, which is causally bypassed in the case that God causes the relevant cognitive act directly; and there is no need for a mental word to supply the content of the act, since that is provided directly by the object:

> The blessed will not find [God] in a [mental] word that is really different from the divine essence; but they will find the divine essence in themselves, which is therefore said to be a concept belonging to the mind, like a [mental] word. . . . The divine essence . . . is not only related to us as a word (on the grounds that it is apprehended and is something found in itself), but also related as something formed in us, as the Apostle says to the Galatians, c. 4: "My little children, with whom I am in labour again until Christ be formed in us again", that is, until is beauteous one (*formosus*) appears in us. Then God will be formed in us, because the beauteous one appears in us.[24]

Giles's intellect, it must be said, is altogether better set up for beatific cognition than Aquinas's is. But the consequence is that Giles rejects Aquinas's immediate-union theory and replaces it with an activity theory.

Giles's account has a very striking semantic consequence. In standard cases, the mental word is what is signified by a spoken word.[25] Words about God uttered in the beatific vision signify the divine essence directly: "If we could then express the concept of our intellect by a noun, and impose one noun on it, that noun, which would sound externally, would be significative and representative of the divine essence itself."[26]

---

23. Giles, *Quod.* V, q. 9 (fol. 60ra).
24. Giles, *Quod.* V, q. 9 (fol. 60ra).
25. Giles, *Quod.* V, q. 9 (fol. 59rb).
26. Giles, *Quod.* V, q. 9 (fol. 60ra–rv).

"Imposition" here is the act of dubbing or baptizing an object with a term: in the beatific vision, if we are able to give God a spoken name, that name signifies God directly.

Giles's account of beatific union has a further turn to it. Aquinas locates the highest human good in cognition. Supposing Aquinas is an immediate-union theorist, he holds that cognition of God requires and presupposes the antecedent union of God with the intellect. And Aquinas's account of beatific cognition—as requiring the real presence of God in the intellect—gives him a good reason for holding that the highest human good requires cognition. But if Giles's critique is correct, there is an explanatory gap here, since there is no account of how God gets to be present to the intellect prior to the act of cognition. Rather, presence is explained by activity, not *vice versa*; and if this is the case, then the motivation for supposing that the relevant act need be cognitive is undermined. Indeed, while Giles, as we have seen, maintains that the cognitive act makes God intimately *present* to the mind, it does not strictly speaking *unite* the mind to God, or bring about a union with the divine. (Contrast Aquinas's claim that "from the form by which the intellect understands and the intellect itself there is made one thing in cognizing.") In line with the Franciscan tradition so much admired by McCord Adams, Giles argues that what unites the soul to God is an *appetitive* act.

Giles's reason is that appetitive acts in general are unitive in a way that cognitive acts are not. To start with, appetitive acts require real union in a way that intellectual acts do not: "it is sufficient to the one who understands that they have an intelligible likeness, and that they have the formal expression [of the thing]."[27] And, Giles adds, if "the intellect, as such, wills the presence of the intelligible object, this is for the sake of the intellection, because it perhaps cannot understand it fully other than through its presence."[28] The intellect "wills" the presence of the object merely because that presence renders the object more intelligible. It does not will it for the sake of the object itself. ("Wills," here, I take it means something like "inclines to.") Unity with its object, in other words, is not what intellection is essentially aimed at, so to speak.

According to Giles, the situation in the case of will is quite different. The whole purpose of love is that "the lover wants themselves to be joined to the beloved, and wants to make themselves what the beloved is, and as

---

27. Giles, *Quod.* V, q. 9 (fol. 56vb).
28. Giles, *Quod.* V, q. 9 (fol. 56vb).

far as is possible transforms themselves into the beloved."[29] Thus, unlike the case of intellect, the lover wills the presence of the beloved for its own sake, and not just for the sake of improving the act of love:

> The lover, as such, does not will the presence of the beloved solely for the sake of love, but also for the sake of the beloved itself, to which, as far as they can, they will to join themselves; indeed, as such they will to transform themselves into the beloved, to the extent that this is possible.... For this reason, love transforms, because it moves the lover outside themselves, and locates them in the beloved.... Therefore divine love, that is, the love by which we love God, causes ecstasy, that is, it places the lovers outside themselves, not permitting them to love themselves, but making them to be lovers of the beloved.[30]

Knowledge is desired for the sake of knowledge; the beloved is desired for the sake of the beloved. And the Aristotelian psychology—according to which the object of knowledge is somehow made to be internal to the knower—provides another stark point of contrast: love, rather than unite the beloved to the lover by taking the beloved into the lover, unites the lover to the beloved by ecstatically taking the lover into the beloved. It is, indeed, not a case of the believer claiming God; rather, God claims the believer. And this is the highest kind of beatific union.

Giles makes much the same point a little later in the discussion too:

> If God, even in heaven, will be understood as he is in us, and loved by us as he is in himself, it follows that we will be united to God, by means of understanding, as he will be in us, and according to our manner, but that we will be united to him, through love, as he is in himself, and in the divine manner.[31]

None of this is to deny the unifying power of beatific cognition. But it to render beatific cognition less potently or effectively unifying than love.

Overall, Giles's account of union with God is clearly an activity theory, not an immediate-union theory. That he should adopt such a theory follows simply from what he takes to be the explanatory gap in Aquinas's immediate-union theory. But in the next section I will try to show how a different response might be developed, one that makes sense

---

29. Giles, *Quod.* V, q. 9 (fol. 56vb). Aquinas hints at something like this in *ST* I-II, q. 28, a. 1 ad 1, but does not develop the insight further.

30. Giles, *Quod.* V, q. 5 (fol. 57ra).

31. Giles, *Quod.* V, q. 5 (fol. 57va).

of immediate union without presupposing any created activity at all. To do so, I shall draw on some of the ways in which some Christological insights of Aquinas's were developed in seventeenth-century Thomism.

3. CHRISTOLOGICAL POSTSCRIPT, WITH A THOMISTIC ACCOUNT OF IMMEDIATE BEATIFIC UNION

McCord Adams is one of the few recent scholars to have written at length about Giles of Rome.[32] Perhaps she was fond of him; I do not know. But I do know that she loved Christ, and she loved Christology. And one of the most interesting by-products of Aquinas's view of beatific union—particularly in its early form—is its use in the Christological discussions of some Renaissance and Baroque Thomists. Thus far, I have focused on problems in Aquinas's account, and shown how Giles attempts to respond to them. Here I shall attempt to find some different solutions, guided by Christological insights of Aquinas's, as inherited by his later successors. And whereas these successors used the question of beatific union to cast light on the hypostatic union, I shall take the opposite approach, using insights from a Thomist theology of the Incarnation to cast light on the question of beatific union.

According to Aquinas's Christology—at least according to one standard interpretation—the divine *esse* is immediately united to Christ's human nature, and this union grounds the hypostatic union between the divine and human natures.[33] The latter union, the relation between the two natures, is something created, over and above the two natures. But the former, the immediate communion of the divine *esse* with the human nature, involves no metaphysical component over and above the nature and the *esse*. Christology, then, is an instance of immediate union, and in this respect just like the case of the beatific vision.

This immediate Christological union has to confront at least the first and the third of the three problems that Aquinas's account of beatific union raises, the presence worry and the composition worry. Aquinas himself deals with the first of these objections to his Christology. The act

---

32. See McCord Adams, *Some Later Medieval Theories of the Eucharist*, ch. 4.

33. See Aquinas, *ST* III, q. 2, a. 6 ad 2; for the interpretation, see Cajetan, *Commentaria in Summam Theologicam* [= *In ST*] III, q. 4, a. 2 (in Aquinas, *Opera omnia*, XI, 77a).

of uniting the human nature to the divine person is just that—an act; and corresponding to this act is a categorial passion in the human nature.[34] But once united the nature and the person require no further medium to unite them: it is the intrinsic metaphysical structures, so to speak, of the two components, the human nature and the divine *esse*, that secure their continued union and presence to each other.

Perhaps beatific union could be treated in a similar way: God immediately unites God's self to the intellect, not merely "as an intelligible form" but really, antecedent to any role God might have in beatific cognition—just as the communion of the divine *esse* with Christ's human nature is not union just "as an intelligible form" but really, the *ipsissimum* divine *esse* communicated to the human nature. The beatific union I am attempting to characterize involves a divine action, and a correlative passion in the human nature. Once united, however, the divine essence and the human intellect require no further bit of metaphysical machinery, over and above essence and intellect, to secure their continued unity. Aquinas, of course, supposes that the union thus described results in a cognitive activity. But this activity is not part of the explanatory mechanism that secures unity in the first place. We have to suppose that the intellect is appropriately "God-shaped," apt to have God immediately united to it as a kind of form.

The analogy between the two cases—beatific union and hypostatic union—is first made by Thomas de Vio Cajetan in the early sixteenth century:

> If we talk of "actuating" and "being actuated" within the whole range of its meanings ... then it is not removed from divine philosophy to say that God can actuate a created thing. In evidence of this, both theologians and philosophers say that the divine essence is the act of any intellect that sees him. Since therefore we say that the human nature in Christ is perfected by divine personhood and divine *esse*, it is not inappropriate (*absonum*) to say also that it is actuated in some way by the divine personhood and *esse*.[35]

---

34. Aquinas, *ST* III, q. 2, a. 8 c.
35. Cajetan, *In ST* III, q. 17, a. 2 (XI, 228a).

I propose taking literally what Cajetan takes merely as an analogy: in beatific union, the divine essence literally becomes a form of the human person.[36]

I shall put a bit more flesh on these bones in a moment. For now, I want to address the second worry, the composition problem. One thinker who takes composition seriously in both of these contexts is the seventeenth-century Thomist Vincent Contenson (1641–74), one of the French Dominicans of the second half of the seventeenth century especially interested in combining Scholastic theology with specifically spiritual and mystical concerns. It is not controversial, in Thomistic circles, to think about the Incarnation as a case of composition; what is distinctive about Contenson's account is that he considers the case of beatific union likewise to be a case of composition.

Contenson holds that the Incarnation consists in the communication of the divine person's subsistence (i.e., the divine person's personal property, filiation) to the human nature, and he construes the relation between a nature and its subsistence as analogous to a formal cause—and thus as something like a form belonging to a nature. Personhood belongs to nature "as a kind of formal cause,"[37] and "a formal cause does not prevail other than by communicating its entity; its formal effect is the communicated form."[38] While the subject of these claims is created personhood, the context requires the claim to be generally true: Contenson is trying to show that a created personhood (unlike a divine one) cannot belong to more than one nature on the grounds that such belonging is a variety of formal causation, and created formal causes are inherently restricted to just one subject.

Here is what Contenson says in response to the composition worry:

> It does not belong to the notion of a composite that it consists of parts, but from several extremes that come together into one thing to constitute a whole. For example, from the intellect of the blessed and the divine essence there is made one thing in the intelligible order, without the divine essence's having the character of a part. For this reason, when theologians assert with St Thomas that God cannot enter into composition, they speak of a

---

36. I deal in detail with early modern Christology, both Catholic and Protestant, in my *Christology and Metaphysics in the Seventeenth Century*.

37. Contenson, *Theologia mentis et cordis* [= *Theol.*] IX, diss. 3, c. 2, spec. 1 (II, 35a).

38. Contenson, *Theol.* IX, diss. 3, c. 1, spec. 3 (II, 34a).

> composition in which the extremes have the character of an incomplete part. And if you contest that by "part" you understand nothing other than an extreme that is a co-cause (*concurrens*) in the composition of some whole, you will be making a question about a word, and will be speaking improperly, because by "part" we are accustomed to understand an incomplete being in which there is brought about, with another, a more perfect whole. For God, who is the extreme of this composition, has the fullest and most complete perfection.[39]

The definition of "part" as such implies something necessarily incomplete: the kind of thing that coalesces with another to make a complete thing. But there are composites that do not consist of parts in this sense. Beatific union is an example of such a composition: a composition "in the intelligible order," a composition of a created intellect and a form—the divine essence—considered as an intelligible object. Aquinas himself, as Contenson makes clear, must be committed to denying that any such union is a case of composition, for just the reason Contenson gives—namely, that composition entails imperfection, for which reason God cannot enter into composition with a creature.[40] But Contenson evidently thinks that the presence of God as a form of the intellect is sufficient for composition, else appealing to it would not help defuse the objection to Christological composition. Likewise he supposes that the presence of divine subsistence as a formal cause of the subsistence of Christ's human nature is a case of composition too. But note one important feature of these compositions: they do not involve any third thing over and above the components themselves. Not only do they not involve some kind of ontologically freighted *relation* between the two; they do not involve any third substance emerging from or supervening on them. All the composition amounts to is the immediate union of the components—just the kind of thing that we require for beatific union. To borrow another distinction often drawn by the baroque Thomists, there is no composite *from* the two, or *out of* the two; there is merely a composition of the two things *with* each other.

So how might these insights apply to the question of beatific union? The initial worry is that there is no account of immediate union that does not entail God's entering into composition with a creature. Contenson's response: bite that particular bullet, and try to show that such

---

39. Contenson, *Theol.* IX, diss. 3, c. 1, spec. 1 (II, 29a).
40. See Aquinas, *ST* I, q. 3, a. 8.

composition is compatible with divine aseity. In the Christological case, composition is secured by the mutual adaptability of a particular human nature (Christ's) and the divine *esse*. What is required in the case of beatific union is the analogous mutual adaptability of a particular human *person* (the blessed) and the divine *essence*.

Whatever this adaptability is, it must preclude the possibility of either the human person's changing into the divine nature, or the divine nature into the human person.[41] Its resulting in incarnation is automatically ruled out: as Aquinas understands it, incarnation requires the communication of *esse* in such a way as to preclude the independent subsistence of a human nature. And beatific union as such is neither of these: it is essence, not *esse* that is communicated; and the object of communication is not an anhypostatic nature but a person.

But I think we can say something more positive too. Just as the divine subsistence actualizes Christ's human nature "as a kind of formal cause," so we might think of the divine essence as something like a (contingent) form of the created substance. If it seems odd to think of the divine essence in this way—as a form or property of something created— we might recall Aquinas's claim that God is both concrete and subsistent, on the one hand, and also abstract and formal, on the other.[42] And if it seems odd to think of the divine essence being immediately united to a human person as a kind a form, recall that Aquinas (or at least some of his followers) holds that the divine *esse* or subsistence can be immediately united to a human nature as a kind of form; and if the divine *esse* can be such, surely the divine essence can be too.

Now, if it is to be the case that the human nature is informed without in that process *becoming* God, we need some ground for supposing that the human nature can *bear* the divine essence without thereby being *characterized* by it—without it being the case that "God" and the divine attributes can be predicated of the human substance. There are, indeed, useful philosophical and theological examples of bearing without being characterized (of being informed, without being denominated, in the technical medieval jargon): matter bearing substantial form without being characterized by it (since it is the substance itself, not the matter, that is characterized by the form), or the body bearing the soul without

---

41. See Aquinas, *ST* III, q. 2, a. 1 c.

42. See Aquinas, *ST* I, q. 3, a. 3 (for God as a subsistent form); and I, q. 13, a. 1 ad 2 (for the identity of concrete and abstract).

being characterized by it;[43] or Christ's human nature bearing the divine subsistence without thereby becoming God or the divine person; or the intellect's bearing an intelligible species (or mental word) without being characterized by its contents—receiving the form without matter, in the Aristotelian language: which takes me back to the text from Aquinas with which I started. But what blocks predication in this latter case is precisely that the contents of the species are *representations* of their external object: *similitudines*, likenesses, in Aquinas's language. What would block predication in the beatific case, I suppose, is simply that a created substance cannot become God, or *vice versa*—just as what blocks predication in the matter–form or body–soul case is simply that matter or body cannot become form or soul: they are not the appropriate kinds of thing to be characterized by the predicates associated with the item they bear.

This view of God's role in beatitude would truly amount to a kind of uncreated grace. To the extent that I understand his view, I take myself to be defending something akin to Karl Rahner's account of uncreated grace in terms of God's acting as a "quasi-formal" cause in relation to the person in beatific union with God.[44] Rahner's *quasi*-formal causality is supposed to secure divine transcendence:

> It cannot be impossible in principle to allow an active formal causality . . . of God upon a creature without thereby implying that this reactively impresses a new determination upon God's Being in itself one which would do away with his absolute transcendence and immutability. . . . All this "quasi" implies is that this "forma", in spite of its formal causality, which must be taken really seriously, abides in its absolute transcendence.[45]

In my view this *desideratum* (if such it be) would be satisfied by the view that the uniting is simply a divine action (with a correlative passion in the human nature). To the extent that divine activity in general is compatible with divine immutability, this action (beatifically uniting a human person to the divine) is so compatible—and Rahner is thus making a relatively easy matter harder than it need be. Equally, Rahner is interested in expounding those of Aquinas's claims with which I started (from the *Sentences* commentary), and so is fundamentally concerned with beatific acts of cognition and volition: "The causality precisely under

---

43. See, e.g., Aristotle, *Physica*, I, c. 7 (190a36).
44. See Rahner, "Some Implications."
45. Rahner, "Some Implications," 331.

discussion here is one which determines the finite spirit in the direction of the object which it is to know and love."[46] I am interested in union with the divine antecedent to such activities—an immediate-union theory, not an activity theory. So I would be inclined to develop the insight about formal causality in a rather different way from that proposed by Rahner. My suggestion: we take God as, quite literally, a non-denominating (non-characterizing) form of the beatified human person. My "quasi" is merely God's (the form's) *non-denomination*. God is truly a form, but without being strictly speaking a formal cause.

On the view of beatific union I am considering here, then, the divine essence is borne by the human person without characterizing that person; it is a form of the human person, immediately united to that person, or entering into immediate communion and composition with that person, without denominating that person. God is as intimate to the person as a body's size or shape is to the body; with the proviso that the person does not become God (whereas as the body is indeed its size and its shape). As in Giles's account, what we have is a case of God *claiming* the human person: becoming the person's form. So there it is: a broadly Thomistic account of beatific union, Christologically inspired, and dedicated to Marilyn McCord Adams—though I fear she won't like it.

---

46. Rahner, "Some Implications," 332.

12

Carnal Knowledge of God

REBECCA VOELKEL

IN MARCH OF 2017, I flew from Minneapolis to New York and boarded an Amtrak train at Penn Station bound for Princeton. When I got off the train, Bob, Marilyn's beloved husband, picked me up and drove me to their home. It had been less than a year since I was last there but the circumstances couldn't have been more different. Then, I had brought my nine-year-old daughter to spend time with Marilyn and Bob, to be around Marilyn's energy, her cooking, her office filled with so many books. Then, I had wanted the child I had carried in my body to know this mentor whose love and genuine interest in me and my scholarship had guided me at pivotal points in my life. Then, I had wanted my voracious reader child to meet a kindred spirit. Now, I was in her home because she was dying and I was joining the community of her mentees to help midwife her into Love's eternal embrace. And maybe the two trips weren't actually all that different, because both were powerfully and palpably about bodies and physical presence.

In retrospect, it seems exactly as it should be, given that most of my relationship with Marilyn was rooted in our shared exploration of how we know and claim God through embodied reality. In fact, when I was working under Marilyn's tutelage to write my first book, I had a working title of *Called to Be Lovers in the Name of God*. But as we spent hours together, talking and editing, she finally suggested that *Carnal Knowledge of God: Embodied Love and the Movement for Justice* was more fitting.[1]

And so, in honor of Marilyn McCord Adams, whose own seeking after carnal knowledge of God has blessed me and so many, I want to offer a few reflections on how it came to be so. In order to do that, I want to share a few stories.

1. FROM DREADED ANSELM WOMAN TO BLESSED ANSELM WOMAN

In the Fall of 1993, I entered Yale Divinity School as a first year Master of Divinity student. Born and raised in the Midwest, I came to YDS from Seattle where I had lived for the previous two years. One of the first official events of the school year was the Opening Convocation in which the newest faculty member was invited to address the gathered academic community. As I sat in Marquand Chapel on a hot September day, I was nearly giddy for what lay ahead in my seminary education. But my excitement quickly turned to deflation and then seething anger as Rev. Dr. Marilyn McCord Adams stood in the high pulpit dressed in academic robes and an ecclesial collar and spoke on and on and on about Anselm's theology of atonement.

My friends and I dubbed Marilyn "The Dreaded Anselm Woman" and referred to her that way for the next two months. Our attitude was borne of several things: the fact that she appeared as if she understood herself superior to all of us; the inaccessible, and seemingly disembodied, language she employed; and the subject matter which struck us as arcane.

But my early conclusions were proven wrong and my relationship with Marilyn changed dramatically.

2. BLESSED ANSELM WOMAN

What changed was that shortly after the semester began, Marilyn asked if she could serve as the faculty advisor to the LGBTQ (Lesbian, Gay, Bisexual, Transgender, Queer) student group. Although Marilyn did not identify as LGBTQ, she had come to New Haven and Yale from Los Angeles where she had served a parish. In the preceding years, she had journeyed with, and borne witness to the deaths of, dozens of gay men

---

1. Voelkel, *Carnal Knowledge of God*.

from HIV/AIDS. And she had been completely transformed by the love and faithfulness of the men's partners in the face of their dying processes. She had allowed her lived, embodied experience to transform her heart and her theology.

When she arrived at YDS, she was an outspoken LGBTQ advocate and ally. We learned this during the first LGBTQ student-sponsored worship service in which Marilyn was invited to preach. Her sermon went deep into Trinitarian theology and the meaning of the creedal affirmation that the persons of the Trinity are *homoousios*. She then moved seamlessly to the conclusion that all three persons of the Trinity are male, and therefore the Trinity can best be understood as a Gay Love Triangle. The entire sermon was preached from memory without a single note. She wore her robe and stole with clerical collar and walked amongst us as she passionately embodied what I would come to recognize as classic Marilyn—a combination of orthodox and progressive understandings and interpretations, drawing from an intellectual brilliance that was simultaneously aware of its practical application to real lives and actual bodies. Unlike her convocation speech, this Marilyn was very embodied. She used her body as one of her most powerful illustrations. She moved toward each of us, looking us in the eye and inviting us into consecrating our own queer bodies through God's queerness.

In addition to her support of LGBTQ students, she and I began to have conversations about the experience of being Midwesterners who had lived on the West Coast and then found ourselves on the East Coast. For those of us newly-arrived in New Haven and at Yale, we were struck by the coldness, meanness and elitism of some. In response, I started making chocolate chip cookies and bringing them with Good Earth tea to Marilyn's office. She returned the favor often. This chocolate chip ministry helped us both get through our first years in a delicious way. And it signaled a shared strategy that helped cement our relationship: tangible, concrete attention to bodies and their needs and desires in order to deal with larger-scale suffering, oppression or pain.

In our second year, Marilyn invited three of us to co-lead a chapel service on the Feast of the Immaculate Conception. Marilyn brought her cope and insisted that all three of us (women, two of whom were lesbian, one of whom was Roman Catholic) wear it as we spoke. Her insistence was rooted in her desire to sacralize our female and queer bodies as we preached about God honoring Mary's young, female body. This was another example of classic Marilyn: orthodox and progressive, aware of the embodied implications.

Around that same time, I took my only Marilyn class—on theodicy. What struck me the most about the experience was her genuine desire to empower the theological hearts, minds, bodies and voices of all of us. She presented several of her writings on theodicy—all of which were brilliant. But she did this not so that we would be able to parrot her, but as an example of how she used her theological heart, mind, body and voice so that we could begin to hone ours. I discovered that the question of theodicy was one of my most pressing theological projects. And I was affirmed in my desire to have my intellectual work be closely tied to the reality of what many parishioners were facing: sexual abuse, homo-, bi- and transphobia, domestic violence, disease, racial injustice, aging, hunger, homelessness. One way to embody these commitments that began to emerge from my time in seminary and with Marilyn as a mentor was that my ministry primarily sits in the hybrid space between the academy, the church (and other religiously rooted communities) and movements for justice.

In the nearly thirty years since, twenty-four as an ordained pastor, it has been in this hybrid space of Academy-Church-Movement that I have done my work. I have spent close to fifteen years as a congregational pastor in the United Church of Christ, spent more than a decade helping to facilitate the national pro-LGBTQ multifaith movement and have taught in a seminary context. In each of these roles, I have sought to hold academic rigor in the same body as open-heartedness, resistance to injustice wherever it lives, and daily, weekly and liturgical season-based spiritual practice.

3. THEOLOGICAL GROUNDEDNESS

Over the course of my life and ministry, I have come to understand that the context in which we live is paradoxical. On the one hand, I affirm that the Holy One, the Divine Creativity, the Mystery created a world and filled it with abundance and love. On the other, the daily reminders of the power of systemic oppression, violence and death make me take sin and evil seriously. How ought we live amidst this paradox? How might we respond in ways faithful and liberative? How do we claim God? These are some of the questions that animate my life of faith. In order to offer some answers, let me first elaborate on the paradox.

4. THE PARADOX OF EVIL: BLESSING

Every morning when my partner and I take a walk beside the flowing waters of the Minnehaha Creek, under the canopy of trees and in sight of eagles and hawks and multiple species of ducks, I am reminded in palpable ways that God loves us. God is a lover of beauty and is constantly seeking to grab our attention and solicit our praise.

In fact, I affirm that God's essence is knit throughout all of creation. God has the deepest of connections, the most real of relationships with the entire universe. One way to describe this immanence is that God has carnal knowledge of humanity. In the act of creation, God uses God's own essence and imbues God's self within creation. God knows intimately creation's embodiment. God understands, and is in deep relationship with, our flesh and bones. God creates in order to be in passionate relationship with creation. "Let us make humankind in our image, according to our likeness" (Gen 1:36 NRSV) is one way God articulates, names into being this carnal relationship. And, because of God's creative actions, humanity has carnal knowledge of God through the very bodies into which God pours God's essence. We can have some understanding of God's body, God's longings, God's desires because of how God created us. Alice Walker captures some of this in her exquisite theological work, *The Color Purple*.

> Listen, God love everything you love—and a mess of stuff you don't. But more than anything else, God love admiration.
> You saying God vain? I ast.
> Naw, she say. Not vain, just wanting to share a good thing. I think it pisses god off if you walk by the color purple in a field somewhere and don't notice it.
> What it do when it pissed off? I ast.
> Oh, it make something else. People think pleasing God is all God care about. But any fool living in the world can see it always trying to please us back.[2]

Carnal knowledge is an intentionally provocative term. It claims the fact that the breadth and depth of embodiment is sacralized. There isn't any part of our embodied experience that God doesn't bless. There isn't any part of our embodied experience that God doesn't experience, too.

God's carnal knowledge of us and ours of God means that I am invited into enjoying God. For me, enjoying God, practicing my carnal

---

2. Walker, *The Color Purple*, 196.

knowledge of God, claiming God, happens in many ways. When I am lustily singing hymns, full voiced and in community, I am enjoying, claiming, practicing carnal knowledge of God. When I am worshiping with an open-heart: in lament or praise or deep silence, I am enjoying, claiming, practicing carnal knowledge of God. I also claim and practice and carnally know God when I am belly laughing or sweating from a workout or making love.

Marilyn affirmed this very understanding throughout her writings and in her living. One of Marilyn's favorite things was to cook and bake. Besides our chocolate chip cookie ministry, many of us at Yale Divinity School were guests at the epic dinner parties Marilyn would throw at her home on St. Ronan Street. With tables laden with food, Marilyn would welcome us into her home for an extravagant communion. Often, these feasts happened after a particularly difficult experience of homo-hatred. Preceding one such feast, the dean of the Episcopal seminary affiliated with Yale had signed onto a letter that ran in the *Wall Street Journal* and claimed, among other things, that "homosexuals" were pedophiles and that when LGBTQ folx made love they were "suboptimal linkages." In response to this harmful, dangerous, and corrosively bad theologizing, hundreds of LGBTQ folx worshipped and protested and Marilyn showed up and stood in solidarity. And then, she threw a feast and invited all those whom the church would condemn to her table. In many ways she was embodying what she wrote and talked about:

> Being in the world with God person-to-person is just as multifaceted as children's growing up in their parents' home and life partners' sharing a household. Here below, togetherness sometimes takes the form of wordless presence (as with mother and child, or lovers staring into one another's eyes) and carnal knowledge (as with a mother nursing her baby or the lover's invasive and enfolding touch) . . . life together takes the form of joint activities: digging the garden and planting the flowers, raking leaves and cleaning the gutters, hiking in the woods, throwing a party, organizing with others for political action.[3]

In this orientation, Incarnation and incarnations are understood together. God not only has carnal knowledge of humanity because of the person of Jesus Christ but God's presence is incarnate throughout all of creation, immanent in plants, animals and individual human beings. And

---

3. McCord Adams, "Prayer as the 'Lifeline of Theology,'" 272.

God is present in communities of resistance and resilience, too. Feasts like the one Marilyn threw are writ through with God's immanent presence that is both in the individual bodies and the communal body of the feast.

5. THE PARADOX OF EVIL: THE CAGE

At the very same time, there is the very real presence of systemic oppression, violence and death which permeates our collective life. For those of us who live in the United States, understanding our current context in light of the Doctrine of Discovery helps create a container in which to respond in faithful and liberative ways.

On June 18, 1452, Pope Nicholas V issued the papal bull *Dum Diversas*. It instructed and authorized Alfonso V of Portugal to reduce any "Saracens (Muslims) and pagans and any other unbelievers" to perpetual slavery. Dum Diversas was followed on January 5, 1455, by a second papal bull called *Romanus Pontifex*. It read in part:

> We weighing all and singular the premises with due meditation, and noting that since we had formerly by other letters of ours granted among other things free and ample faculty to the aforesaid King Alfonso—to invade, search out, capture, vanquish, and subdue all Saracens and pagans whatsoever, and other enemies of Christ wheresoever placed, and the kingdoms, dukedoms, principalities, dominions, possessions, and all movable and immovable goods whatsoever held and possessed by them and to reduce their persons to perpetual slavery, and to apply and appropriate to himself and his successors the kingdoms, dukedoms, counties, principalities, dominions, possessions, and goods, and to convert them to his and their use and profit—by having secured the said faculty, the said King Alfonso, or, by his authority, the aforesaid infante, justly and lawfully has acquired and possessed, and doth possess, these islands, lands, harbors, and seas, and they do of right belong and pertain to the said King Alfonso and his successors.[4]

And in 1493, Pope Alexander VI issued the bull *Inter Caetera* stating one Christian nation did not have the right to establish dominion over lands previously dominated by another Christian nation, thus establishing the Law of Nations. Taken together, these papal bulls create what is known as the Doctrine of Discovery. Indigenous scholars and

---

4. Indigenous Values Initiative, "Dum Diversas."

documentarians Sheldon Wolfchild and Steven Newcomb refer to the Doctrine of Discovery as the Doctrine of Christian Dominance. In their film, *Doctrine of Discovery: Unmasking the Domination Code*, Newcomb and Wolfchild examine how the Doctrine of Discovery continues to distort and infect the lives of indigenous peoples around the world. One of the most powerful reasons for this ongoing influence is the ways in which the Doctrine of Discovery is codified in US (and international) law. In 1823, Chief Justice John Marshall wrote the opinion for the Supreme Court in Johnson vs. McIntosh which cited the Doctrine of Discovery as the legal basis for the fact that Native peoples cannot own land. And, as recently as 2005, Supreme Court Justice Ruth Bader Ginsburg cited the Doctrine of Discovery in one of her rulings.

In this theological understanding, one had to be European and Christian in order to be human. The Africans that were murdered or enslaved by King Alfonso's army were "heathens" and the indigenous peoples encountered by European colonizers in the Americas were "savages." Neither were human. And because the orders to enslave, colonize and commit genocide were sent by a series of popes, they were baptized as sacred. The colonizers claimed God as their legitimizing force and justified all they did with a violent and toxic theology. The result was an interlocking cage of oppression: extractive capitalism, white supremacy and Christian supremacy woven together by empire. This cage is not only historical. It is our present reality. And for those of us who are non-Native, white Christians, it creates a particular and pointed responsibility.

Liturgically, the Doctrine-of-Discovery-rooted cage of oppression requires confession, repentance, and repair from those of us who are non-Native, white and Christian. Indigenous leaders have been calling for the repudiation of the Doctrine of Discovery for years as a first step of confession-repentance-reparation. I first began to really understand this ask when I was at Standing Rock over the course of three visits in the Fall of 2016.

Lakota and other indigenous leaders of the Oceti Sakowin camp had lit a sacred fire from which emanated the life of the resistance to the Dakota Access Pipeline.[5] Over the course of several months, the camp swelled to ten thousand people with tribal representatives from hundreds

---

5. Oceti Sakowin is the proper name for the indigenous people commonly known as Lakota or Sioux. Oceti Sakowin means Seven Council Fires and refers to the seven different communities that make up the Lakota/Dakota/Nakota peoples.

of nations around the world. The sacred fire was a place of education, ceremony and sacred kinship.

In early November, over five hundred non-Native clergy were invited to Standing Rock for a solidarity ceremony and action. The first day of our time together was dedicated to Native elders teaching about the ways in which the Doctrine of Discovery continues to do violence to Native nations and peoples. They also spoke about the ways in which the Dakota Access Pipeline cutting across Lakota burial grounds and under Lake Oahe, the source of drinking water for millions downstream, was first and foremost a manifestation of the Doctrine of Discovery. Coming from this place of deep listening to the teaching of the elders, representatives of the Christian denominations that had done the work of educating themselves on the Doctrine of Discovery and passing resolutions of repudiation were invited to step forward and offer confession, repentance and repudiation. After each had done so, a ceremonial copy of the papal bulls was placed in a metal container and coals from the sacred fire were used to burn it.

Having confessed and started the process of repentance and repudiation, we were then invited to participate in the day's action of protesting the Dakota Access Pipeline by marching to the construction site. The two days were a very powerful liturgical arc: listening to the elders engage in truth-speaking, participating in sacred ceremony of confession, repentance and repudiation, and then acting as followers of indigenous leadership in protest and solidarity.

But in order to make the needed liturgical moves, we must begin by claiming God as healer, liberator, and destroyer of cages. We must profess and embody theologies that counter the violence and toxicity with healing and justice. What made it possible for those five hundred non-Native religious leaders to participate in the liturgical act of repudiating the Doctrine of Discovery is that they had done the preparatory theological work of claiming the solidarity of God.

6. CLAIMING THE SOLIDARITY OF GOD: THEOLOGY

When I was working with Marilyn to write *Carnal Knowledge of God*, we spent a week together at her home in Princeton. For each of the days I was there, we had a pattern of eating breakfast together with Bob, working several hours in the morning, eating lunch with Bob, working in the afternoon, taking a walk, making dinner and eating with Bob and working a bit in the evening. (It wasn't lost on me that our *way* of work was very much in keeping with the *subject* on which we were working.) On one of our walks, we were talking about Marilyn's belief that, given the horrendous evils in the world, we couldn't make do with vague and unspecific notions of God. Instead, we needed specific, particular, embodied stories of God's concrete answer to evil's power. God's carnal knowledge wasn't a theoretical knowledge, it was borne out of presence in the very places where violence and oppression occurred. God wasn't vaguely with us, God was with us amidst it all. And this led us to talking about using the lens of solidarity to articulate what God is up to in Jesus Christ.

God incarnate in the person of Jesus chose to live a life with the poor and marginalized, resisting oppression and working for justice. Because of the kind of life Jesus led, and the systems of oppression in which he lived it, he was arrested, tried and executed by the religious and political authorities of his day. This narrative shows that God is radically with us and for us. Because of what God did in the person and life of Jesus, God stands in solidarity when any person or persons oppressed or marginalized by religious, economic and political authorities.[6]

This solidarity of the cross resonates deeply with me because of my own life experience. In 1987, I was part of a delegation that spent a week in Santa Marta, El Salvador. We were part of the "Accompaniment Movement" that sought to have a religious presence to protest the death squads and violence of the US-backed Salvadoran government.[7] One of the most important moments of that trip, one that marked my coming to an adult faith, occurred when I met a woman who was a "delegate of the Word."

6. Williams, "Re-Imagining Jesus."

7. In December of 1980, four US churchwomen were raped and killed by the Salvadoran government. At the time, El Salvador was second only to Israel in the amount of US aid it received. In response to the killings, the Carter Administration cut off aid to El Salvador. When the Reagan Administration came into office, it restored the aid but the warning of what happened when US citizens were killed was felt. Knowing this, many in the Central American solidarity movement in the US took note and the strategy of "accompaniment" was born. Acting in collaboration with Salvadoran colleagues, Witness for Peace, the Chicago Religious Task Force on Central America and many other groups arranged for US citizens to be physically present to accompany Salvadoran villagers as they returned home from refugee camps in Honduras to their former villages that had been wiped out by death squads. Although the returnees were harassed and threatened (bombing nearby so that the ground would shake was one such tactic), the presence of US citizens in the villages provided enough of a disincentive to the Salvadoran forces to refrain from killing anyone.

These Bible study leaders were often the ones whom the death squads targeted in order to terrorize an entire community. While describing her work, she shared that she had lost five children to the civil war, one of whom she had seen tortured to death. When I asked her how it was that she had survived, she said:

> I have been able to survive because I know that in Jesus Christ, God knows in His body what it means to be tortured to death. So my son did not die alone, but being held in God's arms. And in the resurrection, God has said, once and for all, that life and love are stronger than death. So, it doesn't matter what they try to do to me. Even if they kill me, I know that God will resurrect me. And that makes me powerful.[8]

This understanding that the crucifixion of Jesus is an act of God's radical solidarity with the victims of colonization is critically important as we examine the Doctrine of Discovery and the cage of oppression, violence and death. It places God squarely with the oppressed and powerfully for the marginalized. It highlights that the cross represents another aspect of God's carnal knowledge.

In the crucifixion, God knows through the bodily experience of Jesus, what it means to be tortured to death by the empire's representatives. Roman soldiers (the representatives of the colonizing empire) seek to annihilate Jesus and the movement he has inspired. He is tortured and hung on a cross outside the city/body politic with criminals. Empire makes a travesty of his messianic mission. His body is violated—he is beaten, mocked and sexually abused.[9] This bodily violation, this torture, this sexual abuse is what happens to the colonized every day. In the crucifixion, God has firsthand empathy and embodied solidarity with the reality of this omnipresent suffering in peoples' lives, particularly that suffering which is caused by colonization and the present-day representatives of empire.[10]

---

8. Co-Madre of the Mothers of the Disappeared, interview by author, San Salvador, El Salvador, December 28, 1987.

9. There are several places where scholar David Tombs makes the deeply compelling argument that Jesus was sexually abused. One of those is the volume he edited with Jayme R. Reaves and Rocio Figueroa: *When Did We See You Naked?*. The introduction begins, "at the heart of this book is a surprising, even scandalous, claim: that Jesus was a victim of sexual abuse." Although there is no explicit reference to this abuse in the biblical text, I agree with Tombs' conclusion and know Marilyn did too.

10. Fox, "Moving Beyond a Cross Fetish."

In light of these realities of blessing and Empire's cage of sin, my reflections on theodicy these days are shifting away from "why did this happen?" toward questions of "how might we be called to respond?" More and more, I am leaving the why questions unanswered and, instead, focusing on how? How might we claim God and our carnal knowledge of God? And how are we led to act by this claiming?

In response, liturgy and activism are two strategies for claiming the solidarity of God that are both embodied and rooted in carnal knowledge.

7. CLAIMING THE SOLIDARITY OF GOD: LITURGY

Because of the incredible resilience and adaptability of the Doctrine-of-Discovery-cage of oppression and its penchant for wearing down our hope and extinguishing our resistance, it is important that our religious liturgy have strong eschatological roots.[11] We must create liturgy that matters. We must re-ground ourselves through our praying and our ritualizing, in the reality of God's dream for the world. We must practice a sacrament that allows us to embody, if only for the length of our ritual, the eschaton's justice-love.

Amidst Covid, Lyndale United Church of Christ used the following communion liturgy:

> We remember that on the night before Jesus was killed by those who feared him. . . .
> On the night before he was beaten to death by those chanting China virus because he was Asian American. . . .
> On the night before he was suffocated by the knee of a policeman. . . .
> On the night before her trans* body was murdered. . . .
> On the night before he was infected inside an ICE facility. . . .

---

11. In much of my work and ministry, I rely heavily on eschatology. Because of this, I want to be clear about how I understand this critical theological "locus." Eschatology is the systematic reflection on our Christian hope and what is at risk when we do not attain what our hope holds out to us. It is focused on the promised reign of God in all human experience and in all creation. It has powerful implications for both the individual and the community. Eschatology is not primarily concerned with what lies beyond death and outside of history. Eschatology is a practical and vital hope for the world as it is right now and in which we are all participating (Hellwig, "Eschatology," 349). This "here and now" roots our Christian hope in what God is doing to create a more just and liberated world. Nevertheless, precisely because justice is a major part of what we are hoping for, a sense of the timing and pacing of the eschaton is key. Because of this, I align myself with a tradition that celebrates an inaugurated eschatology.

On the night before her body was destroyed by a pipeline....
On the night before he was arrested and crucified....

Jesus sat at table with those he loved. And as they gathered, they did so with laughter and love, they told stories and remembered all they had done together—healing and blessing, creatively resisting, worshiping and celebrating. And as they were celebrating, Jesus took some bread and blessed it and broke it. And to remind them of all that had been and to give them strength for what lay ahead, He said "this is my body, broken open and shared with you. Each time you eat this ordinary bread, remember the extraordinary, transformative power of our lives when they are broken open for justice and love." [Will you lift up whatever food you have and break it and bless it?]

Then he took the cup, the cup that had been raised in toasts and celebration of all the good and great they had done, or at least attempted, and he said, "this is the cup of blessing. Each time you drink of this cup you participate in the promise of new life, here and now, in communion with God." [Will you raise up your glasses and let us toast one another?]

My friends, even as we partake around individual tables, we are united together in the mystical communion that God offers to us. This is a table that is open to all. You do not need to be a member of this church, or any church; For Christ is the host, Christ sets the table and Christ welcomes all.[12]

Highlighting liberating liturgy seems particularly important in a book that honors Marilyn McCord Adams. So much of the time I spent with Marilyn in seminary was planning liturgies or sharing worship. Even as she continued to grapple with theodicy and never stopped asking the why questions, daily prayer and ritual grounded her entire life. And liturgy, prayer and ritual were the things that sent her into the street in joyful protest with her LGBTQ beloveds.

8. CLAIMING THE SOLIDARITY OF GOD: ACTIVISM

After the dean at the Episcopal seminary at Yale signed onto the article in the *Wall Street Journal* titled "Morality and Homosexuality," many

---

12. Rev. Ashley Harness and Rev. Dr. Rebecca Voelkel, Lyndale United Church of Christ Communion Liturgy, Minneapolis, 2020.

LGBTQ folx and allies shared worship with the dean in the mansion that served as the offices for Berkeley Divinity School at Yale.[13] Students had dubbed the worship space "Martha Washington's Living Room" because of the ornate architecture and decorations; the attempts at dialogue only added to the farcical feeling of the whole thing. The dean continued to assert that his heterosexual marriage was threatened by LGBTQ folx and no amount of humor, theologizing, or personal testimony could move him. After this dialogue, the LGBTQ and allied folx moved outside into the snow and the dean and his supporters stayed inside and sipped sherry. With Marilyn in our ranks and embodying the long-standing tradition in LGBTQ settings for camp, the crowd started chanting "sub-optimal linkages" in a mocking tone. Using humor as an embodied way to shift the power dynamic by making fun of that which sought to harm us helped the gathered queer body metabolize the grief and pain caused by one who held power over many of us publishing the article and reinscribing tropes that continued to cause real suffering. Much of good activism serves this dual purpose: to shift the power dynamics and metabolize grief and pain.

9. MY BOOK: *CARNAL KNOWLEDGE OF GOD*

I saw Marilyn a few times after I graduated and began my tenure as a parish pastor, but it was infrequent. So I was surprised and delighted when I was reconnected with her some fifteen years later. The intervening time included her tenure at Oxford and my pastorate and decade-plus work as a leader in the national, multifaith pro-LGBTQ movement. In the intervening time, we had both experienced treachery at the hands of those we had trusted and learned from it. And we had emerged from the experiences still spiritually grappling with theodicy and the call to engender hope and resistance both academically and in pastoral, priestly and prophetic ways.

I asked Marilyn if she might advise me on writing a book on queer, feminist, and liberation theology and movement building. Her response

---

13. A group called The Ramsey Colloquium, of which the dean was a part, first published an article titled "The Homosexual Movement" in a conservative Christian journal. A shortened version of this work was then published in the *Wall Street Journal*, exposing to a wider audience the Colloquium's embrace of discrimination based on sexual orientation. The Ramsey Colloquium, "The Homosexual Movement," 18; The Ramsey Colloquium, "Morality and Homosexuality," sec. 1, 18.

was almost immediate: yes! And, to my heart's delight, she said that what I'd proposed was something she'd always wanted to see written.

We re-engaged almost where we'd left off. In place of a chocolate chip cookie ministry, Marilyn invited me to the home she shared with her beloved, Bob, in Princeton for a week of conversation, writing and editing interwoven with delicious food she'd prepared and walks throughout town. I left with a solid outline and understanding of where I was headed. And in the subsequent five months, I sent Marilyn chapter after chapter. Each would take me several weeks but in each case she would receive, edit and send it back to me within a twenty-four hour period.

There is a kind of intimacy in writing something together and I will always cherish the time I shared with Marilyn. As we, her former students and mentees, honor Marilyn McCord Adams, there are many things on which to focus. But, for me, her primary lesson was that of holding our scholarship in ongoing conversation with the priestly, pastoral and prophetic roles of church leadership. In order to hold this conversation, she demanded an academic rigor that was not just informed by the bodily realities of real-life Christians but an academic rigor that lived in service to and was guided by Christian community. Don't get me wrong, Marilyn did not suffer fools lightly. She was one of the smartest people I've ever met, but she kept her mind deeply attached to and embedded in her body and allowed her heart and soul to guide her.

Carnal Knowledge of God: Embodied Love and the Movement for Justice came out about two weeks after Marilyn died. I still hold grief that she didn't live to see that I dedicated the book to her. In the dedication, I quote her as telling me often, "be outrageous for the gospel's sake and fiercely trust in the goodness of God in the face of evil." My prayer is that my continued grappling, delighting, en-joying carnal knowledge of God and the justice and love-making to which it calls me is a fitting embodiment of outrageousness for the gospel's sake and a claiming of God's goodness in the face of evil.

Contributors

Michael Barnwell is Professor of Philosophy and Director of the University Honors Program at Niagara University. He earned both a Master of Divinity (1999) and a dual PhD in Philosophy and Religious Studies (2005) from Yale University. At Yale, he met Marilyn McCord Adams and was privileged to pursue his doctoral studies under her direction. McCord Adams served as his dissertation supervisor, even after she left Yale for Oxford University. The thesis was eventually published as a book titled *The Problem of Negligent Omissions: Medieval Action Theories to the Rescue* (Brill, 2010). He has published numerous articles on action theory, soul-making theodicy, and medieval philosophy with special focus on Anselm and Aquinas. Recently, he has begun to innovate "Philosophical Business Consulting" in which the tools of philosophy can be applied in the business world.

Wendy Petersen Boring is Associate Professor of History and Religious Studies at Willamette University. She teaches courses on medieval history, women and gender studies, environmental ethics, climate change, embodiment, contemplative studies, and the inner life of activism. She holds a PhD from Yale University in Religious Studies and a Master of Arts in Religion from Yale Divinity School.

Shannon Craigo-Snell is Professor of Theology at Louisville Presbyterian Theological Seminary, Kentucky, where she teaches systematic and constructive theologies. She has authored and co-authored several books, including *No Innocent Bystanders: Becoming an Ally in the Struggle for Justice* (Westminster John Knox, 2017), written with Christopher Doucot, and *The Empty Church: Theater, Theology, and Bodily Hope* (Oxford University Press, 2014). She has also published numerous articles, book chapters, and essays. She is an ordained minister in the Presbyterian Church (USA).

Richard Cross is John A. O'Brien Professor of Philosophy at the University of Notre Dame, a post he has held since 2007. Prior to that, he was a Fellow of Oriel College, Oxford. He specializes in medieval philosophy and theology, with a particular focus on Duns Scotus. He is currently completing a sequence of five volumes on the metaphysics of the Incarnation in Western thought from 1050 to 1700, which includes the recent *Communicatio Idiomatum: Reformation Christological Debates* (Oxford University Press, 2019), and hopes to do something similar for the doctrine of the Trinity during the same period, in relation to different theories of unity and identity.

Jesse Couenhoven is Professor of Moral Theology in the Humanities and Theology departments at Villanova University. His books *Stricken by Sin, Cured by Christ* (Oxford University Press, 2013) and *Predestination: A Guide for the Perplexed* (T. & T. Clark, 2018) offer historical and constructive perspectives on the limits of human agency and its relation to divine agency. His work engages moral and medical perspectives on sin and disorders, and normative and therapeutic perspectives on freedom and forgiveness. He is currently directing the "Collaborative Inquiries in Christian Theological Anthropology" grant, which is funding science-engaged research projects and educational workshops from 2020–23. He studied under Marilyn McCords Adams during the course of two degrees at Yale, where her work was for him a model of analytically rigorous and historically informed feminist theology.

Christine Helmer holds the Peter B. Ritzma Chair of Humanities at Northwestern University, where she is also Professor of German and Religious Studies. She is the recipient of an honorary doctorate in theology from the University of Helsinki (2017). She is the author of numerous publications in the area of her theological interests, including biblical theology, German intellectual history, and philosophical theology, most recently two edited volumes: *The Medieval Luther* (Mohr Siebeck, 2020) and *Truth-Telling and Other Ecclesial Practices of Resistance* (Lexington/Fortress, 2021). Her most recent book, *How Luther Became the Reformer* (Westminster John Knox, 2019) was awarded a gold medal in theology in the Illuminations Book Awards 2020 Competition.

Ruthanna B. Hooke is Associate Dean of Students and Associate Professor of Homiletics at Virginia Theological Seminary, and Program Director of "Deep Calls to Deep," a program to strengthen Episcopal preaching. She has published numerous articles on preaching and the body, and is the author of *Transforming Preaching* (Church Publishing, 2010). Her current book project is *Sacramental Presence: An Embodied Theology of Preaching*, which explores the preacher's bodily presence in dialogue with sacramental theology. She is a member of the planning committee of the Homiletics and Biblical Studies Section of the Society of Biblical Literature. A Designated Linklater Voice Teacher, she teaches courses in homiletics, voice, performance, and biblical storytelling. An ordained Episcopal priest, she serves as affiliated clergy at Immanuel Church-on-the-Hill, Alexandria, Virginia, and leads voice workshops for liturgical leaders.

JT Paasch teaches math, logic, and philosophy for the School of Continuing Studies at Georgetown University. He has published articles on medieval philosophy and theology, and is the author of *Divine Production in Late Medieval Trinitarian Theology* (Oxford University Press, 2012). He is also a computer scientist working in formal methods and programming languages. His current research focuses on the intersection of type theory and modality in ancient and medieval logical systems.

Sarah K. Pinnock received her PhD in Philosophy of Religion from Yale University supervised by Marilyn McCord Adams. She is currently the Jennie Farris Railey King Professor of Religion at Trinity University, and she received a Fulbright fellowship at the University of Latvia Faculty of Theology in 2006–7. Her book length publications include *Beyond Theodicy: Jewish and Continental Thinkers Respond to the Holocaust* (SUNY Press, 2002), and two edited volumes, *The Theology of Dorothee Soelle* (Trinity Press International, 2003), and *Facing Death: Confronting Mortality in the Holocaust and Ourselves* (University of Wisconsin Press, 2017).

Danielle Tumminio Hansen is an Episcopal priest and the Assistant Professor of Practical Theology and Spiritual Care at Emory University. She is the author of *Conceiving Family: A Practical Theology of Surrogacy and Self* (Baylor University Press, 2019), *Expecting Jesus: Meditations for Advent and Christmas* (Forward Movement, 2014), and *God and Harry Potter at Yale: Teaching Faith and Fantasy Fiction in an Ivy League Classroom* (Unlocking Press, 2010), as well as a forthcoming book on language and sexual violations (Routledge). Her articles on the intersection of theology and contemporary life have appeared in a wide range of academic and popular outlets, including *Modern Theology*, *Journal of Pastoral Theology*, *The Guardian*, and CNN's Belief Blog.

Rebecca Voelkel is an ordained minister in the United Church of Christ and currently serves as the Director of the Center for Sustainable Justice. She is the author of numerous books, *Carnal Knowledge of God: Embodied Love and the Movement for Justice* (Fortress, 2017); *To Do Justice: A Study of Welcoming Congregations* (www.welcomingresources.org/To_Do_Justice.pdf); *A Time To Build Up* (www.welcomingresources.org/ATimeToBuildUp.pdf); and *Preventing Sexual Abuse: A Course of Study for Teenagers* (Pilgrim, 1996), as well as numerous articles and sermons, which have been published in journals such as *Spirit Currents*, *The Journal of Religion and Abuse*, *Creating Change*, and *Parenting for Peace and Justice*.

Scott M. Williams (DPhil, Oxford) is Associate Professor of Philosophy at the University of North Carolina Asheville. His publications focus on medieval philosophy and theology, and the philosophy and theology of disability. He is currently working on a book, *Henry of Ghent on the Trinity*, and has published recently on the Trinity in contemporary philosophy of religion and in patristic theology. He co-edited a recent issue of the journal *TheoLogica* (2020) on Conciliar Trinitarianism, and edited *Disability in Medieval Christian Philosophy and Theology* (Routledge, 2020). He is also an avid gardener.

Marilyn McCord Adams's Bibliography

BOOKS

Christ and Horrors: The Coherence of Christology. Current Issues in Theology. Cambridge: Cambridge University Press, 2006.
Horrendous Evils and the Goodness of God. Cornell Studies in the Philosophy of Religion. Ithaca, NY: Cornell University Press, 1999.
Housing the Powers: Medieval Debates about Dependence on God. With Cecilia Trifogli. Edited by Robert Merrihew Adams. Oxford: Oxford University Press, 2022.
Opening to God: Childlike Prayers for Adults. Louisville: Westminster John Knox, 2008.
Some Later Medieval Theories of the Eucharist: Thomas Aquinas, Giles of Rome, Duns Scotus, and William Ockham. Oxford: Oxford University Press, 2010.
What Sort of Human Nature? Medieval Philosophy and the Systematics of Christology. The Aquinas Lecture, 1999. Milwaukee: Marquette University Press, 1999.
William Ockham. 2 vols. Notre Dame: University of Notre Dame, 1987.
Wrestling for Blessing. London: Darton, Longman, & Todd, 2005.

EDITED, TRANSLATED, AND ANNOTATED WORKS

Guest editor. *Faith and Philosophy: Journal for the Society of Christian Philosophers* 13.4 (1996). Theological Contributions to Theodicy.
McCord Adams, Marilyn, and Robert Merrihew Adams, eds. *The Problem of Evil*. Oxford: Oxford University Press, 1990.

Ockham, William. *Predestination, God's Foreknowledge, and Future Contingents.* Translated with introduction, notes, and bibliographies by Marilyn McCord Adams and Norman Kretzmann. New York: Appleton-Century-Crofts, 1969. Second edition with new introduction by Marilyn McCord Adams. Indianapolis: Hackett, 1983.

Paul of Venice. *On the Truth and Falsity of Propositions and On the Significatum of a Proposition.* Edited by Francesco del Punta. Translation and annotations by Marilyn McCord Adams. Oxford: Oxford University Press, 1977.

Wolter, Allan B. *The Philosophical Theology of John Duns Scotus.* Edited by Marilyn McCord Adams. Ithaca, NY: Cornell University Press, 1990.

ARTICLES AND BOOK CHAPTERS

"Aesthetic Goodness as a Solution to the Problem of Evil." In *God, Truth, and Reality: Essays in Honor of John Hick*, edited by Arvind Sharma, 46–61. London: Macmillan, 1993.

"Afterword." In *Encountering Evil*, edited by Stephen T. Davis, 191–203. 2nd ed. Louisville: Westminster John Knox, 2001.

"Afterword." In *The Call for Women Bishops*, edited by Harriet Harris and Jane Shaw, 193–96. London: SPCK, 2004.

"Aquinas on the Soul: Some Intriguing Conundrums." In *Aquinas's Summa Theologiae*, edited by Jeffrey Hause, 88–110. Cambridge: Cambridge University Press, 2018.

"Arguments from Tradition." In *Christian Holiness and Human Sexuality: A Study Guide for Episcopalians*, edited by Gary R. Hall and Ruth A. Meyers, 13–16. New York: Church Publishing, 2011.

"Aristotle and the Sacrament of the Altar: A Crisis in Medieval Theology." *Canadian Journal of Philosophy Supplementary Volume* 17 (1991) 195–249.

"Biting and Chomping Our Salvation! Eucharistic Presence, Radically Understood." In *Redemptive Transformation in Practical Theology*, edited by Dana Wright and John D. Kuentzel, 69–94. Grand Rapids: Eerdmans, 2004.

"Bodies in Their Places: Multiple Location according to John Duns Scotus." In *Johannes Duns Scotus, 1308–2008: Die Philosophisches Perspektiven Seines Werken, Proceedings of the Quadruple Congress on John Duns Scotus, Part III*, edited by Ludger Honnefelder et al., 139–49. Münster: Aschendorff, 2010.

"Can Creatures Create?" *Philosophia* 34 (2006) 101–28.

"Chalcedonian Christology: A Christian Solution to the Problem of Evil." In *Philosophy and Theological Discourse*, edited by Stephen T. Davis, 173–98. London: Macmillan, 1997.

"The Coherence of Christology: God Enmattered and Enmattering." *Princeton Seminary Bulletin* 26 (2005) 157–79.

"Common Nature and Instants of Nature: Ockham's Critique of Scotus Reconsidered." *Veritas* 14 (1995) 55–67.

"Courtesy, Human and Divine." *Sewanee Theological Review* 47 (2004) 145–63.

"*Cur Deus Homo*? Priorities among the Reasons." *Faith and Philosophy* 21 (2004) 1–18.

"Did Ockham Know of Material and Strict Implication? A Reconsideration." *Franciscan Studies* 33 (1973) 5–37.

"Dissolution and Integrity in the Fourteenth Century." In *Tradition and Ecstacy: Agony in the Fourteenth Century*, edited by Nancy van Deusen, 99–108. Ottawa: Institute of Mediaeval Music, 1997.

"Divine Justice, Divine Love, and the Life to Come." *Crux* 13 (1976–77) 12–18.

"Duns Scotus on the Dignities of Human Nature." In *Interpreting Duns Scotus: Critical Essays*, edited by Giorgio Pini, 122–48. Cambridge: Cambridge University Press, 2022.

"Duns Scotus on the Female Gender." In *The Oxford Handbook of Theology: Sex and Gender*, edited by Adrian Thatcher, 255–70. Oxford: Oxford University Press, 2015.

"Duns Scotus on the Goodness of God." *Faith and Philosophy* 4 (1987) 486–505.

"Duns Scotus on the Will as Rational Potency." In *Via Scoti: Methodologica ad mentem Joannis Duns Scoti*, edited by Leonardo Sileo, 839–54. Roma: PAA–Edizioni Antonianum, 1995.

With Allan B. Wolter. "Duns Scotus' Parisian Proof for the Existence of God." *Franciscan Studies* 42 (1982) 248–321.

"Elegant Necessity, Prayerful Disputation: Method in *Cur Deus Homo*." *Studia Anselmiana* (1999) 367–96.

"The Episcopacy of All Believers." *Modern Believing* 51 (2010) 9–28.

"Essential Orders and Sacramental Causality." In *Proceedings of "The Quadruple Congress" on John Duns Scotus, Part I*, edited by Mary Beth Ingham and Oleg Bychov, 191–205. Münster: Aschendorff, 2010.

"Eucharistic Drama, Rehearsing for a Revolution." In *Theatrical Theology: Explorations in Performing the Faith*, edited by Wesley Vander Lugt and Trevor A. Hart, 203–23. Eugene: Cascade, 2014.

"Eucharistic Real Presence: Some Scholastic Background to Luther's Debate with Zwingli." In *The Medieval Luther*, edited by Christine Helmer, 65–90. Studies in the Late Middle Ages, Humanism, and the Reformation 117. Tübingen: Mohr Siebeck, 2020.

"Evil and the God Who Does Nothing in Particular." In *Religion and Morality*, edited by D. Z. Phillips, 107–31. London: Macmillan, 1996.

"Evil as Nothing: Contrasting Construals in Boethius and Anselm." *The Modern Schoolman* 89 (2012) 131–45; Reprinted in *Anselmo e la 'Nuova' Europa*, edited by Guilio Cipollone and Maria Silvia Boari, 57–75. Miscellanea Historiae Pontificiae 70. Rome: Gregorian Biblical Press, 2014.

"Faithfulness in Crisis: The Follies of the Windsor Report." In *Gays and the Future of Anglicanism*, edited by Andrew Lindzey and Richard Kirker, 70–80. Winchester: O Books, 2005.

"Fides Quaerens Intellectum: St. Anselm's Method in Philosophical Theology." *Faith and Philosophy* 9 (1992) 409–35; Slightly revised version reprinted as "Anselm on Faith and Reason." In *The Cambridge Companion to Anselm*, edited by Brian Leftow and Brian Davies, 32–59. Cambridge: Cambridge University Press, 2004.

"Final Causality and Explanation in Scotus' *De Primo Principio*." In *Nature in Medieval European Thought: Some Approaches East and West*, edited by Chumaru Koyama, 153–83. Leiden: Brill, 2000.

"For Better for Worse Solidarity." In *Christ and the Created Order*, edited by Andrew B. Torrance and Thomas H. McCall, 167–78. Grand Rapids: Zondervan, 2018.

"Forgiveness: A Christian Model." *Faith and Philosophy* 8 (1991) 277–304; Reprinted in *Christian Theism and Moral Philosophy*, edited by Michael Beaty et al., 77–106. Macon: Mercer University Press, 1998.

"Friendliness: Human and Divine." In *Rethinking the Medieval Legacy for Contemporary Theology*, edited by Anselm K. Min, 43–70. Notre Dame: University of Notre Dame Press, 2014.

"Genuine Agency, Somehow Shared: The Holy Spirit and Other Gifts." *Oxford Studies in Medieval Philosophy* 1 (2013) 23–60.

"God and Evil among the Philosophers." *Proceedings and Addresses of the APA* 85 (2011) 65–80; Reprinted in *Portraits of American Philosophy*, edited by Stephen Cahn, 129–50. Lanham: Rowman & Littlefield, 2013.

"God and Evil: Polarities of a Problem." *Philosophical Studies* 69 (1993) 167–86.

"God Because of Evil: A Pragmatic Argument from Evil for Belief in God." In *The Blackwell Companion to the Problem of Evil*, edited by Justin McBrayer and Daniel Howard-Snyder, 160–73. Chichester: Wiley-Blackwell, 2013.

"Hell and the God of Justice." *Religious Studies* 11 (1975) 433–47.

"History of Philosophy as Tutor to Christian Philosophy." In *The Question of Christian Philosophy Today*, edited by Francis J. Ambrosio, 37–60. New York: Fordham University Press, 1999.

"Horrendous Evils and the Goodness of God." *Proceedings of the Aristotelian Society, Supplementary Volume* 63 (1989), 299–310; Reprinted in *The Problem of Evil*, edited with an Introduction by Marilyn McCord Adams and Robert Merrihew Adams, 209–21. Oxford: Oxford University Press, 1990; Reprinted in *Readings in the Philosophy of Religion*, edited by Kelly James Clark, 219–26. Toronto: Broadview, 2000.

"Horrors in Theological Context." *Revista Portuguesa de Filosofia* 57 (2001) 871–80; Also published in *Scottish Journal of Theology* 55 (2002) 468–79.

"Horrors: To What End?" In *Alternative Concepts of God: Essays in the Metaphysics of the Divine*, edited by Yujin Nagasawa and Andrei Buckareff, 128–44. Oxford: Oxford University Press, 2016.

"Hurricane Spirit, Toppling Taboos." In *Ourselves, Our Souls & Bodies*, edited by Charles Hefling, 129–41. Cambridge, MA: Cowley, 1996.

"Ignorance, Instrumentality, Compensation, and the Problem of Evil." *Sophia* 52 (2013) 7–26.

"The Immaculate Conception of the Blessed Virgin Mary: A Thought Experiment in Medieval Philosophical Theology." *Harvard Theological Review* 103 (2010) 133–59.

"The Indwelling of the Holy Spirit: Some Alternative Models." In *Christian Philosophical Perspectives on Human Nature*, edited by J. Prudhomme and Peter Weigel, 83–99. New York: Lang, 2015.

"In Praise of Blasphemy." *Philosophia* 36 (2003) 1–17.

"Introduction." In *Peter Abelard: Ethical Writings—Ethics and Dialogue between a Philosopher, a Jew, and a Christian*, translated by Paul V. Spade, vii–xxvi. Indianapolis: Hackett, 1995.

"Intuitive Cognition, Certainty, and Skepticism in William Ockham." *Traditio* 26 (1970) 389–98.

"Is the Existence of God a 'Hard' Fact?" *Philosophical Review* 76 (1967) 492–503; Reprinted in *God, Foreknowledge, and Freedom*, edited with an introduction by John Martin Fischer, 74–85. Stanford: Stanford University Press, 1989; Reprinted in *Readings in Philosophy of Religion*, edited by Baruch A. Brody, 437–45. 2nd ed. Hoboken, NJ: Prentice Hall, 1992.

With Rega Wood. "Is To Will It as Bad as To Do It? The Fourteenth Century Debate." *Franciscan Studies* 41 (1981) 5–60.

"Julian of Norwich on the Tender Loving Care of Mother Jesus." In *Our Knowledge of God: Essays on Natural and Philosophical Theology*, edited by K. J. Clark, 203–19. Dordrecht: Kluwer Academic, 1992.

"Julian of Norwich: Problems of Evil and the Seriousness of Sin." *Philosophia* 39 (2011) 433–47.

"Liberal and Proud of It!" *Modern Believing* 55 (2014) 331–34.

"Love of Learning, Reality of God." In *Philosophers Speak of God*, edited by Thomas V. Morris, 137–61. Oxford: Oxford University Press, 1994.

"Mascot or Judge: God and the Mores of Church and Society." In *God and the Moral Life*, edited by Myriam Renaud and Joshua Daniel, 171–84. New York: Routledge, 2018.

With Allan B. Wolter. "Memory and Intuition: A Focal Debate in Fourteenth Century Cognitive Psychology: Introduction, edition, and translation of Scotus' Ordinatio IV, d.45, q.3." *Franciscan Studies* 53 (1993) 175–230.

"The Metaphysical Size Gap." *Sewanee Theological Review* 47 (2004) 129–44.

"The Metaphysics of the Incarnation in Some Fourteenth Century Franciscans." In *Essays Honoring Allan B. Wolter*, edited by William A. Frank and Girard J. Etzkorn, 21–57. St. Bonaventure, NY: Franciscan Institute, 1985.

"The Metaphysics of the Trinity in Some Fourteenth Century Franciscans." *Franciscan Studies* 66 (2008) 101–68.

"Mit dem Gott zurechtkommen, den wir haben." In *Logische Brillanz—Ruchlose Denkungsart? Möglichkeiten und Grenzen der Diskussion des Problems des Übels in der analytishen Religionsphilosphie*, edited by Oliver J. Wiertz, 273–98. Münster: Aschendorff, 2021.

"A Modest Proposal? Caveat Emptor! Moral Theory and Problems of Evil." In *Ethics and the Problem of Evil*, edited by James Sterba, 9–26. Bloomington: Indiana University Press, 2017.

"Neglected Values, Shrunken Agents, Happy Endings: A Reply to Rogers." *Faith and Philosophy* 19 (2002) 487–505.

"Ockham on Final Causality: Muddying the Waters." *Franciscan Studies* 56 (1998) 1–46.

"Ockham on Identity and Distinction." *Franciscan Studies* 36 (1976) 5–74.

"Ockham on the Soul: Elusive Proofs, Dialectical Persuasions." *American Catholic Philosophical Quarterly* 75 (2002) 55–97.

"Ockham on Truth." *Medioevo* 16 (1990) 143–72.

"Ockham on Will, Nature, and Morality." In *Cambridge Companion to Ockham*, edited by Paul Vincent Spade, 245–72. Cambridge: Cambridge University Press, 1999.

"Ockham's Individualisms." In *Die Gegenwart Ockhams*, edited by W. Vossenkuhl and R. Schonberger, 3–24. Weinheim: VCH Verlagsgesellschaft, 1990.

"Ockham's Nominalism and Unreal Entities." *Philosophical Review* 86 (1977) 144–76.

"Ockham's Theory of Natural Signification." *Monist* 61 (1978) 444–59.

"The Ordination of Women: Some Theological Implications." In *Looking Forward, Looking Backward: Forty Years of Women's Ordination*, edited by Fredrica Harris Thompsett, 64–73. New York: Morehouse, 2014.

"Philosophy and the Bible: The Areopagus Speech." *Faith and Philosophy* 9 (1992) 135–50.

"Plantinga on 'Felix Culpa': Analysis and Critique." *Faith and Philosophy* 25 (2008) 123–40.

"Powerless Causes: The Case of Sacramental Causality." In *Thinking about Causes: From Greek Philosophy to Modern Physics*, edited by Peter Machamer and Gereon Wolters, 47–76. Pittsburgh: University of Pittsburg Press, 2007.

"Powers versus Laws: God and the Order of the World according to Some Late Medieval Aristotelians." In *The Divine Order, the Human Order, and the Order of Nature: Historical Perspectives*, edited by Eric Watkins, 3–26. Oxford: Oxford University Press, 2013.

"Prayer as 'the Lifeline of Theology.'" *Anglican Theological Review* 98 (2016) 271–83.

"Praying the Proslogion." In *The Rationality of Belief and the Plurality of Faith*, edited by Thomas Senor, 13–39. Ithaca, NY: Cornell University Press, 1995.

"The Primacy of Christ." *Sewanee Theological Review* 47 (2004) 164–80.

"The Problem of Hell: A Problem of Evil for Christians." In *Reasoned Faith: A Festschrift for Norman Kretzmann*, edited by Eleonore Stump, 301–27. Ithaca, NY: Cornell University Press, 1993; Reprinted in *Readings in the Philosophy of Religion*, edited by Kelly James Clark, 317–27. Toronto: Broadview, 2000.

"Problems of Evil: More Advice to Christian Philosophers." *Faith and Philosophy* 5 (1988) 121–43.

"Questioning and Disputing Authority: Medieval Methods for Modern Preaching." *The Expository Times* 17 (2006) 231–36.

"Re-reading *De Grammatico*, or Anselm's Introduction to Aristotle's *Categories*." *Documenti e Studi sulla Tradizione Filosofica Medievale* 11 (2000) 83–112.

"Recent Developments in the Anglican Communion, or Ecumenism Misapplied." *Modern Believing* 52 (2011) 4–14.

"Redemptive Suffering: A Christian Solution to the Problem of Evil." In *Rationality, Religious Belief, and Moral Commitment*, edited by Robert Audi and William Wainwright, 248–67. Ithaca, NY: Cornell University Press, 1986; Reprinted in *The Problem of Evil: Selected Readings*, edited by Michael L. Peterson, 210–32. 2nd ed. Notre Dame: University of Notre Dame, 2017.

"Relations, Subsistence, and Inherence, or Was Ockham a Nestorian in Christology?" *Nous* 16 (1982) 62–75.

"The Resurrection of the Body according to Three Medieval Aristotelians: Thomas Aquinas, John Duns Scotus, William Ockham." *Philosophical Topics* 20 (1992) 1–33.

"Reviving Philosophical Theology: Some Medieval Models." In *Miscellanea Mediaevalia, Band 26: Was ist Philosophie im Mittelalter?*, edited by Jan A. Aertsen and Andreas Speer, 60–68. Berlin: de Gruyter, 1998.

"The Role of Miracles in the Structure of Luke–Acts." In *Hermes and Athena*, edited by Eleonore Stump and Thomas Flint, 235–73. Notre Dame: University of Notre Dame, 1993.

"Romancing the Good: God and the Self according to St. Anselm of Canterbury." In *The Augustinian Tradition*, edited by Gareth Matthews, 91–109. Berkeley: University of California Press, 1998.

"Sanctifying Matter." In *Knowing Creation*, edited by Andrew B. Torrance and Thomas H. McCall, 171–80. Grand Rapids: Zondervan, 2018.

"Satisfying Mercy: Anselm's *Cur Deus Homo* Reconsidered." *The Modern Schoolman* 72 (1995) 91–108.

"Sceptical Realism: Faith and Reason in Collaboration." In *Fides et Ratio: Friends or Foes in the New Millenium*, edited by Anthony Fisher and Hayden Ramsey, 1–18. Adelaide: Australasian Theological Forum, 2004.

"Scotus and Ockham on the Connection of the Virtues." In *John Duns Scotus: Metaphysics and Ethics*, edited by Ludger Honnefelder et al., 499–522. Leiden: Brill, 1996.

"Scotus on the Metaphysics of Habits." In the *Proceedings of the ACPA* 88 (2014) 71–83.

"Separation and Reversal in Luke–Acts." In *Philosophy and the Christian Faith*, edited by Thomas Morris, 92–117. Notre Dame: University of Notre Dame, 1988.

"Sex and the Sins of the Fathers: Fertility Religion versus Human Rights." In *Radical Christian Voices and Practice: Essays in Honour of Christopher Rowland*, edited by Zoë Bennett and David B. Gowler, 241–55. Oxford: Oxford University Press, 2012.

"Sexuality without Taboos." In *The Bible, the Church, and Homosexuality*, edited by Nicholas Coulton, 36–48. London: Dartman, Longman, & Todd, 2005.

"Shaking the Foundations: LGBT Bishops and Blessings in the Fullness of Time." *Anglican Theological Review* 90 (2008) 713–32.

"A Shameless Defense of a Liberal Church." *Modern Believing* 48 (2007) 25–37.

"Showings to Share: The Mystical Theology of Julian of Norwich." In *The Renewal of Mystical Theology: Essays in Memory of John N. Jones (1964–2012)*, edited by Bernard McGinn, 88–108. New York: Herder & Herder, 2017.

"Sin as Uncleanness." *Philosophical Perspectives* 5 (1991) 1–27; Reprinted in *A Reader in Contemporary Philosophical Theology*, edited by Oliver Crisp, 254–77. London: T. & T. Clark, 2009.

"Some Paradoxes of Pain for Rational Agency." In *Philosophy of Suffering: Metaphysics, Value, and Normativity*, edited by David Bain et al., 278–94. London: Routledge, 2019.

"St. Anselm on Evil: De Casu Diaboli." *Documenti e Studi sulla Tradizione Filosofica Medievale* 3 (1992) 423–51.

"St. Anselm on the Goodness of God." *Medioevo* 13 (1987) 75–102.

"St. Anselm on the Goodness of God." In *St. Anselm and His Legacy*, edited by Giles E. M. Gasper and Ian Logan, 360–84. Toronto: Pontifical Institute for Medieval Studies, 2012.

"St. Anselm on Truth." *Documenti e Studi sulla Tradizione Filosofica Medievale* 1 (1990) 353–72.

"The Structure of Ockham's Moral Theory." *Franciscan Studies* 46 (1986) 1–35.

"Symbolic Value and the Problem of Evil: Honor and Shame." In *Interpretation in Religion*, edited by Shlomo Biderman and Ben–Ami Scharfstein, 259–82. Leiden: Brill, 1992.

"Theodicy without Blame." *Philosophical Topics* 16 (1988) 215–45.

"Things versus 'Hows,' or Ockham on Predication and Ontology." In *How Things Are: Studies in Predication and the History of Philosophy and Science*, edited by James Bogen and James E. McGuire, 175–88. Dordrecht: Reidel, 1985.

"Trinitarian Friendship: Same Gender Models of Godly Love in Richard of St. Victor and Aelred of Rievaulx." In *Theology and Sexuality: Ancient and Contemporary Readings*, edited by Eugene F. Rogers Jr., 322–39. Hoboken, NJ: Blackwell, 2001.

"Truth and Reconciliation." In *The Theologians in Their Own Words*, edited by Derek Nelson et al., 15–33. Minneapolis: Fortress, 2013.

"Unfit for Purpose, or Why a Pan-Anglican Covenant Is a Very Bad Idea." *Modern Believing* 49 (2008) 23–45.

"Universal Salvation: A Reply to Mr. Bettis." *Religious Studies* 7 (1971) 245–49.

"Universals in the Early Fourteenth Century." In *Cambridge History of Medieval Philosophy*, edited by N. Kretzmann and A. Kenny, 411–39. Cambridge: Cambridge University Press, 1982.

"Was Anselm a Realist? The Monologium." *Franciscan Studies* 32 (1972) 5–14.

"Was Ockham a Humean about Efficient Causality?" *Franciscan Studies* 39 (1979) 5–48.

"What about Hylomorphism? Some Medieval and Recent Ruminations on Swinburne's Dualism." In *Reason and Faith: Themes from Richard Swinburne*, edited by Jeffrey Brower and Michael Bergmann, 220–43. Oxford: Oxford University Press, 2016.

"What Does Ockham Mean by 'Supposition'?" *Notre Dame Journal of Formal Logic* 28 (1976) 375–91.

"What Wideness, Whose Strictness? The Scope and Limits of Divine Love for Humankind." In *Love Divine and Human: Contemporary Essays in Systematic and Philosophical Theology*, edited by Oliver D. Crisp et al., 113–26. London: T. & T. Clark, 2020.

"What's Metaphysically Special about Supposits? Some Medieval Variations on Aristotelian Substance." *Aristotelian Society Supplementary Volume* 79 (2005) 15–52.

"What's Wrong with the Ontotheological Error?" *Analytic Theology* 2 (2014) 1–12.

"Which Is It? Religious Pluralism or Global Theology?" In *Religious Pluralism and the Modern World: An Ongoing Engagement with John Hick*, edited by Sharada Sugirtharaja, 34–44. London: Palgrave Macmillan, 2011.

"Why Bodies as Well as Souls in the Life to Come?" In *The Science of Being as Being: Metaphysical Investigations*, edited by Gregory T. Doolan, 264–97. Washington, DC: Catholic University of America Press, 2012.

"William Ockham on Making the Most of Morality, While Keeping Morality in Its Place." *Ex Corde* 1 (2009) 28–50.

"William Ockham: Voluntarist or Naturalist." In *Studies in Medieval Philosophy*, edited by John Wippel, 219–48. Washington, DC: Catholic University of America Press, 1987.

With Cecilia Trifogli. "Whose Thought Is It? The Soul and the Subject of Action in Some Thirteenth and Fourteenth Century Philosophers." *Philosophy and Phenomenological Research* 85 (2012) 624–47.

ENCYCLOPEDIA AND DICTIONARY ARTICLES

"Anselm of Canterbury, St." In *The Cambridge Dictionary of Philosophy*, edited by Robert Audi, 26–28. Cambridge: Cambridge University Press, 1995.

"Anselm of Canterbury, St." In *Companion to Metaphysics*, edited by E. Sosa and J. Kim, 12–13. Oxford: Basil Blackwell, 1995.

"Anselm of Canterbury, St." In *The Oxford Companion to Philosophy*, edited by Ted Honderich, 37–38. Oxford: Oxford University Press, 1995.

"Hell." In *Routledge Encyclopedia of Philosophy*, edited by Edward Craig, 4:329–33. Routledge & Kegan Paul, 1998.

"Hylomorphism." In *The Oxford Companion to Philosophy*, edited by Ted Honderich, 384–85. Oxford: Oxford University Press, 1995.

"Ockham's Razor." In *The Oxford Companion to Philosophy*, edited by Ted Honderich, 633. Oxford: Oxford University Press, 1995.

"Ockham's Razor, Parsimony, Principle of." In *The Cambridge Dictionary of Philosophy*, edited by Robert Audi, 545. Cambridge: Cambridge University Press, 1995.

"Ockham, William." In *The Cambridge Dictionary of Philosophy*, edited by Robert Audi, 543–45. Cambridge: Cambridge University Press, 1995.

"Ockham, William." In *Companion to Metaphysics*, edited by E. Sosa and J. Kim, 371–73. Oxford: Basil Blackwell, 1995.

"Ockham, William of." In *Companion to Epistemology*, edited by Jonathan Dancy and Ernest Sosa, 313–14. Oxford: Basil Blackwell, 1992.

"The Problem of Evil." In *Routledge Encyclopedia of Philosophy*, edited by Edward Craig, 3:466–72. New York: Routledge & Kegan Paul, 1998.

"William Ockham." In vol. 2 of *Handbook of Metaphysics and Ontology*, edited by Hans Burkhardt and Barry Smith, 939–43. Munich: Philosophia, 1991.

"William Ockham." In *The Oxford Companion to Philosophy*, edited by Ted Honderich, 633. Oxford: Oxford University Press, 1995.

SERMONS, PRAYERS, AND BIBLICAL COMMENTARY

"Amos 6:1a, 4–7." In *Feasting on the Word: Additional Essays, Year C*. Louisville: Westminster John Knox, 2013. https://www.wjkbooks.com/Content/Site117/Basics/59975YearCaddit_00000032209.pdf.

"And Finally . . . Really Present Relationship!" *Expository Times* 126 (February 2015) 258.

"And Immediately." *Questioning and Disputing*, November 24, 2016. https://questioninganddisputing.wordpress.com/2016/11/24/and-immediately/.

"Arranged Marriage." *Questioning and Disputing*, November 24, 2016. https://questioninganddisputing.wordpress.com/2016/11/24/arranged-marriage/.

"The Backside of God." *The Expository Times* 116 (September 2005) 418–20.

"The B-I-B-L-E." *Questioning and Disputing*, November 22, 2016. https://questioninganddisputing.wordpress.com/2016/11/22/the-b-i-b-l-e/.

"Blessed Fruit." *The Expository Times* 123 (November 2012) 79–80.

"Blessed Trinity, Society of Friends." *The Expository Times* 117 (May 2006) 331–32.

"Brazen Deference." *Questioning and Disputing*, November 23, 2016. https://questioninganddisputing.wordpress.com/2016/11/23/brazen-deference/.

"Bullying." *Questioning and Disputing*, November 23, 2016. https://questioninganddisputing.wordpress.com/2016/11/23/bullying/.

"A Child's Christmas." *The Expository Times* 123 (November 2011) 83–84.

"Confession." In *Race and Prayer: Collected Voices, Many Dreams*, edited by Malcolm Boyd and Chester Talton, 3. Harrisburg, PA: Morehouse, 2003.

"Consenting Adults!" *The Expository Times* 117 (January 2006) 156–57.

"Courtesy as Sacrifice." *Questioning and Disputing*, November 24, 2016. https://questioninganddisputing.wordpress.com/2016/11/24/courtesy-as-sacrifice/.

"Courting a Crisis." *Princeton Seminary Bulletin* 13 (1992) 199–203.

"Crossing over Jordan." *Expository Times* 126 (October 2014) 30–32.

"Crucified Leaders." *Berkeley at Yale* 20 (2000) 16–17.

"Death and Horrors." *The Expository Times* 120 (September 2009) 596–98.

"Death and Memory." *The Episcopal Café*, November 13, 2016. https://web.archive.org/web/20210729152605/https://www.episcopalcafe.com/death-and-memory/.

"Death-Bed Reality." In *When Two or Three are Gathered: Spiritual Stories for Contemporary Episcopalians*, edited by Danielle Elizabeth Tumminio and Kate Malin, 7–10. Cincinnati: Forward Movement, 2013.

"Deep Waters." *The Expository Times* 116 (July 2005) 340–41.

"Diagnostic Discipleship." *The Expository Times* 117 (September 2006) 509–10.

"Eucharistic Prayer for Coming Out Day Liturgy." Lecture, Marquand Chapel, Yale Divinity School, October 7, 1993.

"Eucharistic Prayer for the Powerless, the Oppressed, the Unusual." In *Equal Rites: Lesbian and Gay Worship, Ceremonies, and Celebrations*, edited by Kittredge Cherry and Zalmon Sherwood, 111–13. Louisville: Westminster John Knox, 1995.

"Eucharistic Prayer for St. Francis Day Liturgy." Lecture, Marquand Chapel, Yale Divinity School, October 4, 1996.

"Exodus 32:7–14." In *Feasting on the Word: Additional Essays, Year C*. Louisville: Westminster John Knox, 2013. https://www.wjkbooks.com/Content/Site117/Basics/59975YearCaddit_00000032209.pdf.

"Faith and Works, or How James Is a Lutheran!" *The Expository Times* 117 (May 2006) 462–64; Reprinted in abridged form in *Luther Digest* 17 (2009) 13.

"Fallen Idols." *The Expository Times* 119 (November 2007) 85–87.

"Fiery Trials, Realistic Surprises." *The Expository Times* 122 (May 2011) 389–91.

"Figs from Thistles." *The Expository Times* 116 (June 2005) 309–10.

"Forgiving Discipline." *The Expository Times* 116 (August 2005) 379–81.

"Fulfilling All Righteousness." *The Expository Times* 125 (December 2013) 127–29.

"'Getting Real'!" *The Expository Times* 125 (February 2014) 237–39.

"God's Friends!?!" *The Expository Times* 117 (April 2006) 291–92.

"Good Shepherd?" *The Expository Times* 119 (March 2008) 287–88.

"Gospel Compulsion." *The Expository Times* 120 (January 2009) 183–85.

"Healing Judgment." *The Expository Times* 117 (February 2006) 196–97.

"Holy Conflict." *The Living Pulpit* 3 (1994) 40–41.

"House-building." *The Expository Times* 117 (June 2006) 378–80.

"Housing the Holiness." *The Expository Times* 117 (December 2005) 112–13.

"Imaginative Faith, Surprising Hope!" *The Expository Times* 117 (November 2005) 74–75.

"'In Between' Faithfulness." *Questioning and Disputing*, November 27, 2016. https://questioninganddisputing.wordpress.com/2016/11/27/in-between-faithfulness/.

"Intense Encounters, Living Bread." *The Expository Times* 117 (July 2006) 419–20.

"Interrupted Resurrection, Resurrecting Interruption." *The Expository Times* 121 (March 2010) 299–300.

"Joshua 24:1–3a, 14–25." In *Feasting on the Word: Additional Essays, Year A*. Louisville: Westminster John Knox, 2013. https://www.wjkbooks.com/Content/Site117/Basics/59975YearAaddit_00000032207.pdf.

"Keeping Faith at the Polls." *Questioning and Disputing*, November 24, 2016. https://questioninganddisputing.wordpress.com/2016/11/24/keeping-faith-at-the-polls/.

"Kneading Light into Clay." *Faith & Leadership*, December 19, 2011. https://faithandleadership.com/marilyn-mccord-adams-kneading-light-clay.

"Lenten Work." *Faith & Leadership*, February 8, 2011. https://faithandleadership.com/lenten-work.

"The Love of Christ Controls Us!" *Trinity College Bulletin* 14 (1997) 60–64.

"Mark 1:9–15." In *Feasting on the Word*, edited by David L. Bartlett and Barbara Brown Taylor, Year B, 2:44–49. Louisville: Westminster John Knox, 2013.

"Mark 9:2–9." In *Feasting on the Word*, edited by David L. Bartlett and Barbara Brown Taylor, Year B, 1:428–33. Louisville: Westminster John Knox, 2013.

"Matthew 6:1–6, 16–20." In *Feasting on the Word*, edited by David L. Bartlett and Barbara Brown Taylor, Year B, 2:20–25. Louisville: Westminster John Knox, 2013.

"No Thanks!" *The Expository Times* 121 (September 2010) 615–17.

"Omnibus Benediction." *Questioning and Disputing*, November 23, 2016. https://questioninganddisputing.wordpress.com/2016/11/23/omnibus-benediction/.

"Once and Future Rescue: Psalm 85." *Interpretation* 68 (2014) 69–71.

"Out-of-bounds Power." *Questioning and Disputing*, November 25, 2016. https://questioninganddisputing.wordpress.com/2016/11/25/out-of-bounds-power/.

"Praying Angry and Surviving Abuse." *Reverberations*, October 22, 2013. https://forums.ssrc.org/ndsp/2013/10/22/praying-angry-and-surviving-abuse/.

"Prologue to Celebration of the Holy Eucharist." Lecture, Marquand Chapel, Yale Divinity School, October 9, 1998.

"Psalm 113." In *Feasting on the Word: Additional Essays, Year C*. Louisville: Westminster John Knox, 2013. https://www.wjkbooks.com/Content/Site117/Basics/59975YearCaddit_00000032209.pdf.

"Psalm 78:1–7." In *Feasting on the Word: Additional Essays, Year A*. Louisville: Westminster John Knox, 2013. https://www.wjkbooks.com/Content/Site117/Basics/59975YearAaddit_00000032207.pdf.

"Real Authority." *The Expository Times* 123 (June 2012) 446–47.

"Realistic Re-creation." *Spectrum Magazine of Yale Divinity School* (Spring 2002) 2–3.

"Resurrecting the Cosmos." *Questioning and Disputing*, November 25, 2016. https://questioninganddisputing.wordpress.com/2016/11/25/resurrecting-the-cosmos/.

"The Resurrection of the Body." *The Expository Times* 117 (March 2006) 251–52.

"A Serious Call to a Devout and Holy Life." *Theology* (July 2006) 243–51.

"The Slaughter of the Innocents." *Episcopal Café*, December 17, 2012. https://web.archive.org/web/20210801113244/https://www.episcopalcafe.com/the_slaughter_of_the_innocents/.

"Speaking to the Soul: The Coming Judgment." *Episcopal Café*, December 18, 2014. https://web.archive.org/web/20210802062411/http://www.episcopalcafe.com/speaking-to-the-soul-the-coming-judgment/.

"Spirited Peace." *The Expository Times* 116.7 (April 2005) 237–38.

"Strange Exorcists." *Episcopal Café*, October 1, 2012. https://web.archive.org/web/20210618031535/https://www.episcopalcafe.com/strange_exorcists/.

"The Substance of Faith." *The Expository Times* 124 (July 2013) 496–97.

"Understanding Mind, Heart of Wisdom." *Questioning and Disputing*, November 24, 2016. https://questioninganddisputing.wordpress.com/2016/11/24/understanding-mind-heart-of-wisdom/.

"Uprooting Trees." *The Expository Times* 124 (September 2013) 594–96.

"Violent Devotion." *The Expository Times* 116.8 (May 2005) 271–73.

"Wahrheit und Toleranz." *Orientierung* 69 (2005) 47–48. [German translation of sermon delivered for the BBC broadcast of matins commemorating 300th anniversary of Locke's death, November 7, 2004.]

"What Sort of King?" *The Expository Times* 117 (October 2005) 27–28.

"What Sort of Victory?" *Episcopal Café*, May 10, 2011. https://web.archive.org/web/20210729061039/https://www.episcopalcafe.com/what_sort_of_victory/.

"Which Shepherd?" *The Expository Times* 124 (March 2013) 289–91.

"The Wild Ones." *The Living Pulpit* 9 (2000) 14–15.

REVIEWS

Commentary on Anselm's De Grammatico, by D. P. Henry. *Archives Internationales d'Histoire des Sciences* (1976) 311–17.

Confessions of a Rational Mystic: Anselm's Early Writings, by Gregory Schufreider. *Speculum* (1996) 242–45.

The Dissolution of the Medieval Outlook: An Essay on the Intellectual and Spiritual Change in the Fourteenth Century, by Gordon Leff. *Journal of the History of Philosophy* 18 (1980) 83–87.

Lectura Secunda, vols. 1–3, by Adam de Wodeham, edited by Rega Wood and Gedeon Gál. *Philosophical Review* 102 (1993) 588–94.

"Metaphysics and Eschatology: A Response to Tonstad." *Conversations in Religion and Theology* (2010) 34–36.

Opera Philosophica II, by G. de Ockham, edited by Gedeon Gál et al. *Philosophical Review* (1980) 129–37.

Opera Theologica IV, by G. de Ockham, edited by G. Etzkorn and F. Kelly. *Philosophical Review* (1983) 93–97.

Opera Theologica IX, by G. de Ockham, edited by J. Wey. *Philosophical Review* 92 (1983) 98–103.

Opera Theologica V–VI, by G. de Ockham. Vol. V edited by Gedeon Gál and Rega Wood. Vol. VI edited by G. Etzkorn and F. Kelly. *Philosophical Review* (1986) 474–80.

Opera Theologica VII, by G. de Ockham, edited by Rega Wood and Gedeon Gál. *Philosophical Review* (1988) 417–24.

Peter Abelard's Ethics, with an introduction, translation, and notes by D. E. Luscombe. *Philosophical Review* (1973) 404–9.

The Philosophy of William of Ockham in the Light of Its Principles, by Armand Maurer. *University of Toronto Quarterly* 71 (2001/2) 202–5.

Scriptum in Librum Primum Sententiarum: Ordinatio. Vol. I, *Prologus*, by William Ockham. Edited by Gedeon Gál and Stephen Brown. *Philosophical Review* (1970) 268–74.

Scriptum in Librum Sententiarum: Ordinatio. Vol. III, by William Ockham, edited by G. Etzkorn. *Philosophical Review* (1979) 117–21.

William Ockham: The Metamorphosis of Scholastic Discourse, by Gordon Leff. *Journal of the History of Philosophy* 15 (1977) 334–39.

NEWS MEDIA

"Born of Outrage, This Is Just Confusion." *The Church Times*, March 18, 2011.

"How to Quench the Spirit!" *The Church Times*, October 29, 2004.

"Leaven in the Lump of Lambeth: Spiritual Temptations and Ecclesial Opportunities." *The Church Times*, April 27, 2007.

"Silence on Sex Is No Answer." *The Guardian*, March 5, 2004. https://www.theguardian.com/world/2004/mar/06/religion.gayrights.

Bibliography

Adams, Robert Merrihew. "Existence, Self-Interest, and the Problem of Evil." *Noûs* 13 (1979) 53–65.

———. "Love and the Problem of Evil." *Philosophia* 34 (2006) 243–51.

———."Must God Create the Best?" *The Philosophical Review* 81 (1972) 317–32.

Alcoff, Linda Martín. *Rape and Resistance*. Cambridge: Polity, 2018.

Anselm of Canterbury. *S. Anselmi Cantuariensis Archiepiscopi Opera Omnia, Ad fidem codicum recensuit Franciscus Selesius Schmitt*. Stuttgart: Friedrich Frommann. 1968.

Aquinas, Thomas. *Opera omnia*. Rome: Leonine Commission, 1882–.

———. *Scriptum super Sententiis*. https://www.corpusthomisticum.org/snp0000.html.

———. *Summa contra Gentiles*. https://www.corpusthomisticum.org/scg1001.html.

———. *Summa Theologiae*. https://www.corpusthomisticum.org/sth0000.html.

Aristotle. *Physics*. In vol. 1 of *The Complete Works of Aristotle*, edited by Jonathan Barnes, translated by R. P. Hardie and R. K. Gaye, 315–446. Bolingen Series 71. Princeton: Princeton University Press, 1991.

Augustine. *On the Trinity*. Translated by Edmund Hill. New York: New City, 1991.

———. *De Trinitate, libri I–XII*. Edited by W. J. Mountain and Fr. Glorie. Turnholt: Brepols, 1968.

Averroes. *Long Commentary on "De Anima" of Aristotle*. Translated by Richard C. Taylor and subedited by Thérèse-Anne Druart. New Haven: Yale University Press, 2009.

Barnes, Michel R. "De Régnon Reconsidered." *Augustinian Studies* 26 (1995) 51–79.

Barnwell, Michael. "The 'Harder Problem' of the Devil's Fall Is Still a Problem: A Reply to Wood." *Religious Studies* 53 (2017) 521–43.

———. "Soul-Making Theodicy and Compatibilism: New Problems and a New Interpretation." *International Journal for Philosophy of Religion* 82 (2017) 29–46.

Berry, Wendell. "Faustian Economics." *Harper's Magazine*, May 2008. https://harpers.org/archive/2008/05/faustian-economics/.

Beste, Jennifer. *God and the Victim: Traumatic Intrusions on Grace and Freedom*. AAR Academy Series. Oxford: Oxford University Press, 2007.

Black, Deborah. "*Cognoscere Per Impressionem*: Aquinas and the Avicennian Account of Knowing Separate Substances." *American Catholic Philosophy Quarterly* 88 (2014) 213–36.

Bonaventure, St. *Bonaventure: The Soul's Journey into God, the Tree of Life, the Life of St. Francis*. Translated by Ewert Cousins. Mahwah, NJ: Paulist, 1978.

———. *Commentary on the First Book of Sentences: Opera Omnia*. 4 vols. Paris: University of Paris, 1250–52.

Boring, Wendy Petersen. "Ecclesiology and Climate Change: Church at the Margins in the Anthropocene." Paper presented at Pax et Bonum, a workshop in honor of Marilyn McCord Adams, Rutgers University Center for the Philosophy of Religion, February 2018.

———. "Sustainability and the Western Civilization Curriculum: Reflections on Cross-Pollinating the Humanities and Environmental History." *Environmental History* 15 (2010) 288–304.

Boring, Wendy Petersen, and Emily L. Boring. "God's Self-Diffusing Goodness: Bonaventure, Evolutionary Biology, and Cosmic Order." Paper presented at the Society of Christian Philosophers session in honor of Marilyn McCord Adams, American Academy of Religion Annual Meeting, Boston, November 2017.

Brenet, Jean-Baptiste. "Vision béatifique et séparation de l'intellect au début du XIVe siècle." *Freiburger Zeitschrift für Philosophie und Theologie* 53 (2006) 310–42.

Brison, Susan. *Aftermath: Violence and the Remaking of a Self*. Princeton: Princeton University Press, 2002.

Buber, Martin. *The Eclipse of God: Studies in the Relation between Religion and Philosophy*. New York: Harper & Row, 1952.

———. *I and Thou*. Translated by Ronald Gregor Smith. New York: Macmillan, 1987.

———. *The Prophetic Faith*. Translated by Carlyle Witton-Davies. New York: Collier, 1949.

Burke, Edmund. "The Big Story: Human History, Energy Regimes, and the Environment." In *The Environment and World History*, edited by Edmund Burke III and Kenneth Pomeranz, 33–53. California World History Library 9. Berkeley: University of California Press, 2009.

Burke, Megan. *When Time Warps: The Lived Experience of Gender, Race, and Sexual Violence*. Minneapolis: University of Minnesota Press, 2019.

Cajetan, Tommaso de Vio. *Commentaria in Summam Theologicam Sancti Thomae Aquinatis*. Lyrae, 1892.

Christensen, Jen. "Climate Anxiety Is Real, but There's Something You Can Do about It." *CNN*, May 7, 2019. https://www.cnn.com/2019/05/07/health/climate-anxiety-eprise/index.html.

Contenson, Vincent. *Theologia mentis et cordis*. Lyon, 1687.

Couenhoven, Jesse. *Predestination: A Guide for the Perplexed*. Guides for the Perplexed. London: Bloomsbury, 2018.

———. "The Problem of God's Immutable Freedom." In *Free Will and Theism: Connections, Contingencies, and Concerns*, edited by Kevin Timpe and Daniel Speak, 294–311. New York: Oxford University Press, 2016.

———. *Stricken by Sin, Cured by Christ: Agency, Necessity, and Culpability in Augustinian Theology*. New York: Oxford University Press, 2013.

Craigo-Snell, Shannon. "Wrestling with God: The Lived Theology of Marilyn McCord Adams." *Anglican Theological Review* 100 (2018) 339–54.

Cross, Richard. "Deification in Aquinas: Created or Uncreated." *Journal of Theological Studies* (2018) 106–32.

———. *Duns Scotus on God*. Ashgate Studies in the History of Philosophical Theology. New York: Routledge, 2005.

———. "Medieval Theories of Haecceity." In *The Stanford Encyclopedia of Philosophy*, edited by Edward N. Zalta. https://plato.stanford.edu/archives/sum2014/entries/medieval-haecceity/.

———. "Two Models of the Trinity?" *Heythrop Journal* 43 (2002) 275–94.

———. *Christology and Metaphysics in the Seventeenth Century*. Changing Paradigms in Historical and Systematic Theology. Oxford: Oxford University Press, 2022.

Duns Scotus, John. *Quodlibet*. In vol. 12 of *J. Duns Scotus, Opera Omnia*, edited by Luke Wadding, 205–6. Hildesheim: Olms, 1968.

———. *Ordinatio*. Edited by C. Balić et al. Vol. 6. Vatican: Typis Polyglottis Vaticanis, 1963.

———. *Ordinatio*. In *Opera Omnia*. Vatican ed. Civitas Vaticana: Typis Polyglottis Vaticanis, 1950–.

Episcopal Church. *The Book of Common Prayer and Administration of the Sacraments and Other Rites and Ceremonies of the Church: Together with the Psalter or Psalms of David according to the Use of the Episcopal Church*. New York: Seabury, 1979.

Faith Climate Action Week. "Religious Statements on Climate Change." https://www.faithclimateactionweek.org/resources/religious-statements-on-climate-change/.

Fletcher, Jeannine Hill. *The Sin of White Supremacy: Christianity, Racism, and Religious Diversity in America*. Maryknoll, NY: Orbis, 2017.

Folke, Carl. "Respecting Planetary Boundaries and Reconnecting to the Biosphere." In *State of the World 2013: Is Sustainability Still Possible?*, edited by Linda Starke, 19–37. Washington, DC: Island, 2013.

Fox, Matthew. "Moving beyond a Cross Fetish: The Empty Tomb and Creation Spirituality." *Tikkun*, October 26, 2012. https://www.tikkun.org/moving-beyond-a-cross-fetish-the-empty-tomb-and-creation-spirituality/.

Frankl, Viktor E. *Man's Search for Meaning: An Introduction to Logotherapy*. Translated by Ilsa Lasch. New York: Simon & Schuster, 1984.

Gardiner, Stephen M. *A Perfect Moral Storm: The Ethical Tragedy of Climate Change*. Environmental Ethics and Science Policy Series. New York: Oxford University Press, 2011.

Giles of Rome. *Quodlibeta*. Venice, 1502.

Greenberg, Irving. "Cloud of Smoke, Pillar of Fire: Judaism, Christianity, and Modernity after the Holocaust." In *Auschwitz: Beginning of a New Era*, edited by Eva Fleischner, 7–55. New York: KTAV, 1977.

Greggs, Tom. *Barth, Origen, and Universal Salvation: Restoring Particularity*. New York: Oxford University Press, 2009.

Harrison, Nonna Verna. "The Trinity and Feminism." In *Oxford Handbook of the Trinity*, edited by Gilles Emery and Matthew Levering, 519–30. Oxford: Oxford University Press, 2011.

Hasker, William. "Can a Latin Trinity Be Social? A Response to Scott M. Williams." *Faith and Philosophy* 35.3 (2018) 356–66.

———. "God and Gratuitous Evil: A Response to Klaas Kraay." In *Oxford Studies in the Philosophy of Religion*, edited by L. Buchak et al., 9:54–67. Oxford: Oxford University Press, 2019.

———. "Is the Latin Social Trinity Defensible? A Rejoinder to Scott M. Williams." *Faith and Philosophy* 38.4 (2021)(forthcoming).

———. "The Necessity of Gratuitous Evil." *Faith and Philosophy* 9 (1992) 23–44.

———. "O'Connor on Gratuitous Natural Evil." *Faith and Philosophy* 14 (1997) 388–94.

Heil, John. *From an Ontological Point of View*. Oxford: Clarendon, 2003.

Hellwig, Monika K. "Eschatology." In *Systematic Theology: Roman Catholic Perspectives*, edited by Francis Schüssler Fiorenza and John P. Galvin, 2:347–72. Minneapolis: Fortress, 1991.

Helmer, Christine. "Marilyn McCord Adams: How a Theologian Works." *Anglican Theological Review* 100 (2018) 327-38.

Henry of Ghent. *Summa (Quaestiones ordinariae): Art. XLVII–LII*. Edited by M. Führer. Henrici de Gandavo Opera Omnia 30. Leuven: Leuven University Press, 2007.

———. *Summa (Quaestiones ordinariae): Art. LX–LXII*. Edited by G. A. Wilson et al. Henrici de Gandavo Opera Omnia 33. Leuven: Leuven University Press, 2018.

Herman, Judith. *Trauma and Recovery: The Aftermath of Violence—From Domestic Abuse to Political Terror*. New York: Basic, 1997.

Hick, John. *Evil and the God of Love*. 2nd ed. Basingstoke: Palgrave MacMillan, 2010.

Indigenous Values Initiative. "Dum Diversas." *Doctrine of Discovery Project*, July 23, 2018. https://doctrineofdiscovery.org/dum-diversas/.

Jenkins, Willis. *The Future of Ethics: Sustainability, Social Justice, and Religious Creativity*. Washington, DC: Georgetown University Press, 2013.

Kant, Immanuel. *Groundwork for the Metaphysics of Morals*. Translated by Christopher Bennet et al. Oxford World's Classics. Oxford: Oxford University Press, 2019.

Keller, Catherine. *Political Theology of the Earth: Our Planetary Emergency and the Struggle for a New Public*. Insurrections: Critical Studies in Religion, Politics, and Culture. New York: Columbia University Press, 2018.

Kraay, Klaas. "Theism, Pro-Theism, Hasker, and Gratuitous Evil." In *Oxford Studies in the Philosophy of Religion*, edited by L. Buchak et al., 9:31–53. Oxford: Oxford University Press, 2019.

Krause, Katja. "Albert and Aquinas on the Ultimate End of Humans: Philosophy, Theology, and Beatitude." *Proceedings of the American Catholic Philosophical Association* 86 (2013) 213–29.

Langer, Lawrence L. "The Dilemma of Choice in the Death Camps." In *Holocaust: Religious and Philosophical Responses*, edited by John K. Roth and Michael Berenbaum, 222–32. St. Paul, MN: Paragon, 1989.

Lathrop, Gordon. *Holy Things: A Liturgical Theology*. Minneapolis: Fortress, 1993.

The Leap Manifesto. "The Leap Manifesto." https://leapmanifesto.org/en/the-leap-manifesto/.

Levinas, Emmanuel. "Useless Suffering." In *The Provocation of Levinas: Rethinking the Other*, edited by Robert Bernasconi and David Wood, translated by Richard Cohen, 156–67. Warwick Studies in Philosophy and Literature. London: Routledge, 1988.

Lewis, C. S. *The Problem of Pain*. New York: Macmillan, 1962.

Leys, Ruth. *Trauma: A Genealogy*. Chicago: University of Chicago Press, 2000.

Lombard, Peter. *The Sentences, Book 1: The Mystery of the Trinity*. Translated by Giulio Silvano. Toronto: Pontifical Institute of Medieval Studies, 2007.

———. *Textus Magistri Sententiarum*. In *Ioannis Duns Scoti Commentaria Oxoniensia ad IV. Libros Magistri Sententiarum*, edited by Fernandez Garcia, 1122–23. Quaracchi, 1912.

Marandiuc, Natalia. *The Goodness of Home: Human and Divine Love and the Making of the Self*. AAR Academy Series. New York: Oxford University Press, 2018.

McFague, Sallie. *The Body of God: An Ecological Theology*. Minneapolis: Fortress, 1993.

———. *Life Abundant: Rethinking Theology and Economy for a Planet in Peril*. Minneapolis: Fortress, 2001.

Metz, Johann Baptist. *The Emergent Church: The Future of Christianity in a Postbourgeois World*. Translated by Peter Mann. New York: Crossroad, 1981.

———. "Facing the Jews: Christian Theology after Auschwitz." *Concilium* 175 (1984) 26–33.

———. "Theology as Theodicy?" In *A Passion for God: The Mystical-Political Dimension of Christianity*, edited and translated by J. Matthew Ashley, 54–71. New York: Paulist, 1998.

Mildenberger, Matto, et al. "The Spatial Distribution of Republican and Democratic Climate Opinions at State and Local Scales." *Climate Change* 145 (2017) 539–48.

Moore, Kathleen Dean, and Michael P. Nelson. *Moral Ground: Ethical Action for a Planet in Peril*. San Antonio: Trinity University Press, 2010.

Morley, Janet. *All Desires Known*. London: SPCK, 1994.

Nixon, Rob. *Slow Violence and the Environmentalism of the Poor*. Cambridge: Harvard University Press, 2011.

Ó' Tuama, Padraig. "Belonging Creates and Undoes Us." *On Being* (podcast), April 11, 2019. https://www.youtube.com/watch?v=5DKB0QTxPQY.

———. *In the Shelter*. Dublin: Hachette, 2015.

Oreskes, Naomi. *The Collapse of Western Civilization: A View from the Future*. New York: Columbia University Press, 2014.

Paasch, JT. *Divine Production in Late Medieval Trinitarian Theology*. Oxford: Oxford University Press, 2012.

Pew Research Center. "Religion and Views on Climate and Energy Issues." *Pew Research Center*, October 22, 2015. https://www.pewresearch.org/science/2015/10/22/religion-and-views-on-climate-and-energy-issues/.

Pini, Giorgio. "Scotus on Universals: A Reconsideration." *Documenti e studi sulla tradizione filosofica medievale* 18 (2007) 395–409.

Pinnock, Sarah K. *Beyond Theodicy: Jewish and Continental Thinkers Respond to the Holocaust*. SUNY Series in Theology and Continental Thought. Albany: State University of New York Press, 2002.

Plantinga, Alvin. "Supralapsarianism, or 'O Felix Culpa.'" In *Christian Faith and the Problem of Evil*, edited by Peter van Inwagen, 1–25. Grand Rapids: Eerdmans, 2004.

Rahner, Karl. "The 'Commandment' of Love in Relation to Other Commandments." In *Theological Investigations*, translated Karl-H. Kruger, 5:439–59. Baltimore: Helicon, 1966.

———. *The Love of Jesus and the Love of Neighbor*. Translated by Robert Barr. New York: Crossroad, 1983.

———. *Prayers for a Lifetime*. Edited by Albert Raffelt. New York: Crossroad, 1997.

———. "Some Implications of the Scholastic Concept of Uncreated Grace." In of *Theological Investigation*, translated by Cornelius Ernst, 1:279–346. London: Darton, Longman & Todd, 1961.
Rambo, Shelly. *Spirit and Trauma: A Theology of Remaining*. Louisville: Westminster John Knox, 2010.
The Ramsey Colloquium. "The Homosexual Movement." *First Things* 41 (1994) 15–21.
The Ramsey Colloquium. "Morality and Homosexuality." *Wall Street Journal*, February 24, 1994.
Reaves, Jayme R., et al., eds. *When Did We See You Naked? Jesus as a Victim of Sexual Abuse*. London: SCM, 2021.
Richards, John F. *The Unending Frontier and Environmental History of the Early Modern World*. California World History Library 1. Berkeley: University of California Press, 2003.
Roberts, David. "Why Climate Change Doesn't Spark Moral Outrage, and How It Could." *Grist*, July 27, 2012. https://grist.org/article/why-climate-change-doesnt-spark-moral-outrage-and-how-it-could/.
Rohr, Richard. "A New Way of Thinking." *Center for Action and Contemplation*, October 3, 2019. https://cac.org/daily-meditations/a-new-way-of-thinking-2019-10-03/.
Rohr, Richard, with Mike Morrell. *The Divine Dance: The Trinity and Your Transformation*. New Kensington, PA: Whitaker, 2016.
Rosenfeld, Alvin H. "The Holocaust according to William Styron." *Midstream* 25 (1979) 43–49.
Roth, John K. "A Theodicy of Protest." In *Encountering Evil: Live Options in Theodicy*, edited by Stephen T. Davis, 1–37. Louisville: Westminster John Knox, 1981.
Rowe, William L. "The Problem of Evil and Some Varieties of Atheism." *American Philosophical Quarterly* 16 (1979) 335–41.
Rubenstein, Richard L. *After Auschwitz: Response to a Catastrophe in Modern Jewish Culture*. Indianapolis: Bobbs-Merrill, 1966.
Russell, Bertrand. *The Problems of Philosophy*. New York: Oxford University Press, 1969.
Saliers, Don E. *Worship as Theology: Foretaste of Glory Divine*. Nashville: Abingdon, 1994.
Scott, Mark S. M. *Pathways in Theodicy: An Introduction to the Problem of Evil*. Minneapolis: Fortress, 2015.
Sigurdson, Ola. *Heavenly Bodies: Incarnation, the Gaze, and Embodiment in Christian Theology*. Translated by Carl Olsen. Grand Rapids: Eerdmans, 2016.
Soelle, Dorothee. *The Silent Cry*. Translated by Barbara Rumscheidt and Martin Rumscheidt. Minneapolis: Fortress, 2001.
———. *Suffering*. Translated by Everett R. Kalin. Minneapolis: Fortress, 1975.
Spade, P. V. *Five Texts on the Mediaeval Problem of Universals: Porphyry, Boethius, Abelard, Duns Scotus, Ockham*, 57–113. Indianapolis: Hackett, 1994.
Surin, Kenneth. *Theology and the Problem of Evil*. Oxford: Basil Blackwell, 1986.
Taylor, Richard. "Arabic/Islamic Philosophy in Thomas Aquinas's Conception of the Beatific Vision in IV *Sent.*, d. 49, q. 2, a. 11." *Thomist* 76 (2012) 509–50.
———. "Deification in Aquinas: Created or Uncreated." *Journal of Theological Studies* 69 (2018) 106–32.
Tumminio Hansen, Danielle. "Absent a Word: How the Language of Sexual Trauma Keeps Survivors Silent." *Journal of Pastoral Theology* 30 (2020) 136–49.

---. "Do People Become More Religious in Times of Crisis?" *The Conversation*, May 5, 2021. https://theconversation.com/do-people-become-more-religious-in-times-of-crisis-158849.

---. "Remembering Rape in Heaven: A Constructive Proposal for Memory and the Eschatological Self." *Modern Theology* 37 (2021) 662–78.

University of California Berkeley. "Greater Good Science Center." https://ggsc.berkeley.edu/.

Vargas, Manual R. "The Runeberg Problem: Theism, Libertariansism, and Motivated Reasoning." In *Free Will and Theism: Connections, Contingencies, and Concerns*, edited by Kevin Timpe and Daniel Speak, 27–47. New York: Oxford University Press, 2016.

Vitale, Vincent Raphael. "Horrendous Evils and the Ethical Perfection of God." PhD diss., Worcester College, 2012.

Voelkel, Rebecca M. M. *Carnal Knowledge of God: Embodied Love and the Movement for Justice*. Minneapolis: Fortress, 2017.

Walker, Alice. *The Color Purple*. New York: Harcourt, 2003.

Wallace-Wells, David. "When Will the Planet Be Too Hot for Humans? Much Sooner Than You Imagine." *Intelligencer*, July 10, 2017. https://nymag.com/intelligencer/2017/07/climate-change-earth-too-hot-for-humans.html.

Weil, Simone. "The Love of God and Affliction." In *Waiting for God*, translated by Emma Craufurd, 117–36. New York: Harper & Row, 1951.

Wiesel, Elie. *Night*. Translated by Marion Wiesel. New York: Hill & Wang, 2006.

---. *The Town beyond the Wall*. Translated by Stephen Becker. New York: Schocken, 1982.

Williams, D. C. "On the Elements of Being: I." *Review of Metaphysics* 7 (1953) 3–18.

---. "On the Elements of Being: II." *Review of Metaphysics* 7 (1953) 171–92.

Williams, Delores. "Re-Imagining Jesus." Lecture, Re-Imagining: A Global Theological Conference by Women: For Men and Women, Minneapolis, November 4–7, 1993.

Williams, Scott M. "Augustine, Thomas Aquinas, Henry of Ghent, and John Duns Scotus: On the Theology of the Father's Intellectual Generation of the Word." *Recherches de Théologie et Philosophie médiévales* 77 (2010) 35–81.

---. "Discovery of the Sixth Ecumenical Council's Trinitarian Theology: Historical, Ecclesial, and Theological Implications." *Journal of Analytic Theology* 10 (2022) (forthcoming).

---. "Gregory of Nyssa, Conciliar Trinitarianism, and the Latin Social Trinity: Response to William Hasker." *Faith and Philosophy* 38.4 (2021) (forthcoming).

---. "In Defense of a Latin Social Trinity: A Response to William Hasker." *Faith and Philosophy* 37.1 (2020) 96–117.

---. "Indexicals and the Trinity: Two Non-Social Models." *Journal of Analytic Theology* 1 (2013) 74–94.

---. "Unity of Action in a Latin Social Model of the Trinity." *Faith and Philosophy* 34.3 (2017) 321–46.

Williams, Terry Tempest. "Gods among Us: Erosion and Resurrection of Belief." *Orion Magazine*, September 23, 2019. https://orionmagazine.org/article/gods-among-us/.

---. "The Liturgy of Home." *Harvard Divinity Bulletin*, Spring/Summer 2018. https://bulletin.hds.harvard.edu/the-liturgy-of-home/

Wolfchild, Sheldon, and Steven Newcomb, dir. *The Doctrine of Discovery: Unmasking the Domination Code*. 38 plus 2 Productions, 2008.

Zagzebski, Linda. "The Dignity of Persons and the Value of Uniqueness." *Proceedings and Addresses of the American Philosophical Association* 90 (2016) 55–70.

———. "The Uniqueness of Persons." *The Journal of Religious Ethics* 29 (2001) 401–23.

Index

Accompaniment Movement, 201
Activism, 203–5
Adams, Robert Merrihew, vii, 57, 61, 67–69, 70, 90n64
AIDS, 8, 48, 89, 97, 141, 194
Alexander VI, Pope, 198
Alfonso V of Portugal, 198–99
Angels, 37–44, 147, 154
Anselm of Canterbury, 4, 5, 28–30, 37–44, 132, 193
Appelfeld, Aharon, 23, 25
Appetitive act, 176, 183
Aquinas, Thomas 10, 157, 160–62, 164–65, 169, 175–91
Aristotle, 110, 112, 174, 180–81, 184, 190
Attachment, 75, 76, 83–86, 92–93, 129, 131
Assimilation, 77–79
Augustine, 61, 71, 157–61, 168
Auschwitz, 12–16, 18, 24–26
Averroes, 175, 177–78

Barnes, Michel, 156
Barth, Karl, 5
Best of all Possible Worlds, 6
Beste, Jennifer, 91

Book of Common Prayer, 10, 133, 144–45, 147–49
Bonaventure, 77, 95, 102n33, 130
Buber, Martin, 14, 26–28

Cajetan, Thomas de Vio, 185n33, 186–87
Chocolate Chip Cookies, 11, 80, 194, 197, 206
Climate, 10, 94–100, 102, 106–9
Compatibilism, 57, 60–67, 70–71
Constantinople. *See* Sixth Ecumenical Council
Contenson, Vincent, 187–88
Courtesy, 105–8, 131
Covenant, 14, 22, 82, 100, 104–5, 108, 148
Cross, 22, 27, 100, 105, 149, 201–2
Cross, Richard, 10, 112n2, 112n3, 155n2, 153, 156, 162n11, 163, 170
Crucifixion, 8, 15, 24, 97, 99, 149, 202, 204
Cultic Drama, 138–39

Dakota Access Pipeline, 199–200, 204
Determinism, 61, 63, 70
Devil, 30, 37, 39n27

Divine essence, 155, 157–58, 160–67, 169, 171–72, 175–76, 178–79, 181–82, 186–89, 191, 196
Divine *esse*, 185–86, 189
Doctrine of Discovery, 198–200, 202–3

Ecclesiology, 135–38
Eschatology, 69, 75, 91, 146–47, 203
Essential acts, 155, 160–64, 169
Eucharist, 4, 82, 133–34, 137–40, 141n21, 142–45, 174, 203–4
Evil, gratuitous, 30–37, 41–44
Evil, horrendous, 6–7, 10, 12–13, 15–17, 19–24, 26, 28, 29–31, 44, 45, 47, 49–50, 52, 54–55, 59, 64, 67, 71, 79–80, 89, 91, 98–99, 146, 201
Evil, moral, 33, 62
Evil, natural, 33, 62

Fletcher, Jeannine Hill, 27
Frankl, Viktor, 24
Free Will Defense 6, 16, 56–58, 59, 64, 66–67
Friendship, vii, 4, 7–8, 10–11, 45, 51–55, 75–78, 80, 82–84, 86–93, 137, 143, 148, 154–55, 157–59, 163–64, 168, 174, 204

Giles of Rome, 10, 176–77, 180–85, 191
Ginsburg, Ruth Bader, 199
God our Mother, 87, 90, 97
God the Father, 77, 97, 131n40, 154–56, 158–60, 162–68, 170–73
God the Holy Spirit. *See* Holy Spirit
God the Son, 110–11, 131n40, 142, 149, 154–56, 158–60, 162, 164–74
Greenberg, Irving, 26
Gregory of Nazianzus, 156–57
Gregory of Nyssa, 156–57
Gruber, Dean, 14

Habitual knowledge, 165
Habitus, 142–43, 145
Haecceity, 111, 115, 125, 128–29
Hasker, William, 30, 32–37, 41–44, 173n27
Hebrew Bible, 14, 21–22
Hegel, Georg Wilhelm Friedrich, 5

Henry of Ghent, 153, 157–58, 164–70, 174
Hick, John, 40–42, 44, 66
Hitler, Adolph, 15, 18–19, 25
Holocaust, 10, 12–20, 22–28, 53
Holy Spirit, 77, 131n40, 133–37, 141, 147, 148, 154–55, 158–62, 164–73
Holy Spirit as Zeal, 166–69, 174
Horror defeat, 8, 10, 16, 45, 52–54, 70, 81–82, 91–92, 99, 140, 146

Incarnation, 7, 65, 80, 103, 149, 154, 158, 163–64, 174, 185, 187, 189, 197

Jenkins, Willis, 99
Job, 6, 14–15, 27, 141, 145
Julian of Norwich, 54, 87, 130

Kant, Immanuel, 91, 126–27
Keller, Helen, 69
Kierkegaard, Soren, 5, 85
Kraay, Klaas, 30, 32–37, 41–44

Langer, Lawrence, 16
Lathrop, Gordon, 145
Legacy, 45, 52–55
Levinas, Emmanuel, 12, 22–23, 84n37
LGBTQ community, 3, 8, 48, 132, 135, 142, 148, 193–95, 197, 204–5
Libertarianism, 56–57, 60–61, 63, 65–67
Lindbeck, George, 12
Liturgy, 9–11, 89, 97, 99–100, 103, 105, 107–8, 133–34, 136–48, 195, 199–200, 203–4, 209
Lombard, Peter, 159–60
Luther, Martin, 7, 209
Luck, 22, 68

Marshall, John, 199
Marandiuc, Natalia, 75, 83–86, 89–93
Metaphysical mismatch, 78, 80
Metaphysical size-gap, 18, 26, 48, 79, 87, 99, 100, 129–31, 131n40
Metz, Johan Baptist, 26–27

Newcomb, Steven, 199
Nicaea I, Council of, 154

Nicholas V, Pope, 198
Notional acts, 160–62
Numerical Oneness, 114, 119–20, 123–24

Occurrent knowledge, 165–66
Ockham, William, 3–4, 126, 153
Ontology, 15, 48, 111, 123, 125–26, 129, 137, 171
Origen, 65

Problem of evil, 6, 12, 30, 56–57, 71, 97, 174
Problem of evil, evidential, 31–32
Problem of evil, logical, 5, 30n4
Propositional knowledge, de re, 155, 166, 170
Propositional knowledge, de se, 155–56, 158, 163–64, 166–67, 169–72

Queerness, 142–45, 194

Recognition, 20, 53, 84, 86, 88–90
Rahner, Karl, 75, 83–86, 91–93, 190–91
Richard of St. Victor, 76–77
Ritschl, Albrecht, 4
Roth, John, 12, 15–16, 24
Rubenstein, Richard, 12, 14–15
Russell, Bertrand, 46

Sacrifice, 8, 82, 89, 104–6, 108, 148–49
Schleiermacher, Friedrich, 7
Scotus, John Duns, 10, 110–31, 153–55, 157, 161–66, 169–70
Scripture/Bible, 5, 6, 8, 10, 14, 47, 103, 130n39, 134–35, 202
Sexual trauma/sexual abuse, 45–46, 48–51, 55, 64, 195, 202
Sexuality, 8, 134, 142, 144
Sigurdson, Ola, 143–44

Singleton, 111, 113–17, 120–25, 128–29, 131
Sixth Ecumenical Council/Third Council of Constantinople, 156–57, 173
Skeptical theism, 32, 65
Soelle, Dorothee, 28
Solidarity, 53, 80, 197, 200–203
Soul-making theodicy, 40–41, 44, 59–60, 62
Styron, William, 16–17
Supersessionism, 22, 28

Taboos, 8, 134, 136, 139–40, 143–45
Taylor, Charles, 84
Teresa of Avila, 28
Theodicy, 4–7, 12–13, 15–16, 21, 23, 26–27, 29, 31n5, 40–41, 44, 45, 48, 52–53, 57, 59–67, 70–71, 79, 140, 154, 195, 203–5
Tillich, Paul, 15
Trinity, 9–10, 75–78, 87, 93, 107, 131n40, 153–59, 163–65, 167–74, 194
Trope, 111–12, 115, 119–25, 128–29, 205
Trauma, 26, 45–47, 49–51, 53, 54n18, 55, 60, 64, 81

Union with God, 62, 66, 77, 86, 204
Union with God, beatific, 11, 175–79, 182–91
Union with God, hypostatic, 78, 80, 85, 154, 159, 185–86, 188
Universals, 111, 118–20, 122–23
Universal Salvation, 7, 65–68

Wiesel, Elie, 15, 24–25, 27
Williams, D.C., 112
Williams, Terry Tempest, 94
Wolfchild, Sheldon, 199

Zagzebski, Linda, 127–28

www.ingramcontent.com/pod-product-compliance
Lightning Source LLC
Chambersburg PA
CBHW051639230426
43669CB00013B/2367